Cornwallis
The Violent Birth of Halifax

Jon Tattrie

Pottersfield Press, Lawrencetown Beach, Nova Scotia, Canada

Library and Archives Canada Cataloguing in Publication

Tattrie, Jon

Cornwallis : the violent birth of Halifax / Jon Tattrie.

ISBN 978-1-897426-48-7

1. Cornwallis, Edward, 1713-1776. 2. Nova Scotia--History--1713-1775.

3. Halifax (N.S.)--History--18th century. 4. Governors--Nova Scotia--Biography.

5. Great Britain. Army--Officers--Biography.

I. Title.

FC2321.1.C67T38 2013   971.6'01092   C2013-900227-8

Cover design by Gail LeBlanc
Cover image of Cornwallis by Jeff Friesen (www.jeff-friesen.com)

We acknowledge the financial support of the Government of Canada through the Canada Book Fund for our publishing activities and the support of the Canada Council for the Arts, which last year invested $157 million to bring the arts to Canadians throughout the country. Nous remercions le Conseil des arts du Canada de son soutien. L'an dernier, le Conseil a investi 157 millions de dollars pour mettre de l'art dans la vie des Canadiennes et des Canadiens de tout le pays. We thank the Province of Nova Scotia for its support through the Department of Communities, Culture and Heritage.

Pottersfield Press
83 Leslie Road
East Lawrencetown, Nova Scotia, Canada, B2Z 1P8
Website: www.PottersfieldPress.com
To order, phone 1-800-NIMBUS9 (1-800-646-2879) www.nimbus.ns.ca

The Canada Council   Le Conseil des Arts
for the Arts   du Canada

NOVA SCOTIA
Communities, Culture and Heritage

Canada

To Marge Ferguson (née Tattrie),
keeper of family lore,
and to Giselle and Xavier

Contents

Prologue:
Stepping on Cultural Landmines

The models gathered for an advertising photo shoot in the south end of Halifax, Nova Scotia, in 2010. Dressed as skimpily as the cold spring air would allow, they clustered on the stone steps of a statue and posed for the camera. The winning shot is amateurish. One young woman looks at the camera while another stares off to the left; a third hides behind dark sunglasses as the fourth throws her head back in laughter. All are proudly holding the item on sale at a local beauty shop: real human hair extensions. The statue of a tall, stern man staring toward England, with his back to Nova Scotia, does not appear in the photo. His name does: Edward Cornwallis, 1713-1776. The short plaque records him as the founder of Halifax.

That detail caught the eye of Daniel Paul, a prominent Mi'kmaq historian. He attached a scan of the ad to his regular group e-mail and described it as "Reprehensible conduct. However, it was probably taken in ignorance of the scalp proclamations he [Cornwallis] issued. If not, it is racism at its worst!"

The e-mail caught the eye of a journalist – me – and my story ran on the front page of *The Chronicle Herald*. The problem was that Cornwallis, as governor of Nova Scotia from 1749 to 1752, had issued a "scalping proclamation," wherein his government paid a cash bounty to anyone who killed a Mi'kmaq person and brought in the top part of their head. The juxtaposition of his statue and the models with real human hair jarred Paul. My editor wondered if it was a publicity stunt.

It wasn't a stunt. The owner of the beauty salon was shocked at the cultural landmine he had detonated. "Who would suspect it? It's a public park. If there's such an offensive connection to it, why is it there? Why aren't there warning signs on it?" he asked me, exasperated.

The Cornwallis controversy burned brightly for the next two years, culminating in the decision to strip his name from Halifax's Cornwallis Junior High. The school board meeting that made the decision was covered by every major Canadian media outlet (including me, this time for the CBC) and sparked numerous radio show debates, opinion pieces and counter-opinion pieces. Cornwallis Junior High became Halifax Central Junior High in 2012.

Paul, who had long campaigned for the removal of the statue and of Cornwallis's name from public buildings and streets, said the statue controversy was a symptom of the province's "hidden history."

"Are we doing a good job of teaching history to our children?" he asked. "If you want to prevent the wrongs of the past from happening again, you have to teach the population about the past."

Others argued Cornwallis lived in a different time and it was foolish to judge him with twenty-first-century minds. Historian Paul Bennett chastised those he saw as cherry picking one incident from the vicious, multi-sided war that ravaged Nova Scotia in the mid-eighteenth century. He described the campaign to remove the Cornwallis name as an attempt to sanitize the past.

"Social justice advocates and special interest groups are usually the instigators and the 'sanitizers' claim to be 'correcting all past wrongs.' Charges of racism, genocide and inhuman cruelty are heaped upon the dead and are too often simply accepted without much scrutiny," he wrote.

He quoted another historian saying, "You can't apply today's standards to people in the past. That just gets silly," and said the statue and school controversy were political correctness run wild.

A vast gulf separated the two ends of the polarizing debate. They agreed on little, but both found common ground in the refrain, "We need more history, not less."

Cornwallis himself was absent from the debate. Like many people, I wanted to learn more about him, but found no biography had been written about him in the three hundred years since his birth. Nothing put his life and his decisions into the context of his times. The most complete account was a seventeen-page overview from an 1899 presentation to the Historical Society of Nova Scotia.

A full, dispassionate biography of Cornwallis was overdue. I realized if I wanted to read it, I'd have to write it first. This book will soon leave behind the twenty-first-century debate to immerse you in Cornwallis's world, from his birth in England in 1713 to his death on Gibraltar in 1776. It is an extraordinary story of a life at the cutting edge of a rapidly expanding British empire, and the wounds that edge left in its wake.

This first biography of Cornwallis includes the slim reports found in other books, but takes its heart directly from the subject himself: Cornwallis. I spent months reading his correspondence from Nova Scotia and the minutes of council meetings he led. I read the diaries and accounts of men who lived and worked with him in England, Scotland, Nova Scotia and Gibraltar. I discovered transcripts of his testimony at the two courts martial that dogged his later career. I read his correspondence from Gibraltar, and the last letters of his friends.

The intention of this book is not to examine the modern debate about Cornwallis's legacy, but to fully investigate his life and present the facts to readers, so they may make up their own minds.

Find a quiet corner and let this book become a time machine transporting you back three centuries to a world of violence, resistance, loyalty and treachery. This is the complete story of Edward Cornwallis, as never told before.

Edward Cornwallis Timeline

February 22, 1713: Cornwallis is born in London, England.

1725-27: Appointed royal page at Windsor and Hampton Court palaces.

May 4, 1731: Made ensign in 47th Foot Regiment, serving under Prince William, Duke of Cumberland.

1738-1743: Cornwallis works in diplomatic service between The Hague and London.

1744: Appointed Member of Parliament for Eye in Suffolk.

1745: Joins his regiment in Flanders, Belgium, for Battle of Fontenoy. He is appointed Groom of King George II's Bedchamber.

1746: Now a lieutenant colonel, fights Jacobite rebels at Culloden and leads soldiers in the Pacification of the Scottish Highlands.

1748: Resigns command of the mutinous 20th Regiment.

May 1749: Commands an expedition to establish a British settlement on the Atlantic coast of Nova Scotia.

June 21, 1749: Arrives in Chebucto harbour and founds Halifax.

October 1752: Resigns command of Nova Scotia and returns to England.

1753: Returns to Parliament. He weds Mary Townshend.

1756: Involved in a failed expedition to relieve Minorca.

1757: Sent on a failed expedition to attack the French port of Rochefort.

March 18, 1762: Appointed commander-in-chief of Gibraltar.

January 23, 1776: Cornwallis dies in office.

Book One:
Born with Kings

Edward Cornwallis, 1713-1776, painted by Sir George Chalmers at Minorca, 1755.

I

Culloden Moor

The exhausted Highland army stood waiting on the foggy moor. Thousands of ghostly warriors hovered in the rain, bonnets dripping over somber faces, dirty kilts rustling in the breeze. It was early morning, April 16, 1746. The sun had not yet risen, but its light bent over the horizon and illuminated the distant mountain range. Tired hands clutched dulled broadswords and battered wooden shields. The rebels had been fighting for months and now stood with their feet on Culloden Moor and their backs to the wall of the Highlands. An ocean and a sea flanked the warriors. Only the Lowlands, and then England, lay before them. There would be no more escaping. They would fight here. Now.

The imperial British army massed unseen on the moor's far end. If the troops of King George II won at Culloden, the rest of the Highlands lay open. A Highlander victory would push the imperial forces south of the border for a generation or two. It could even reopen the road to London and see the downfall of the hated English king.

Charles Edward, better known as Bonnie Prince Charlie, the Stuart contender for the Scottish throne, inspected his ragged troops from his malnourished horse. The Young Pretender shouted words of encouragement. A gust took them into the heather. It had been a long battle since he had arrived on Scottish shores the year before. He was tired.

The Highlanders lived simple, difficult lives, and imperial issues were beyond their concern. But the English boot had choked the Scottish neck for too long. The threat it would press down and destroy the Gaelic race seemed to grow with each year. The Jacobites had rallied around Charles Edward during his exile in France as their best hope for protecting their lives from the invading English. When the prince finally landed in the Highlands in July 1745, he brought with him only seven men on one ship. The Highland chiefs were not awed by their wayward ruler.

"Go home," one told him.

"I am come home," he replied.

He spoke confidently of defeating England. Of working with France – mutual Catholics, and mutual enemies of Protestant England – and making Scotland safe for centuries.

The chiefs believed him. They went home to raise an army. Farmers traded in their plowshares for broadswords. Most of Scotland's able men answered the call, leaving homes in the care of women and children. Many had no choice; their chiefs coerced them into service, or the money was needed to stave off the starvation of their families. Charles Edward told them to gather at Loch Sheil, near Scotland's west coast, in August.

On that drizzly morning, Charles Edward stood alone at Loch Sheil contemplating his failure. He scanned the high horizon, but saw only cloudy sky. Then he heard the bagpipes. Out of those mists arose a ghost army that would become a nightmare for the imperial English. Clan Cameron led the way, the piper stirring eight hundred souls as they marched to their king. More joined. The Jacobite uprising was on.

The rough army marched to Edinburgh and amazed everyone by conquering it as easily as entering the city. The British army holding Edinburgh had gone into the Highlands to cut down the rebel flower before it bloomed. But the Highlands are wide, too: the British forces stumbled up dale and down glen for months and found nothing at all. Their bright red coats were seen by every eye, and word of their approach raced ahead of them. The Scots knew every glen, each thistle, and vanished before every advance. The English felt like they were fighting a fog.

The Highland army slipped south beside them and claimed the unguarded capital. The Lowlanders cheered their strange kin and Scotland celebrated its freedom. The errant English marched back toward Edinburgh and the Scots met them at a nearby field in Prestonpans. The Highlanders had broadswords, daggers and flimsy shields. The well-armed, well-trained

English army rolled its eyes. The Highland warriors sharpened their broadswords that day, and painted their faces blue, with everyone but them expecting a swift slaughter and the end of the Jacobite cause. Using the superior knowledge brought by their home field advantage, the Scots sneaked across a brook and stood invisible in the mist just seven hundred feet to the left of the Red Coats. When the mist cleared, the Scots used their secret weapon: the Highland Charge. Thousands of warriors ran screaming at the imperial soldiers and hacked them down in great numbers. Cannon fire, musket rounds and bayonets drew Highland blood, but the roaring, terrifying Charge overwhelmed the English defences. No matter how many Highlanders the English muskets killed, another wave rolled up behind them and sought revenge.

At first, the imperial troops were not fazed. The stupidity of running straight at guns seemed obvious and it was just a matter of mathematics and physics resolving themselves in victory for the British. But the attack was relentless. The Charge pressed until the English army collapsed on itself. The British dragoons sprinted from the battlefield. A platoon of Scots chased them while others turned to the centre of the army and eviscerated it. It was a rout. The English soldiers ran like scared children; the Highlanders butchered them like sheep. When the last scream fell silent, four hundred government troops were dead and fourteen hundred imprisoned. The Jacobites lost just forty men.

It was a shocking, humiliating defeat for the revered British army. They were well fed, well armed and well trained, and yet routed by savage Highlanders.

The destruction of one of the world's greatest armies by a rabble took just fifteen minutes. Bonnie Prince Charlie was riding high. He invaded England with an army of five thousand in November 1745. He jogged his troops south, claiming Manchester and Derby. Stuart wanted his crown back. The French promised to help. London lay open before them. Rumours swirled across the Channel, exciting the Scots and terrifying the English: the Catholic French were gathering a massive army to invade England in support of the Catholic Highlanders. Spies counted thirty-seven warships, thirty-four transport and fire ships and 6,709 soldiers preparing to invade from France. The man heading the armada was Duc D'Anville, Jean-Baptiste Louis Frédéric de La Rochefoucauld de Roye. If the rumours were even half true, it would be the largest force to ever invade Great Britain. The oppressed Catholic Irish to the west watched with cold eyes.

The nightmare pincer move – Catholic Scots from the north, Catholic French from the east, Catholic Irish from the west – was poised to choke Protestant England dead.

Charles Edward and his army hacked through Carlisle and Manchester before halting in Derby. Poised 130 miles from King George's court in London, the Young Pretender hesitated like Hamlet. There were on-the-field cabinet meetings between the prince and his advisers and the clan leaders. To stay or not to stay? That was the question. While he lingered in Derby, London thickened its defences and assembled an army to confront the threat lurking down the road.

The Highland army slept uneasily, stirred by every broken twig and splash of water. Perhaps Charles Edward was waiting for a Catholic English uprising, or for reinforcements from France, but he was left alone with his five thousand men. And then one night, Charles Edward set his army in motion. The soldiers were baffled when the sun rose on the wrong side of the Earth. But nature was in her place: the army was marching north, not south. It was going back to Scotland. It marched through its shoes down to its bare feet. It exhausted its food and marched its stomach empty. Warriors became menacing beggars, relying on hospitality to get through Dumfries and Glasgow by Christmas. The ghost army disintegrated into the misty mountains.

Duc D'Anville's French fleet had not arrived at Dover. The invasion of England was a ruse; the mission had top-secret orders that were only delivered after the expedition had left France and sailed past England. The famished Irish stayed on the Emerald Isle. The Catholic Scots were retreating.

An uneasy relief breathed life into England. A new song was composed for King George II:

> *May he sedition hush*
> *and like a torrent rush*
> *Rebellious Scots to crush.*
> *God save the king.*

George had been rattled to see the Highlanders advance to the door of London. He was not content to let the Highlanders retreat and rearm for a more favourable day. His orders to his army commanders were clear: take or destroy every Highland warrior and then press on to annoy, distress or kill every Scottish savage who had even daydreamed of supporting the Jacobite cause. The traitors were to be rooted out of the land decisively, and forever.

The vanguard of George's forces entered Scotland in January 1746, led by William, the Duke of Cumberland. The twenty-four-year-old was the king's second son. He would never inherit the crown, so he took up the sword and rose swiftly to the top of the armed forces. When recalled from a European war to fight on the homeland, he brought two of his closest allies: Edward Cornwallis, thirty-two, a childhood friend and comrade in the European wars, and James Wolfe, eighteen, son of an army major general and a rising star. Both would benefit from his patronage throughout their careers, which would criss-cross the continents. Cumberland also brought with him a massive, highly trained army. He decided not to take the fight straight to the retreating Highlanders in the winter, but to march his troops past them north to Aberdeen. He was joined by five thousand Hessian soldiers. Cumberland had heard reports of a weakened, hungry Highland army crawling over mountains and staggering down valleys in search of relief. They were on the run and he did not intend to let them run forever.

Cumberland learned from the mistakes at Prestonpans. He drilled his troops in a new approach to battle. The musketeers learned to fire three shots a minute, instead of two. He drilled them to act as one in the face of the Highland Charge. At Prestonpans, the Charge had crushed them as each British soldier was overwhelmed by the long line of Scots in front of him. Cumberland had a new strategy: each soldier would now bayonet the Scot to his right, not the one straight in front of him. If every soldier trusted the man next to him, he would kill a Scot every time a Highlander lifted his sword and exposed his side. He would have to trust the soldier on his left to slice into the exposed warrior attacking his neighbour. It was a bold move.

Peace would not come until the Jacobite army was dismantled body by body. In April, Cumberland decided it was time. Here, now, Cumberland was ready for revenge. The battle was scheduled for April 16 on Culloden Moor, a dreary bog east of Inverness. Inverness was the last bastion, the dwindling capital, of the Highland forces. Cumberland marched his troops to the moor. The weary Highland army waited for the battle to begin.

*   *   *   *   *

Edward Cornwallis woke early on the morning of April 16. He was tired after spending a restless night on the desolate moor. He hated being away from home. Dreams of his soft bed and well-stocked larder back in London fogged his brain. He shook it clear to better focus on the Scottish mist slipping into his tent. He was in good health and ready to prove his mettle. A role in a decisive victory on this remote Highland bog would mean an end to the exile on the outer extremities of King George's glorious realm and a return to the inner court.

Outside his tent, he heard the British army rousing itself and overrunning the river with their voices. Soldiers cursed the chilly spring air and hawked another drop into the soggy ground. A few nursed hangovers and cursed the Highlanders. Others checked and rechecked their muskets and sharpened their bayonets. Tents were struck. Commanders received their orders in writing. As they prepared to march to the battlefield, the general orders of the day were read to every company in the line.

"If any person taking care of the trainhorses or any other horses loaded with tents or general's baggage should abscond or run from them, he or they should be punished with immediate death. If any officer or soldier does not behave according to his duty in his rank and station during the time of engagement, he should be liable to the same punishment," the orders read. "It is quite necessary and prudent to have a regular and strict order preserved so that a finishing period might be put to the scandalous progress of these rebellious vermin."

Cornwallis led his men in a hoarse-throated cheer. Confidence was returning to the disciplined ranks of Red Coats after the disaster at Prestonpans and the long, hurried flight south. The Duke of Cumberland's return from the European war to defend his father's kingdom boosted their morale. Michael Hughes signed up as an eager recruit to reclaim his country and heaped praise upon the Duke. "The most prudent way to quell this vile rebellion would be to follow the traitors and pursue this prowling monster into the land where he was engendered," Hughes wrote. "And who so proper for this undertaking as the Captain General, his Royal Highness the Duke? In whom centre so many distinguishing virtues: noble generosity and honour, firm courage, great good nature and affability, sagacity, experience, activity and temperance?"[1]

---

1 Hughes, Michael. A Plain Narrative and Authentic Journal of the Late Rebellion. London: Henry Whitridge, 1747. Page 30.

Cumberland's troops agreed. Today they were well fed, well armed and half hopeful, but fear still chilled their bones. It had been a ghastly year tangling with the armies of Charles Edward. Before Prestonpans, the Red Coats had racked up a string of easy wins and began to think themselves categorically better than any opposition. War became a path for glory and promotion. But the ragged Scots had pierced that armour and sent the British running.

On paper, the battle at Culloden Moor read like Goliath versus an infant David. The British troops were some of the best soldiers in the world, confident after a string of victories. The Highlanders were a bedraggled army of tenant farmers, misfits and outcasts. Some Highlanders fought for their would-be king, some for their clan, but just as many had been dragooned into service. They were hungry, but not for war.

To most Englishmen, the Highlanders were a race apart, speaking an incomprehensible, dying Gaelic tongue, worshiping the foreign Pope and armed with primitive swords, rusty guns, dull dirks and thin shields. Isolated from the modern world by the mountains, in 1746 they still fought like it was 746. From their kilts to their red hair to their raucous dances, they were a people apart from modernity. Cornwallis believed his king had offered them peaceable admission to his benign rule and it had been violently rejected. Instead, the Highlanders wanted to force everyone to live in their shabby past. As the Jacobite rebellion dragged on, anti-Highlander views gained currency. They were branded savages, and therefore beyond the protection of the law. A popular song printed in the London *Evening Post* called them "Sons of Murder" and the direct descendants of the original murderer, Cain. The song denigrated men, but was also aimed at Highland women and children.

Cornwallis, stationed at Edinburgh and Stirling, was in the thick of the uprising. Like all the British army, he was sick of the Scots' running to avoid a fair fight and eager to use his muskets, cannon, bayonets and cavalry. Cornwallis heard soldiers cursing the Highlanders and vowing to disembowel the rebellion.

Cornwallis dressed in his uniform and walked outside into the drizzly dawn. He spotted his commander, the Duke of Cumberland, barking orders to his subordinates. Sitting atop his stout horse, the portly duke lifted his hat above his wig. It had been his twenty-fifth birthday yesterday and he had celebrated with copious brandy, bread and cheese for all the men.

He had slept like a stone in a nearby home loaned to him by the local earl.

"My brave boys, we have but one march more and all our labour is at an end. Sit down at your tent doors and be alert to take your arms," Cumberland called out as soldiers came to attention.

The men cheered him on, tossing their hats on their bayonets.

Cumberland had not fought at Prestonpans, but he had suffered a stinging defeat of his own that same year during the Battle of Fontenoy in Belgium. On May 11, 1745, Cumberland had entered the battlefield in Flanders with Cornwallis and Wolfe at his side. They joined the 50,000 British, Dutch and Hanoverian troops to take on the 70,000-strong French army. It had been a disaster. Cornwallis was fighting under a Colonel Craig, but Craig was killed early and Cornwallis had taken over. The Dutch and the Hanoverians quickly gave up and fled the field, leaving the British to cover their retreat. Cornwallis's troops staved off total annihilation, but there were no parades awaiting them in England. Of the 18,000 British soldiers who fought, 2,800 were killed and 4,000 wounded. Cornwallis's regiment, the 20th, lost Craig, seven other officers and 385 men. An expensive failure. The troops were scorned back in England. People wanted miracles – they wanted 18,000 English soldiers to outnumber 70,000 French. The streets were aflutter in chapbooks mocking Cornwallis, Cumberland and the other commanders.

Cornwallis reasoned that at least those who knew about war appreciated what they had accomplished in trying circumstances. He was summoned before the king and given a prominent position in George's court as Groom of His Majesty's Bedchamber. By the end of the year, he was promoted to lieutenant colonel of the 20th Regiment and that fall was posted to Scotland under the command of Cumberland to handle the Jacobite uprising.

Cumberland had learned his lesson from the disaster at the retreat from Flanders. He ran a tight army in Scotland. There was no gambling and the duke frequently had men flogged for selling parts of their uniform and threatened them with hanging if they sold any of their food rations. Women were banned from the camp and sentries were ordered to stand at their posts, rather than sit as was the custom. Any signs of disobedience were dealt with swiftly. Three soldiers defied orders and broke into a home in Aberdeen, robbing the occupant. Two were hanged and the third escaped only by playing his politics right and getting a pardon as he stood on the scaffolding. Any soldier who left the camp without permission faced execution.

When a boy of seventeen loitering around the camp was discovered to be a rebel spy, he was dragged to the scaffolding and a noose placed round his neck. The floor gave away and as he dangled and strangled, a Scottish Protestant minister raced into the encampment and pleaded with the duke to spare the boy's life.

"He had not lately been acquainted with the rebels and was naturally but a poor, simple youth whom they deluded away," the minister pleaded.[2]

Cumberland, in a show of mercy, ordered the boy be spared. He had already hung for ten minutes, but the executioner cut him down and stupidly watched as he crashed to the ground. The boy was cut in the fall and bled profusely, but sprang to his feet and staggered away from the scaffold.

When it came time for battle on Culloden Moor, the English troops were a disciplined force under Cumberland. Cornwallis watched as rays of sunlight broke through the clouds in shafts, sending beams of light roving over the mountaintops. It was as if God Himself were scanning the hills in search of the ghostly rebel army. The bog squished under his feet. He was glad he wouldn't be on the front lines.

As Cornwallis discussed the battle plan with the other commanders, the Highland army got up to its old tricks. The surprise attack had worked at Prestonpans, so Charles Edward ordered a platoon of Scots on a ten-mile march through the woods to outflank the English. They had left in the middle of the night, intending to secure a sneak attack before dawn that would stagger King George's forces before the battle had begun. In fact, they surprised only themselves. They got lost, fell down, got muddy, lost daggers and ran into stone walls and each other in the dark. In the early morning hours, it became clear the sneak attack wasn't going to work. The platoon marched back to the battlefield.

Exhausted, they rejoined the main army on the moor. Tired, hungry and fatalistic, the rebels stood on a little hill waiting for the Red Coats. The British heard their chilling war cries well before they saw them. Cumberland's soldiers slipped seamlessly into battle formation and advanced. At times the bog rose to their knees, but they marched calmly until the Highlanders were in front of them. English drums beat, battling in the air with the Scottish bagpipes. Flags flew on both sides. Cornwallis

---

2 Hughes, Michael. Page 35.

watched from the rear as the Red Coats took their position on the battlefield. He took pleasure in their professionalism. Everyone was spaced equally distant from the men next to and behind them. If they were scared, it didn't show. They had a job to do, and they'd do it.

Charles Edward, watching from behind the front lines, was banking entirely on the audacity of another hopeful Highland Charge. "I have fully experienced your conduct, loyalty and valour, both at Prestonpans and at Falkirk," Charles Edward shouted to his troops.[3] "I must without flattery assure ye that it is my opinion the affair will be desperate and bloody – bloody, especially, as I am persuaded that you all abhor to be taken prisoners by them."

The would-be king said help was on its way from France and awaiting only fair weather to land. "Therefore if you had rather stay for the reinforcement, I am far from urging what may seem hasty or imprudent. But as your own judgment is to prevail, I entirely depend on your great affection, abilities and courage."

His Highland troops answered by throwing their bonnets in the air and shouting, "God bless the king and Prince Charles!"

There would be no more waiting.

Cumberland, mounted atop a majestic warhorse, spoke to his men at the rear of the English position. The commanders stayed out of the fray to preserve their safety and to hold an overview of the battle.

"My gentlemen and fellow soldiers: Though the time is short, yet I think proper to observe that you are now going to engage in defence of your King and country, your liberties, properties and religion. By the justice of our cause, I make no doubt of leading you onto a sure victory. Stand firm, and your enemies will soon fly before you. But if any among you through fear are diffident of their courage and behaviour, which I have not the least reason to suspect, or if any other through conscience or inclination cannot be zealous or alert in performing their duties, it is my desire that all such would immediately leave us," he said.[4]

The soldiers scanned their ranks for any faint-hearted men. There were none.

"I declare they shall have my free pardon, for I would rather be at the head of 1,000 brave, resolute men than 10,000 among which there are some who by cowardice or misbehaviour may dispirit and disorder the

---

3 Hughes, Michael. Page 43.
4 Hughes, Michael. Page 43.

troops and bring dishonour to an army under my command," Cumberland continued.

No soldier left. Instead, a loud roar lifted their spirits and they cheered their leader. Cumberland retreated to his vantage point commanding the battlefield and gave the order to begin.

At noon, Charles Edward ordered his cannon to fire, starting the fight. The balls roared through the air and spat up dirt at the English feet. King George's forces played for time as they dragged their own cannons through the mud to the front lines. The weather began to clear even as the war smoke filled the air.

The English gunners opened fire on the Highland army. At first, the Jacobite rebels stood still. Balls caved in chests, knocked brains from heads and blew arms from bodies, but the rebel commanders were silent.

"What are they doing? Is this some new tactic? A decoy?" the English wondered.

The British shook their heads as the Scots stood still for fatal minutes, dying in large number. Finally, nerves frayed, and the disturbed Highland army charged without orders. The smooth front line disintegrated as the warriors screamed across the moor toward the impassive government troops, who gunned them down as fast as they could reload: three shots a minute. Cornwallis felt his own nerve shaking as the Highlanders kept charging – if enough Scots could survive the onslaught, they could overrun the British again and win.

But one side of the clan lines hit a bog while the other sprinted across dry land. The far right of the Highland lines ran into a stone wall and soon The Charge churned into itself. The British kept firing. When the swarming Highlanders finally reached the government lines, the new bayonet strategy worked with lethal efficiency and the Scottish wedge was sliced apart. They were no longer an army, but a mob. The government troops kept firing. The Charge collapsed. The Highlanders found themselves stranded without reinforcements, staring down the barrels and bayonets of British guns. The bravest kept charging as individuals, and took their last breaths face down in the bog. The survivors were herded into an enclosing horseshoe of Red Coats and slaughtered. Over the next three minutes, seven hundred were shot. The survivors staggered in the gunsmoke, tripping over fresh corpses. The Highlanders turned and ran. The muskets chased them down, followed by Cumberland's composed men.

Bonnie Prince Charlie watched the slaughter from his command position three miles to the rear of the battle. When it was clear his army would be defeated, he fled. He would eventually elude the British by disguising himself as a woman and slipping away to France. The fate of those left at Culloden was a bad one. After the Highlanders capable of standing had been shot dead, and after the Highlanders capable of fleeing had fled, the Red Coats marched through the smoking fields and murdered everything that moved. Cumberland, patrolling the battlefield and scanning the distance with a spyglass, spotted a group of rebels in consultation. But it soon was clear they weren't planning a rally, but only trying to find a safe retreat.

A deserting Scot staggered out of the smoke and begged for mercy. He was unarmed and of possible intelligence value, so was taken into custody. But the apparent deserter picked up a firearm and shot at a British commander. The gun failed to fire and the Highlander was shot dead on the spot.

"Have mercy," another Highlander pleaded in broken English as he lay bleeding in the mud. Mercy was given: a bayonet to the heart. Red Coats roamed Culloden Moor, stabbing Highlanders to death, shooting them, or kicking them until they stopped twitching.

Cumberland ordered no quarter be given; each injured clansman was to be clubbed or shot to death. His brutal suppression of the rebellion earned him a nickname he cherished: The Butcher.

Two English soldiers stood over a moaning Highlander covered in blood and the rags of his kilt. One was white-faced and his hands trembled as he held the bayonet in the air.

"I can't do it," he whimpered.

"Don't think of them as human beings. You can't think of them as human beings," the older man said. "We know these dogs from Prestonpans. They must be slaughtered or they will rise again."

The young soldier nodded, raised his bayonet, and plunged it into the Highlander's heart.[5] It was just before one p.m. The battle had taken only forty-five minutes.

---

5 "Culloden: The Jacobites' Last Stand." *Battlefield Britain*. Dir. Ian Lilley. Presenters Peter and Dan Snow. BBC Two, April 17, 2004. Television.

Cumberland chased the warriors into the Highlands. The Scots blew up their ammunition stores and abandoned Stirling. The remnant army overran the lightly guarded British barracks in Perth, forcing them to join the rebellion. "They exercised their shocking cruelty upon four soldiers, who being strict to their oath of allegiance and refusing to take arms with the rebels against their own sovereign King George, the Scots forcibly put them down alive into a deep well, where they continued until his Royal Highness came there," Hughes recorded.[6]

Cumberland found the soldiers dead. He retrieved their bodies and buried them.

The Highlanders fled further north.

Cumberland followed. His army destroyed roads, broke bridges, chased off livestock and made life unlivable for every person in northern Scotland. He ordered his troops to press on.

---

6 Hughes, Michael. Page 28.

2

The Pacification of the Scottish Highlands

The road to Inverness was strewn with bodies. Locals had come out to watch the battle on Culloden Moor. Never doubting the Highland army would win, they came out to cheer the victory. When fortune turned on them, so did the English army. Cumberland sent word down: the rebels owed a great debt to King George for months of rape, murder and cruelty. It was time to pay. The unarmed civilians were killed with the same energy as armed soldiers.

Edward Cornwallis commanded an army unit of 320 men into the mountainous region of northern Scotland in what became known as the Pacification. Cumberland made it clear that whether a person had been forced to quarter Charles Edward's soldiers or did so out of loyalty to the Pretender was of no concern to him. Treason was treason. There was no distinction between an active rebel and a passive supporter. One fed the other. The orders came directly from London: the entire Highland way of life was now illegal and punishable by death. Scots were prohibited from wearing or owning kilts, tartans, broadswords, playing music or speaking Gaelic. The clan system was dismantled by gunfire.

Cumberland assigned the task to his most trusted allies: Cornwallis, who had fought with him in Fontenoy; John Campbell, the Earl of Loudon, who later commanded the British army in North America; James Wolfe, who would conquer Quebec; William Blakeney, whom Cornwallis would one day attempt to rescue from Minorca; and Humphrey Bland, whom Cornwallis would eventually replace as governor of Gibraltar.

Loudon, who had strong Highland connections, worried about the indiscriminate punishment. He said he could not tell an armed Jacobite rebel hiding in a home from a loyal Highlander armed to defend his home. "The distinction between these classes of men in point of guilt or innocence is too fine for me to observe," he wrote.[7] But that did not bother most of the English army as it assaulted the Highlands.

In Fort Augustus, Cumberland set up a field headquarters with Loudon. The rebels had destroyed every building they encountered on their hasty retreat, so the British troops constructed a fine hut with doors and glass windows, covered on top with green sods and boughs. "His Royal Highness resembles a shepherd's life more than a courier," Michael Hughes remarked.

As spring warmed the cold hills, the fleeing rebel army was uprooted from the land. Freed from any serious resistance, the British army went from glen to glen, village to village and door to door. Sometimes they knocked, sometimes they kicked the doors in. "Are you a Jacobite?" they'd ask. If the answer was yes, the man was executed on the spot. If he denied it, the house was ransacked. Any sign of disloyalty – a crucifix, a kilt, a look in the eye – and the inhabitants were shot. Whole villages were burned. Clan leaders were hunted down and executed. Rape was used as a punitive measure, and to discourage future rebellion. As Scotland had no standing army, the Highland men could only fight by leaving their families unprotected. They would be less likely to leave home to fight English soldiers if they feared their wives and daughters would be raped while they were away. Both Wolfe and Loudon encouraged sexual assault as the most effective way to force men to abandon Charles Edward.

"A body of troops may make a diversion by laying waste to a country that the male inhabitants have left to prosecute rebellious schemes. How soon must they return to the defense of their property (such as it is), their wives, their children, their houses and their cattle!" Wolfe wrote.[8]

British forces moved into Inverness and liberated imprisoned soldiers, setting them loose for revenge. Inverness had been sure of a rebel win, so the town was well stocked with booze and food intended for the celebration. The British made sure it did not go to waste. Those who had sided with the rebels were rounded up to face a court martial. Thirty prominent

---

7 Plank, Geoffrey. *Rebellion and Savagery*. Philadelphia: University of Pennsylvania Press, 2005. Page 61.
8 Plank, Geoffrey. Page 63.

Jacobites were strung up and hanged for all to see. Lesser men were whipped to death.

English soldiers marauded across the mountains, leaving smoking ruins and screaming children. Still smarting from Prestonpans, they destroyed everything they could find. Barefoot children were ordered off their ancestral land and forced to flee alone across the moors while their fathers were executed and their mothers raped. Grandmothers were run down in the open fields and bayoneted to death. Grandfathers were hacked to pieces and left to rot in bogs. The English drummers marched deeper into the remote regions of Scotland, filling Highland hearts with dark terror. In the end, it didn't matter whether a Scot had fought, been neutral, or staunchly supported the British king: everyone was punished. "The only good Highlander is a dead Highlander," repeated many an English soldier.

A few bands of half-starved clansmen tried to resist, running ineffective ambushes on the imperial troops, but it was rocks against cannon fire and the rebels were slaughtered as quickly as they charged. The millennial-old way of life was cleansed off the land in the Pacification. Near Fort Augustus, a dozen Highlanders – men, women and their children – were herded into a house. The doors were barred and the soldiers set fire to it. The screaming boiled through the crackling inferno as the soldiers helped themselves to the unburned property. Those English soldiers who didn't have the heart for slaughter would sometimes burn damp hay to make it look like the village had been torched. They'd then march back to their commander and hope their faces betrayed nothing.

Cumberland broke up his army into smaller, more agile units. He sent Cornwallis, then a lieutenant colonel, and the 320 men he commanded into the western Highlands to destroy the houses and people in the lands belonging to the Camerons and the MacDonalds of Moidart and Knoidart, from Loch Arkaig to north of the River Lochy. He gave instructions to Cornwallis: "You have my full command to plunder, burn and destroy through all the west part of Invernessshire called Lochaber, from the Glens above Knoidart down to Arafack, Moidart and Swenard. You have positive orders to bring no more prisoners to the camp."

Cornwallis prepared his light brigade for the hills. They carried nothing but guns and ammunition. They would hunt for the rest. This gave the men a strong motivation to sack and pillage each outpost they encountered. He took his troops out of Fort Augustus in the late afternoon of a cloudy, dull summer day. He was instructed to "clear everything" through the area near Fort Williams. In later years, Cornwallis's operation was remembered as one of unrestrained violence.[9] Scottish men were killed merely for looking away when they saw his soldiers coming; it was taken as a sign of guilt. Others were summarily executed because weapons were found in their houses.

The writer and army volunteer Michael Hughes travelled with him. "The mountains here are as high and frightful as the Alps in Italy. We have nothing pleasant to behold except the sky," he recorded. "'Tis rainy, cold and sharp weather for nine months of the year, and the other quarter can never be called good."

Cornwallis's soldiers, still buzzing from the victory, marched through the bogs. He ordered his men to set loose cattle and chase them off to destroy that food resource for any remaining rebels. It destroyed the food source for entire villages, too. The only hope of escape for any Scottish person was full surrender. When the Macdonalds' Clan of Glengarry came to lay down their arms before the duke, all seventy-two were pardoned.

"Cornwallis is a brave officer of great humanity and honour," Hughes wrote as they marched down Old Wade's Road to the southwest.

Cornwallis led his troops through the mountains along a stony path and for a further twenty miles along the shore of Loch Lochy. They intended to march all night, but a great rain brought them to a halt. They made a rough camp among some deserted huts and slept fitfully for two hours before marching on to Mucomir, where the River Spean entered the loch. They turned northeast toward Achnacarry, home of the chiefs of Clan Cameron. As the sun rose on a wet day, the columns of soldiers passed through the tranquil oak groves to the very clearing where Locheil's clan had gathered to start the resistance to Britain.

Cornwallis ordered his men to stop. The morning mist hid sections of the land. Maybe the rebels were hiding in the hills, ready to come down for a grisly vengeance.

"Oh God, it's them!" a young soldier cried as the mist lifted to reveal a mass of Highland warriors clad in plaid with their broadswords glinting in the dawn light. The warriors advanced, before stopping suddenly. Cornwallis's troops tensed for battle. A Highland officer broke ranks and rode over to confer with Cornwallis. He identified himself and Cornwallis smiled. He told his men to stand easy: the red saltires on the Highlander bonnets showed they were the Munros of Culcairn's militia, Scottish

---

9 Plank, Geoffrey. Page 67.

soldiers who had sided with the British king. The difference was not easily spotted. Culcairn's militia had also been rebel hunting. The two detachments joined platoons and marched straight to the heart of the Cameron territory, home to Donald Cameron, the old man who led the rebellion from these hills. The soldiers stormed in the front door and found his residence empty. It was ransacked and Cornwallis ordered the troops to set fire to the entire estate. It burned for days, eating up all of the Cameron wealth. In the grim light that filtered through the falling ashes, Cornwallis instructed his men to dismantle the fruit garden and set fire to the summer house.

As Cornwallis led his men onward, burning houses, driving off cattle and shooting vagrants found in the mountains, a cry came up from the rear ranks.

"Come out here, you dirty Jacobite bastard!" a soldier shouted. Cornwallis turned to look. A filthy old man was hauled out of the blackened stones of a ruined hut. Soon a second was found and both were dragged before Cornwallis. Later sources identified them as Lochiel's gardener and cook.

Lochiel was reputed to be among the richest of the clan leaders, but little of value had been found in the raids. Cornwallis demanded the captives turn over the wealth. One man said there wasn't any wealth left, while the other pleaded for mercy in Gaelic. The old Highlanders shook with fear, but did not or could not tell the Englishman where the gold, silver and jewels were. Cornwallis ordered the old men to be flogged. The two were handed over to the drummers, who took turns whipping them until their flayed backs were more blood than skin. The captives were put in irons and sent to Inverness for a worse fate.

Cornwallis marched his platoon back into the hills, the smoke of Achnacarry still casting a dark cloud over the ruins. All houses and huts on the way were torched, the inhabitants chased into fields and shot. That night, Cornwallis and his men camped at Loch Arkaig. One soldier spotted a boat on the shore and a group investigated but found only a large, black stone and started back for the main camp. On the way, they encountered a scraggly man with a thick beard. The man, aged about sixty, had just turned the bend in the road and acted as though stillness would make him invisible. He had his cap in his hands, as though he were begging for alms. "That they might not return without some gallant action ... they shot him," a Presbyterian minister named John Cameron recorded.[10]

Further down the road, Cornwallis's soldiers encountered an old beggar woman blind in one eye. They demanded money and intelligence about the Highland army. She stared without comprehension before starting to speak in Gaelic. Halfway through the first sentence, she was shoved to the muddy ground. The soldiers lifted her dirty clothes and raped her before murdering her. That story also reached Cameron, a chaplain at Fort William, and made him weak. "What is reported to have been done to her before she was dead, I incline not to repeat – things shocking to human nature," he wrote.

The troops marched on. A scout spotted two young men carrying dung to their sickly fields and ordered them to come before Cornwallis. The men stopped still, dropped the dung, and walked to him. As they approached, one turned to look back at his field. He was shot dead. Later two rebels approached the camp in feigned surrender, but quickly opened fire. They were captured and after thirty minutes ordered executed. They refused to kneel or to cover their faces with caps, so were shot on their feet.

All through that long, dreary summer, Cornwallis's Red Coats marched up and down hills, burning and looting villages, raping and murdering as they went. In Moidart, Cornwallis met up with his old friend, Lord George Sackville, himself at the head of 480 men, and they joined forces. Cornwallis and Sackville celebrated the merger with a convivial evening. The two shared aristocratic roots and a bond that was forged in Fontenoy. Sackville walked with a limp, a leftover gift from Flanders. In fact, Cornwallis noted he was still wearing the coat he had been shot in. As the joined forces marched on, a commotion broke out at the rear of the English lines. A group of Highlanders had emerged from the muck and made off with Sackville's bedding, linen, clothes and provisions. Sackville's men chased them, but they slipped away into the dark hills.

At the next hamlet, Cornwallis and Sackville sent troops in to clear out the houses and assemble the Scots in the open fields. The men were bound and controlled by one group of English soldiers while another handled the women. Their plaid dresses were torn off and they were raped, one by one, in front of their husbands and sons. When the British troops had had their fill, they buttoned up their pants and hauled the weeping

---

10 Prebble, John. *Culloden*. London: Secker & Warburg, 1961. Page 208.

women to their feet. The rapists then held them while their colleagues shot and bayoneted every man and boy in the village. Then they killed the women.

After two weeks, Cornwallis led his men back to Fort Augustus. There was not a living person or head of cattle within fifty miles. His section of the Highlands had been well and truly cleared.

Those who had signed on only to quash the rebellion were discharged; others accepted generous terms to stay on to finish the job. The booty was split and the men were paid and sent back to London to resume their lives. Michael Hughes returned to his old job as a weaver and published his account of the Pacification.

"The rebellion being extinguished by the spirit, vigilance and conduct of our renowned illustrious young hero, this wonderful event must give joy to all who love the Protestant religion and settlement, British laws and British liberty," Hughes wrote in the last paragraph of his notebook. "Record His Royal Highness, William Duke of Cumberland, as another deliverer of his country, a second William, Great Britain's glory and defender."

Cornwallis was appointed one of the judges overseeing the courts martial of the British officers who had surrendered forts in the Highlands in the early stages of the Jacobite uprising. William Blakeney, First Baron of Blakeney, served as presiding judge. Historians have noted that British military officers were under intense pressure to perform and open to severe punishment for a range of misbehaviours. Anyone who had negotiated with the enemy was punished, as were lapses in judgment, incompetence and cowardice. Whether the officers were found guilty or acquitted determined if they would face punishment, but the mere fact that they had faced a court martial was a stinging disgrace that hobbled most of them throughout their careers.

When the Pacification was complete, Cornwallis returned to London. Others stayed behind to set in motion the multi-generational Highland Clearances.

*   *   *   *   *

The events known as the Highland Clearances drove thousands of peasants off their land and stripped them of any wealth. Many boarded boats sailing for the New World, where they arrived as penniless indentured servants, slaves and beggars. The harsh conditions at sea killed many on the bleak ocean crossing. The anti-revolutionary purge continued for decades, destroying the Highland way of life. Culloden would stand as the final land battle fought in Britain.

Sir George MacKenzie of Coul, a landowner in the Highlands, put forward the British rationale for the clearance policy, which he called the Improvements. Writing two generations after the Pacification, Coul said the Improvements allowed landlords to remove human tenants and replace them with profitable sheep. He wrote disparagingly of the Highlanders. "They live in the midst of filth and smoke. That is their choice. They will yet find themselves happier and more comfortable in the capacity of servants to substantial tenants than in their present situation."[11]

The Scottish writer Donald McLeod etched some of the scenes in his 1841 book, *Gloomy Memories in the Highlands of Scotland*. He took a different view of the Clearances. "The consternation and confusion were extreme. Little or no time was given for the removal of persons or property; the people striving to remove the sick and the helpless before the fire should reach them; next, struggling to save the most valuable of their effects. The cries of the women and children, the roaring of the affrighted cattle, hunted at the same time by the yelling dogs of the shepherds amid the smoke and fire, altogether presented a scene that completely baffles description it required to be seen to be believed," he wrote.[12]

"A dense cloud of smoke enveloped the whole country by day, and even extended far out to sea. At night an awfully grand but terrific scene presented itself – all the houses in an extensive district in flames at once. I myself ascended a height about eleven o'clock in the evening, and counted two hundred and fifty blazing houses, many of the owners of which I personally knew, but whose present condition – whether in or out of the flames – I could not tell. The conflagration lasted six days, till the whole of the dwellings were reduced to ashes or smoking ruins. During one of these days a boat actually lost her way in the dense smoke as she

---

11 MacKenzie, Sir George, of Coul. *A General View of the Agriculture of Ross and Cromarty.* London: George Ramsay & Co., 1810.
12 McLeod, Donald. *Gloomy Memories in the Highlands of Scotland.* Glasgow: A. Sinclair, 1841. Page 16.

approached the shore, but at night was enabled to reach a landing-place by the lurid light of the flames."[13]

The Highland Clearances, known to the Highlanders as *Fuadach nan Gaidheal* (the Expulsion of the Gaels), rolled over Scotland in waves until the 1850s. Thousands of Scots were forced to flee. Many made new homes in a distant British colony called Nova Scotia – New Scotland.

---

13 McLeod, Donald. Page 16.

3

Growing up with a King

Edward Cornwallis returned to London in high spirits. Culloden had
been a massive success – better, surely, than even the most optimis-
tic Englishman could have hoped for. While the French still menaced from
across the Channel and troubles were brewing in the colonies overseas, a
relief lightened England. The terror the kilted Highlanders had stirred up
with their march toward London – and the carnage they surely would have
brought with them – had been removed with a summer job. After decades
of unrest, the Jacobite uprising was crushed. After Cornwallis's key role
in putting down the Scottish insurrection, King George again smiled upon
him. He and the other commanders of the North British troops received
the thanks of the government for their work.

For the next three years, Cornwallis served the king faithfully in
Whitehall. He mostly worked as a diplomatic courier travelling between
London and The Hague, though he retained his military rank and post.
While no complaints are recorded regarding his diplomatic service, he ran
into military trouble. His unruly regiment became nearly mutinous and the
physical stress wore him down. He resigned his regimental post in 1748.
The king accepted his resignation and appointed James Wolfe to take his
place. Wolfe soon had the regiment back under control and was highly
commended by the war department.

As Cornwallis contemplated his future, he thought also of his past. His life had started off with such promise he'd hardly been able to keep pace. He was born February 22, 1713, in London, England. His father Charles was the fourth Baron Cornwallis and his mother was Lady Charlotte; both were descended from earls and dukes. King Charles I created the Cornwallis family peerage in 1627. It made the family part of the British nobility and was a reward for the support his fellow Protestants had given him during religiously tumultuous times of near constant wars with Catholic claimants to the throne. The Cornwallis wealth continued to grow with income generated by the large estates they owned in Suffolk and the Channel Islands. The family's Protestant faith kept them in tight with successive royals, except for the Catholic Stuarts. Family fortunes rocketed again when the German Hanoverians pushed the Stuarts off the throne the year after Edward was born. Shortly before Edward was born, his parents had acquired a home in London's Leicester Square to bring them closer to the royal court. The king also had a home on Leicester Square and his sons, including Cumberland, were raised there.

Charles Cornwallis's sixth son didn't come alone. Charlotte gave birth to identical twin boys: Frederick and Edward. Both were described as sallow, unathletic boys. "They are as alike in body and mind and of so marked a resemblance to each other that it was difficult at times to know them asunder," remarked Cole, an antiquary and social historian of the court.[14] They were described as differing in personality. Frederick was always gregarious and outgoing, while Edward was aloof. They both became royal pages at twelve and formed a fraternity with the inner circle of imperial power. The boys worked at Windsor and Hampton palaces for two years. Despite the differences in them, many at the court imagined they were prankster twins. Both were assured of a bright future when their family friend was crowned King George II when the twins were fourteen. At sixteen, the boys went to the private school Eton, training grounds for the rulers of Britain. It was clear at least one of the brothers would go into the military, and the other would likely enter the church, but neither set a particularly high bar for physical prowess to claim the military berth. The matter was decided when Frederick lost his balance, fell, and paralyzed his right arm.

---

14 MacDonald, James. *Hon Edward Cornwallis, founder of Halifax*. Halifax, Nova Scotia: The McAlpine Publishing Company, 1905.

His parents channelled Frederick into the church and Edward went into the army. At eighteen, Cornwallis joined the 47th Foot in Canterbury, where he first served his childhood friend, the Duke of Cumberland. This kept him close to military power, and close to royal power, as his garrison duty meant he rarely left London. At twenty-one, he was made a lieutenant; three years later he obtained his own company and was transferred to the 20th Foot. He worked at Whitehall for five long years, paying his dues in the diplomatic service and regularly ferrying between The Hague and London. When his older brother Stephen died in 1744, Edward was given the family's political seat in Parliament as the member for Eye in Suffolk. That took him right into the heart of power – the War Office.

At thirty-one, his career seemed guaranteed a steady accumulation of power and wealth. His success in Scotland cemented his place near the king. Frederick, meanwhile, was having a grand time in the clerical life. He was ordained a priest at age twenty-nine and married one of London's most sought-after women. In 1746, Frederick became King George II's personal chaplain. The twins' careers seemed destined to mirror each other all the way to the top.

4

Dispatched to the New World to Establish a New City

Cornwallis's next appointment in 1749 was to take him far from the throne. His king was sending him across the ocean to an obscure province rapidly becoming important as the British-French war shifted its focus from Europe to North America. Cornwallis was to found a new fortress city in Nova Scotia to entrench George's claim to the land. Despite the name of "New Scotland," there were in fact few Scots in the province. At the time, the Scots who had made it to the New World were mostly Lowland Protestants and did not sport kilts or Jacobite sympathies, although later phases of the Clearances would populate the northern parts of the province with dispossessed Highlanders. The name was a relic from the reign of King James I. James, the son of Mary Stuart, was a Scot – the Protestant king of Scotland who united the realms upon his accession to the throne of England and Ireland in 1603. He acquiesced to the request of a poet friend, William Alexander, who wished for a New Scotland to join New England and New France. James Latinized it and decried a plot of unseen land to be the rightful property of the men Sir William would gather there. A handful of disastrous missions to plant a colony ended in starvation, plague or massacre. Nothing much came of Nova Scotia, apart from Fort Anne in the southwest.

Cornwallis was briefed on the province's background. The land had long been disputed by France and England, but the matter was largely resolved with the Treaty of Utrecht in 1713. In it, Britain and France officially stated that Nova Scotia was British, and that island off its northern edge, Île Royale (now Cape Breton), was French. But in fact, since France built the powerful fortress Louisbourg on the island, they ruled the whole peninsula. In 1745, a group from New England headed by Captain John Gorham captured the fort. It was an astonishing win for the semi-autonomous colonials and they felt bitterly betrayed when Britain handed their trophy back to France in 1748. To appease the colonialists, and to bolster Britain's claim to Nova Scotia, Cornwallis's job was to build a rival fortress city on the Nova Scotia mainland that would become a bulwark against French aggression and a bastion for King George's domination of the entire continent. For years, King George had been so focused on the immediate threat from Scotland and France that he had neglected his overseas ventures. But since Culloden, the king found himself with too many soldiers and not enough land, so he started sending them to the frontier front lines to fight proxy wars with France in the New World.

Nova Scotia was unlike the colonies in Virginia and Massachusetts, which the British had always viewed as plantations. Nova Scotia was a military outpost, the first land Britain had taken from France in the New World. It had a small British population, a sizable French Acadian population, and an unknown number of Mi'kmaq natives. The intellectual elite of Britain debated how to handle Nova Scotia. Some looked to Ireland, England's colony across the Irish Sea, as a model for military power mixed with an imported settler population. Detractors of that approach said the complicating presence of Acadians and Mi'kmaq made that model untenable. Others argued the Acadians and natives would have to be enslaved or reduced to a tributary people to ensure British control.

The debate had not been resolved when Cornwallis was sent to establish the new capital in May 1749. His masters were reluctant to build alliances with the Acadians and Mi'kmaq, but also reluctant to engage in the costly option of war. So the empire blundered along on its outer reaches, the tiller of state left in the hands of hundreds of local governors, as each sought a mix of violence and friendliness to consolidate King George II's hold on a growing realm.

Where exactly Cornwallis founded this city was to be left to his judgment, but he was made aware that the king favoured the harbour known as Chebucto. The French had often visited the area and had full plans to build a settlement on an island in the harbour in 1711. Those plans didn't get off the drawing board until 1746 with the ill-fated Duc D'Anville expedition.

This was the same D'Anville whose army had massed on the coast of France at the height of the Jacobite rising and threatened to wipe out the Protestant British throne by joining Charles Edward's army as it advanced to Derby. English intelligence had been half right. There was an enormous army at Brest that set sail for Great Britain in May 1746. Every single soldier and sailor on board believed the invasion of England had begun – everyone except Duc D'Anville. He had secret orders to sail past England, past Ireland, and on to the Americas. The plan was for his fleet to rendezvous in Chebucto harbour with a French squadron from the West Indies and support from allies and Indians in Quebec and the local Acadians. The armada would then attempt to capture Fort Anne at Annapolis and sweep along the eastern seaboard to burn Boston to the ground and lay waste to every English settlement on the coast. If successful, D'Anville would have stolen England's American colonies.

Duc D'Anville's flotilla had sailed out of France in full pomp, but out on the Atlantic Ocean, the wind went out of his sails. Becalmed, the fleet bobbed without direction, eating through their supplies, dying of typhus and scurvy. Periodically, the calm turned to storm and spun the ships around, sending more men to their deaths. The fleet spent the entire summer of 1746 inching across the ocean before staggering to Sable Island off the Nova Scotia coast in September. The Graveyard of the Atlantic took a few more ships to its bosom. When the weather finally cleared, less than half of the original fleet was able to sail on for Chebucto. The support from Quebec, led by Du Vignan and the Catholic priest Jean-Louis Le Loutre, had arrived in early summer, as per instructions, and found only water, woods and the Mi'kmaq allies. They all waited, but decided D'Anville was not coming. The Quebec forces went on to France and the Mi'kmaq back to their normal lives. The West Indies contingent turned up later still, found Chebucto unoccupied, and so split up, returning to the islands or to France.

When the D'Anville fleet listed into the harbour on September 10, there was no one to greet them. They sailed through the long entrance to the harbour, spotting only brief glimpses of the Mi'kmaq in the woods. The Frenchmen on board were a starved, diseased rump of the mighty force that had left France four months earlier. On a bitterly cold September 27, 1746, D'Anville's officers were gathered in the expansive basin at the end of the harbour. The situation was desperate. D'Anville had died suddenly at three a.m. His officers said it was due to apoplexy, but crewmen said it was suicide by poison.

Another handful of French ships limped into Chebucto later that day. Their commander, Vice-Admiral D'Estourmel, was given control of the entire mission. He wanted to go home, but others wanted to stay for the winter. D'Estourmel lost the argument and responded by locking himself in his cabin and impaling himself on his sword. "Gentlemen, I beg pardon of God and King for what I have done," he said. (D'Estourmel survived his unsuccessful suicide attempt, and returned to Paris where he died in 1765.) Command dropped down another rung. The fleet crawled to the back of Bedford Basin and huddled at Birch Cove. There, they died in the hundreds. Desperately hungry, weakened by disease and shivering in the cold, men dropped dead on deck and were dumped into the harbour. They died on the stony shores and were pushed underwater. They died in the forests and were buried. In the end, there were too many bodies and too few among the living to bury them, and the bodies rotted where they fell. In October, the last five floating ships were stocked with the living. The abandoned ships were burned in the harbour. The French set sail for Fort Anne, still clinging to plans of invasion. They encountered more bad weather sailing around the southern end of Nova Scotia and along the Bay of Fundy. Only two ships made it to Fort Anne and they were easily defeated by the waiting British ships.

Cornwallis's orders were to sail with soldiers and settlers for Nova Scotia and to succeed where D'Anville failed.

5
War in Europe Drives Refugees to Nova Scotia

The world Cornwallis was leaving behind was in turmoil. The endless religious wars between Catholics and Protestants displaced thousands of Europeans. In the French province of Montbeliard, the Lutheran majority had long tangled with the Catholic minority.[15] The Lutherans had built a church in the village of Chagey, but the French government forced them to build a wall inside the sanctuary and give the better half to the Catholics. Other Protestant churches were routinely desecrated. In 1740, a gang of Catholics marched into a nearby church and sacked it. The final outrage came when Chagey's Lutheran minister died. France's King Louis XV was responsible for approving and sending a new Lutheran minister, but instead sent them a Catholic priest.

The Lutheran men of Chagey resisted and France commanded that their church be turned over to the Catholics. Fifty men gathered in front of the church armed with stones. One of the young leaders of the rebellion was Jean-George D'Attrey, who was joined by his good friend Pierre Mailliard. The two farmers were accustomed to war. (Both would later fight alongside the British in the Protestant Pragmatic Army at the Battle of Fontenoy.) Standing with them were the men of the Bezansons, Bissetts, Bigneys, Boutiliers, Sartys, Doreys, Dauphinees, Brattos, Joudrys, Jollimores, Langilles, Lowes, Mingos, Matatalls, Patriquins and Robars. On August 27, 1740, a detachment of French troops was sent to dislodge them.

---

15 Haliburton, Gordon M. "George Tattrie: A Nova Scotian Pioneer From Montbeliard." *Nova Scotia Historical Review* Vol. 1, No. 2, 1981. Pages 74-90.

They were headed by the new priest. "I warn you – it is useless to resist," the priest shouted to the Montbeliard men.

The men refused to budge.

The priest conferred with the soldiers' commander. A warning volley of musket fire was sent over the resisters. Mailliard gave the retaliatory cry, "Fire!" and his friends threw a volley of stones at the soldiers.

The French soldiers trained their firearms on the Lutherans and began shooting. Panic scattered the resistance. Backed against the church and facing disciplined and well-armed soldiers, the Montbeliard men threw sticks, stones and anything else they could lift. D'Attrey struck one soldier in the head with a good shot, but he turned and shot D'Attrey in the leg. D'Attrey shouted and collapsed; the ball had gone deep into his thigh and he bled badly. It would stay there the rest of his life. Two men fell dead beside him.

The priest ordered the soldiers to stop firing.

"You must surrender," the priest called to the men of Montbeliard over the moaning and through the smoke of gunpowder.

"Never!" was the only reply, followed by a fresh rain of rocks.

The priest called on his detachment to open fire. Twenty-one of the fifty Montbeliard men were shot; three died and the rest fled. D'Attrey's old friend Pierre Mailliard helped him limp away from the advancing troops and the little resistance was snuffed out. The remaining men surrendered; the church D'Attrey's ancestors had built was handed over to the Catholics and Catholicism was re-established by force. The Montbeliard villages of Selemcourt, Bondeval, Lougres, Blamont and Villars-Les-Blamont followed suit. It was obvious there was no future for Protestants in Montbeliard, so the Lutherans looked for any escape from the persecution. Several years later, word came that England was seeking Protestants to settle a place in the New World called Nova Scotia. The refugees of Montbeliard decided to take up the British offer.

*   *   *   *   *

On March 23, 1749, Edward Cornwallis rose during a session of Parliament in London and resigned his family seat of Eye in Suffolk. At the same time, he was named colonel of the 24th Regiment and appointed governor of Nova Scotia.

"Nova where?" asked more than one colleague. Few could see the political advantages of leaving the centre of the world – London, the Parliament, his post as Groom of the King's Bedchamber – to sail into a forest full of savages thousands of miles from civilization.

"The New England colonies are not far," a defender argued.

"As I said – thousands of miles from civilization, surrounded only by wild savages," a fellow parliamentarian joked.

But for Cornwallis – thirty-six years old, still a bachelor – it seemed an immense opportunity. His twin brother Frederick was working the home turf and would keep Edward informed of life in London. Frederick had become a Doctor of Divinity the year before and had been King George's personal chaplain for three years. Frederick was also a canon of Windsor and rumoured to be on the cusp of becoming canon to St. Paul's Cathedral. His steady rise in the church – and in the favour of King George, the head of the Anglican church – seemed assured.

Cornwallis was confident his service in Nova Scotia would give him the opportunity to build his career back home. The king was increasingly convinced that the future security and prosperity of England depended on the security and prosperity of his colonies in the Americas. Cornwallis's city-fortress would anchor British ambitions for the whole continent. Cornwallis was being trusted with the seed to the future. If planted well on Nova Scotia shores, it would grow into a tree that would help his ascent to the highest ranks of empire.

Whitehall was buzzing with plans for the expedition. All of the previously paused energies of war had been transferred to this task. Letters from Governor William Shirley in Massachusetts seemed to arrive every week, imploring London to spare no expense in stocking the Cornwallis mission. At the Board of Trade and Plantations, the government department in charge of the adventure, George Montagu-Dunk, Earl of Halifax, became an ardent supporter of the Nova Scotia mission, and of Cornwallis personally.

By spring, it seemed to Cornwallis that even the people in the streets of London dreamed only of Nova Scotia. He read with a smile an article in *The Gentleman's Magazine* that emphasized the reward awaiting those who boldly invested in Nova Scotia. "Nova Scotia is worth more than Cape Breton and New Found Land together," it boasted.

In March a promotional article ran in *The London Gazette*. "A proposal having been presented unto His Majesty, for the establishing a Civil

Government in the Province of Nova Scotia in North America, as also for the better Peopling and Settling the said Province, and extending and improving the Fishery thereof, by granting Lands within the same and giving other Encouragements to such of the Officers and Private men lately dismissed His Majesty's Land and Sea Service, as shall be willing to settle in the said Province," it began.

Cornwallis was able to read between the lines: there were too many unemployed soldiers hanging around in Britain. Better dispatch them for greater glories in the New World than risk they grow restless and troublesome in the Old World. The king was confident his troops would serve him well in Nova Scotia. But it was not to be a simple military post – the notice went on to say willing pilgrims would be given land grants and invited to bring their families. In fact, every private soldier or seaman would get fifty acres – an unimaginably large holding to most – and it would be tax-free for ten years. Even then, taxes and rents would stay at one shilling a year. Those soldiers and seamen who brought their families would receive an additional ten acres for each family member, "including women and children," and would accrue an additional ten acres for each new member. Officers could get up to eighty acres. Captains claimed 600-acre estates.

The ad recruited surgeons, carpenters, shipwrights, smiths, masons, joiners, brickmakers, bricklayers and anyone else who could make a case for their skills being useful in the building of a new city. London promised to pay for food and other costs of living for an entire year after arrival – plenty of time to establish a local, self-sustaining system. The government would also provide weapons and the tools needed to clear and cultivate the land and also to build houses.

There were regular rumours, stories and the odd theatrical production about the dangers of "Indians" in the New World. To assure the settlers that they would be safe, the *Gazette* article said, "Proper measures will also be taken for their security and protection."

Cornwallis emphasized the importance of this – the settlement would not succeed unless its inhabitants could be confident their homes and land would not be troubled and their lives would not be at risk. The deadline for applicants was noon, April 7, 1749. The ship would be ready to receive the pilgrims on April 10 and would set sail April 20. Nova Scotia became a synonym for Utopia for the unemployed poor of England. The thought of free food for a year – anywhere – made the land seem heavenly.

The *Gentlemen's Magazine* printed a ballad pillorying the government promises for Nova Scotia:

> *Let's away to New Scotland, where Plenty sits queen*
> *O'er as happy a country as ever was seen;*
> *And blesses her subjects, both little and great,*
> *With each a good house, and a pretty estate.*
>
> *No landlords are there the poor tenants to tease,*
> *No lawyers to bully, nor stewards to seize,*
> *But each honest fellow a landlord, and dares*
> *To spend on himself the whole fruit of his cares.*
> *They've no duties on candles, no taxes on malt,*
> *Nor do they, as we do, pay sauce for their salt:*
> *But all is as free as in those times of old,*
> *When poets assure us the age was of gold.*

Cornwallis knew it was meant to be satire and the author assumed his reader recognized the golden days of the past were as false a memory as were the promises of the future, but Cornwallis also knew ordinary people believed the lines as they appeared. This was a land of plenty. A returning ship's captain described an island of pleasure where the rivers ran with wine, streets were paved with mutton pies, walls made of hasty pudding and houses tiled with pancakes. People in pubs read the captain's account with big eyes.

> *There is nothing there but holidays,*
> *with music out of measure;*
> *who can forbear to speak the praise*
> *of such a land of pleasure.*
> *There you may lead a pleasant life,*
> *free from all kinds of labour,*
> *and he that is without a wife,*
> *may borrow of his neighbour.*

Where there is smoke, there is fire, they reasoned. Nova Scotia had to be better than England.

* * * * *

Over the next month, Cornwallis frequently checked in on the ships being loaded with four thousand pounds of gold and silver, stacks of official stationery, hospital supplies, fishing gear, seeds, bricks, blankets and clothes. It felt like he was stocking Noah's Ark. The holds were full of salted meats and sea biscuits, and spiritual sustenance too – Protestant Bibles to share the true word of God with the Catholic Acadians. There were also tubs and tubs of what seemed to him trinkets for the natives.

Not long after *The London Gazette* promotion, eager travellers started arriving, clutching the torn-out advertisement and offering what support they could for their claim to military entitlement. It was a stretch to believe these men had ever served King George II.

Where are the officers, Cornwallis wondered, as pauper after pauper was turned away. But few soldiers came, having read between the lines and understood that their promised "estates" were buried under forests inhabited by hostile French and natives.

That left the very poor of London, whose lives at home were so bleak that the promise of food for a year and a chance to build a new life was a significant step up. The theoretical dangers of the woods paled next to the actual threat of dying at the bottom of British society.

Even the colony's chaplain scorned the settlers. "They are nothing more than a set of profligate wretches debilitated by drink," William Tutty wrote. Later historians derided them as "a shiftless lot, full of complaints, many in rags, others sick or feigning sickness to avoid the labour of clearing the townsite."[16]

Cornwallis watched in amazement as these poor wretches streamed onto his ships. So many came that departure was delayed for a month. Finally, on May 14, Cornwallis boarded the *Sphinx* and, after a little ceremony on the Spithead docks south of London, set sail for the New World. Thirteen ships followed, carrying 1,174 families, including one hundred men retired from the army and four hundred from the Royal Navy. The ships also had thirty-eight medical personnel. There were more than four hundred children, and an almost equal number of servants and enslaved African men and women forced to accompany them. Parliament bankrolled the entire outfit with £40,000, an immense sum for an immense task.

---

16 Raddall, Thomas H. *Halifax: Warden of the North.* Halifax, Nova Scotia: Nimbus Publishing, 2010. Page 25.

They also had one grand dandy, a man as aristocratic as Cornwallis, and a close friend, but an utter mystery to the new governor when it came to personal habits. Captain Richard Bulkeley, a tall, handsome and rich Irishman, shared a suite with Cornwallis on the voyage and while Cornwallis had brought the bare minimum of possessions – clothes, stationery and pens for official business, a few pairs of boots – Bulkeley travelled as though he were moving to his summer palace. Bulkeley and Cornwallis had fought together many times before, and the captain quickly accepted his fast-rising friend's invitation for a tour in the New World. He brought a valet, groom and butler. And three horses. There were other dandies on board fatted by the milk of patronage. Cornwallis tolerated them on the ship, but grew to hate them in Halifax. They were Hugh Davidson, there through a connection to the Duke of Bedford, who would serve as treasurer and secretary, and John Salusbury, there through a connection to Lord Halifax himself, and the colony's register and receiver of His Majesty's rent.

Standing in his quarters on the sloop-of-war *Sphinx*, watching the coast of England disappear to be replaced by open ocean, Cornwallis allowed himself a thin smile. He'd be back soon, and with a remarkable achievement under his belt – a permanent English hold on North America.

Book Two:
Nova Scotia

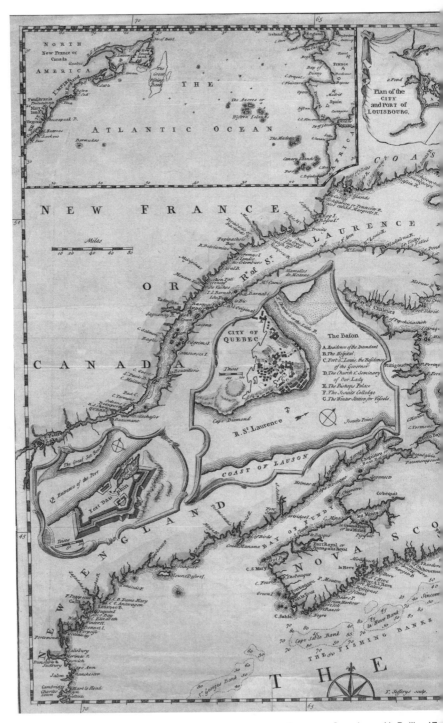

A New Chart of the Coast of New England, Nova Scotia, New France or Canada ..., N. Bellin, 17

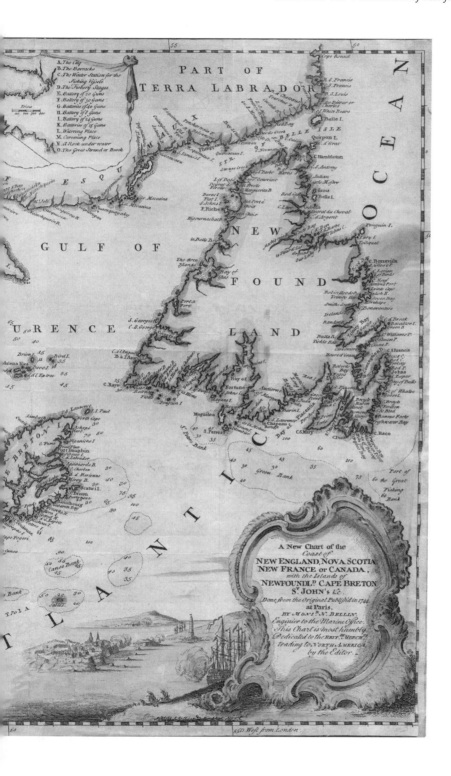

I

Welcome to Mi'kma'ki

The tired sentry of Mi'kmaq warriors stood on the mist-enshrouded meadow. Long black hair dripped over somber faces in the rain, fur robes rustling in the breeze. It was a chilly early morning, summer. The sun had not yet risen, but its light bent over the horizon and illuminated the distant ships.

A few weeks earlier, they had received reports of a lone European ship entering Chibookt, the great harbour. Information trickled in: the ship was English. England, which had claimed all Mi'kmaq Districts for itself a generation earlier, was intent on invading Mi'kma'ki and conquering in practice what they had until then held only in name. Word came from the south, the west and the north: an English invasion meant brutal war. The dwindling Beothuk now lived as refugees on their own island of Ktaqam-kuk, which the English called New Found Land. Mi'kmaq and Maliseet cousins to the south told of scalping bounties issued by the English governor of what they called Massachusetts. More horrors came from the interior of the continent. War was not new, but the systematic attempt to kill every man, woman and child, or to drive them from their homeland, was.

The people had suffered many territorial disputes in their 13,000 years in Mi'kma'ki, but had long ago developed a sophisticated form of interconnected government to peacefully resolve disagreements. The land was divided into the Seven Districts; each was autonomous, but all worked together to resolve disputes and advance collective issues.[17]

---

17 Paul, Daniel. *We Were Not the Savages*. Halifax: Nova Scotia., Fernwood Publishing, 2000. Page 11.

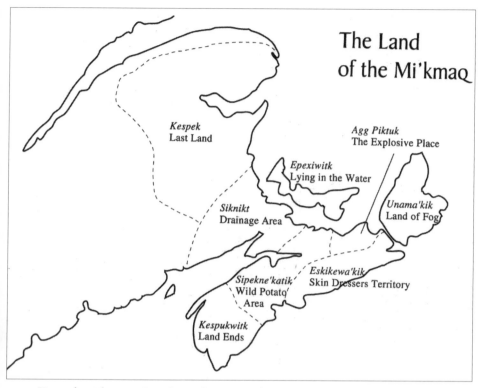

Kespukwitk, or Land Ends, was the southwest territory along the mighty Bay of Fundy. Sipekne'katik, or Wild Potato Area, was next and included the rest of the Fundy coast and the isthmus connecting the peninsula to the mainland. Eskikewa'kik, Skin Dressers Territory, took in the eastern coast from Chibookt up to Canso. Unama'kik, or Land of Fog, was the island the French called Île Royale and the English later called Cape Breton. Agg Piktuk, or the Explosive Place, comprised the remainder of the peninsula. Siknikt, the Drainage Area, was the mainland area occupied by the French. Epekwitk, Lying in the Water, was the island just off the coast (Prince Edward Island). Kespek, Last Land, was the outer frontier of Mi'kmaq territory and went up the mainland to the St. Lawrence River.

In these districts, people lived in villages of fifty to five hundred people and had a district chief and council as the local form of government. The council, including elders and village chiefs, oversaw most of ordinary life. Once a year, the Grand Council of the Mi'kmaq from all Seven Districts assembled to resolve any major problems and to hold celebrations. The Grand Chief, appointed by all of the district chiefs, was the highest office. His power was limited to friendly persuasion, rather than top-down control. That model of leadership was true at all levels of government.

The Grand Council of the Mi'kmaq was loosely associated with a broader military and political alliance called the Wabanaki Confederacy, formed by northeastern countries to promote trade and cooperation and fend off aggression from hostile neighbours such as the Iroquois. Among their allies in the Wabanaki Confederacy, the various political units had a complex land-sharing agreement. Each had a seasonal schedule of access to resources, including fish, meat, plants and vegetables. But on the peninsula, the Mi'kmaq were clear: it was their land and the territorial boundaries were inviolable. Their bands maintained absolute control and exclusive authority over the territory, especially along the Atlantic coast. Villages set up on the coast in the summer and moved inland for the winter. Men were responsible for hunting and fishing and heavy-work chores; women handled small-scale farming, food gathering from the woods and preparation of clothing.

The sophisticated Mi'kmaq government limited war among themselves to rare skirmishes. Death tolls were kept down and if too many lives were lost, the matter could be resolved with a fight to the death between the two chiefs who urged the war. That discouraged warmongering among chiefs.

The first European settlement had arrived nine generations before with the French, and a long, respectful partnership had developed based on trade and intermarriage. Peace with the Acadians, as the French became known, was deep and lasting, and accommodations were made with the fishing Europeans. But those who wanted to claim all of the Mi'kmaq territory met with stiff resistance.

An unanticipated disaster had come in the same Chibookt harbour just a few years before when the French navy sailed in to claim the land from the English. The battered fleet laid anchor in the great basin. It was a traditional stopping place for Mi'kmaq travellers, as it sat between rivers used as water highways, later called the Sackville, Nine Mile and Shubenacadie rivers. The Mi'kmaq had several camps in the area, some marked by ancient petroglyphs.

Seeing the distress of the D'Anville mission in the basin, the Mi'kmaq had helped their old allies. But the French brought scurvy and typhoid along with the gifts. The Mi'kmaq watched hundreds of men die and be buried in shallow graves, or pushed into the water with stones tied at their feet. Bones and skulls could be seen on the shores for many years after the disaster. The French scuttled their unusable fleet before departing on the ill-fated mission to Annapolis, but the ribs and hulls of the sunken ships would remain visible at low tide until the early 1800s. The Mi'kmaq went on their way, unknowingly carrying the seed of death. Typhoid killed up to half of the population in the western territories.

Things had changed a generation before, when the 1713 Treaty of Utrecht between France and England gave the English the French claim to Mi'kma'ki. England built a fort called Annapolis in the southern Kespukwitk District. Relations were tense and there was limited opportunity to trade. The English concept of land ownership was based on force and excluded sharing resources with others. Individual English men could sell parcels of the land to each other, regardless of how it affected others. To Mi'kmaq eyes, the English lacked the permanent sense of land ownership that was the basis of Mi'kmaq life. It was clear England intended to expand its territory in the Seven Districts and the Mi'kmaq warriors had spent much of the past generation attacking the European fort at Annapolis and discouraging them from leaving its walls. Europeans had used the edge of Canso as a temporary landing spot for the fisheries for a century, with the Mi'kmaq's tacit blessing. Thousands of men and hundreds of vessels visited the coastal area each year, but it was attacked if it showed signs of becoming a permanent encampment.

In fact, any time the British attempted to permanently claim the land by building forts anywhere in Mi'kma'ki, they met fierce resistance. In the early 1720s, New Englanders attempted to build a fort on Canso Island – three men were killed in a devastating Mi'kmaq raid. The victors shouted, "Vive le Roi!" as the New Englanders fled – it was never clear if the Mi'kmaq felt they had French backing for the raid, or were just mocking the British.

In one sea battle, British sailors on two ships were entangled in a two-hour skirmish with Mi'kmaq warriors operating captured ships. The British gained the upper hand and set fire to the Mi'kmaq boats and then shot the men in the water. Five corpses washed ashore. The British decapitated them and pierced their heads on pikes to warn others. This sparked a trend for gratuitous, demonstrative violence among the New England fishermen and British settlers and soldiers. Outpowered militarily and reduced to occasional flying victories, the Europeans deployed tactics designed to demoralize the Mi'kmaq: taking and murdering hostages, mutilating corpses and reviving the custom of the scalp bounty that the Massachusetts government had pioneered in 1696.

The fighting with the British had continued itinerantly. The Mi'kmaq warriors were also husbands and hunters, and could only be spared to fight for so long. Spring was fighting season, but winter was a natural ceasefire as the Mi'kmaq moved inland to their winter hunting grounds. France generally stayed out of direct involvement, hoping the Mi'kmaq would drive the British out on their own.

Peace treaties were signed with the British in Maine in 1725 and Annapolis Royal in 1726. The agreements stated the Mi'kmaq would be left to govern themselves, and would cease harassing British settlements. In line with broader policy laid out in the 1713 Treaty of Utrecht, the British treated the "natives of America" as groups, rather than individuals. So if one Mi'kmaq attacked a British soldier, all would be held accountable. The Mi'kmaq ameliorated this arrangement by agreeing to pay compensation. If a rogue warrior killed a British soldier or settler, the band would pay his debt in goods, rather than in blood. One of the rising Mi'kmaq leaders at the time of the treaties was Kopit from the Shubenacadie River band. His name meant "beaver," which was the sign of his family. The Europeans called him Jean-Baptiste Cope. He was twenty-seven and his power was growing.

That uneasy truce held until 1744, when France and Britain's clash on their own continent spilled into Mi'kmaq territory and the restive province the Europeans called Acadia or Nova Scotia again erupted into war.

And now this lone ship was spotted slinking along Mi'kma'ki shores into Chibookt. The vanguard *Sphinx* had sailed slowly past the shores, stopping to talk to some of the French-speaking inhabitants. Word leaked back to their Mi'kmaq allies: the frigate was the head of a vast flotilla holding thousands of Europeans. It wasn't just soldiers coming, but settlers. The lone ship lay anchor off the coast of a prime moose-hunting ground deep inside Chibookt. The settlement would be built on the moose-hunting territory.

No British leader had approached a Mi'kmaq counterpart to inquire about setting up a new fort or settlement. There had been no summits to discuss location, size, or how the treaty could be adjusted to accommodate the new presence. This was an armada. The invasion had begun.

2

Arrival in Chebucto Harbour

On June 14, 1749, after a long journey from England, the *Sphinx* drew within sight of the Atlantic's other edge. The lead ship of the flotilla lingered off the coast for a week, seeking a pilot with local knowledge who could guide them along the unsure route inland. On June 20, a pilot from a passing British sloop running from Louisbourg to New England boarded the *Sphinx* and guided it into Chebucto harbour.

Consulting maps, Edward Cornwallis and his crew navigated the long entry, sailing past endless woods and rocky shores. Cornwallis watched it all with a military eye, assessing the waterway's strengths and weaknesses in the face of French attack.

On June 22, a clear and hot day, he wrote his first report to London. "We had nobody on board that knew anything of the coasts or the Bay of Fundy, so we were to cruise off the coast until we met with a pilot. We made the land of Acadie the 14, but with no pilot," he said.[18]

"The coasts are as rich as they have been represented," Cornwallis remarked approvingly as the *Sphinx* sailed along the verdant land. "We've caught plenty of fish every day since we came within 50 or 60 leagues [150 to 180 miles] of the coast."

He marvelled at the thick woods, accustomed as he was to the sparse forests of England. But here, no houses or fields cut into the rocks and

---

18 From Cornwallis's letter to the Board of Trade, dated June 22, 1749. For ease of reading, all future references to Cornwallis's correspondence will be embedded in the text, rather than in footnotes. All come from the Nova Scotia Archives.

trees. "There's not a clear spot to be seen or heard of." An aide assured him the forest was mostly slender trees and so would not pose a major problem when it came time to clear land for the fortress city.

The destroyed D'Anville mission stayed in Cornwallis's thoughts. "The D'Anville fleet only cut wood to use, not to clear any land," he observed. He jotted down that there were many brooks, but few rivers.

On the way in, the ship dropped anchor in Melgrich Bay and several Acadian families came on board to pay their respects. They told Cornwallis there was a bigger Acadian settlement that would be happy to resupply his men. He ordered a crew to head inland for provisions and to discreetly check out the houses and living conditions to gauge their strength. A man familiar with the territory guided Cornwallis's crew overland via a cattle path; they returned with glowing reports. "Very comfortable houses, sir, covered with bark. They have plenty of cattle and sheep, too, and they have cleared more ground than strictly necessary," a soldier reported.

As the *Sphinx* entered the great harbour, the local pilot pointed to a long, wooded island in the mouth and explained it was to have become the French city in the D'Anville expedition.

The *Sphinx* sailed deep into Chebucto on June 27, as close to the shore as they dared, to give Cornwallis a detailed tour of the coast. He was looking for a spot that could be defended against inland attacks from Quebec or Louisbourg and that could command the harbour without letting enemy vessels sneak up on it. Old plans called for a settlement at the back of the big basin, named in honour of the Duke of Bedford, as it could be easily defended with a battery at the narrows, but Cornwallis decided it was too far into the harbour to be of use to the fishery. He preferred a long finger of land that jutted out past George's Island, near the would-be French island city he named Cornwallis Island (McNabs Island), and that had the long Sandwich River (Northwest Arm) to its west side. Crews started to clear at Sandwich or Pleasant Point (Point Pleasant), but Inigo Bruce, the town planner, objected to the shallow coast and shoals. The land was either stony or swampy.

"It would make a great fort, but an extremely dangerous spot for a town," Cornwallis was told. "And the wind in the ocean winter will be terrible."

Cornwallis settled on a sloping hill on the mainland just west of George's Island. If cleared and fortified, he believed the hill could protect the colonists and at the same time allow the British military to dominate the harbour. A brook running down the hill would supply fresh drinking water and there was plenty of space to expand into.

William Shirley, the governor of Massachusetts and until Cornwallis's arrival the *de facto* leader for Nova Scotia, had previously suggested Chebucto as a good site, but decided against it because of an agreement with the Mi'kmaq. A new settlement was vulnerable enough without directly antagonizing the natives, he reasoned. But Cornwallis did not expect any serious problems from the Mi'kmaq. He believed the sheer power and scale of the British ambitions in Chebucto would overawe the Mi'kmaq and they would accept it without a fight.

The *Sphinx* laid anchor. Cornwallis stayed on board while scouts went inland to explore the area. The shore would accommodate a harbour. The hill could easily be turned into a citadel. The location was far enough into the harbour to be protected, but close enough to the ocean to house the fishery. It was the perfect spot. This would be Halifax.

His ship was soon followed by the thirteen transport ships housing 2,576 colonists. Almost all of them were English, with a few Irish, Scots, Germans and Jews mixed in. Impressively, only one passenger – a child – had died during the trip. Cornwallis credited the new ventilation design for that. It allowed fresh air below decks and vastly improved the health of the people inside the ship.

Cornwallis, having watched them distantly on the voyage, had little good to say about his settlers other than that they were in good health. He was confident he could whip them into shape once they saw the magnitude of the challenge of building Halifax before the winter, and so fall in line behind their commander. He had absolute control over the colony and the colonists.

Meantime, he sent the passing sloop to Boston to notify William Shirley he had arrived. He also helped plan for the British departure from Louisbourg, whose population had swollen as the French arrived to reclaim it. The bitter remnant of the New Englanders who had conquered it in 1745 with the lives of their brothers watched as an English garrison busied itself undoing the damage the New Englanders had done – each gun was restored, each breach of the walls patched, each plank and nail put back in place. All for a distant treaty bettering the interests of Old England. John Gorham, a ranger (a mercenary soldier) who had nearly died in the fight, left for Chebucto in disgust.

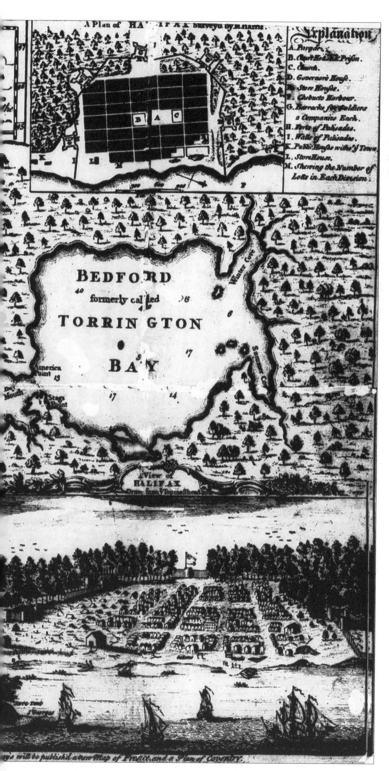

A Map of the South Part of Nova Scotia and its Fishing Banks, published January 25, 1750. The upper right inset is "A Plan of Halifax" and the bottom right inset shows "A View of Halifax."

Another sloop's captain was told to stop at Annapolis Royal to inform its commander, Paul Mascarene, that Cornwallis had arrived; an Acadian was sent overland with the same message. Representatives fanned out to the Mi'kmaq tribes.

Cornwallis prepared to set foot on the territory he now commanded. He landed at a small marshy cove on the western shore, near the brook that would supply the town. The beach was fine gravel, convenient for small boats and with good, deep anchorage not far off shore. "Nothing could be easier than to build wharves right here," he remarked. He stepped ashore next to a giant hardwood tree with Inigo Bruce, his town planner. Bruce laid his blueprints on the ground and stared into the thick woods. He alone seemed to possess an imagination large enough to turn the forest into a city. The town was to begin with a slender trail following the south bank of the brook up the citadel hill. The slim trail was given a grand name – Cornwallis called it George Street, in honour of the king. The first arrivals would settle there; that very day, they began clearing trees and pitching tents along the brook's bank. Bruce measured thirty feet off on each side of the "street." Markers were struck. The initial boundaries of Halifax were established.

As the settlement spread in the coming weeks, a new street name was needed for the path that ran parallel to the harbour just above the beach and swamp. Cornwallis named it Bedford Row in honour of the First Lord of the Admiralty. More huts, more cuts through the woods and more streets named for British gentry: Granville, Sackville, Holles (later Hollis), Grafton and Argyle. He threw in a Prince and Duke to cover a range of ranking men back home.

*　*　*　*　*

Despite his low opinion of the settlers, Cornwallis knew he needed them. The good weather was flying by and there was much work to be done to prepare the settlement to survive a North American winter. He had been briefed on the possibility of a long winter – as many as six months – with the land trapped under snow and providing little food, while the deep cold steadily picked off the weaker members of the new community. His goal was to have each of the settlers in a house before winter. He further planned to put a fort at Sandwich Point and across the entrance on the former French island to protect the settlement. A battery on George's Island would complete the arrangement.

Cornwallis sent the strongest of the men to the base of the hill with axes and saws to start clearing the land. It was hot, ugly work in the summer heat. Mosquitoes plagued the men. Cornwallis used all the carpenters he had brought with him, plus more from Annapolis. They started to build log houses for storage. He was still short of workers and compelled to draw upon the Acadians, the descendents of the original French settlers. Many had roots in the province dating back 150 years. When France ceded the territory to Britain, they became nominally British subjects, but remained friendly with the Mi'kmaq and the colonialists in New France. Cornwallis did not trust their loyalty. That would be a problem to solve another day. Now, he needed labourers, so he hired Acadian workers from Minas at a healthy pay. They promised to send fifty men to work until October. It was expensive, but cheaper than having everyone living on the ships all winter.

He also sent Captain Edward How to the St. John River. How was born in England, but had lived in Nova Scotia for decades. Cornwallis had heard the French were building a fort near the river to menace his new settlement. How met some of the Mi'kmaq chiefs en route and sent a letter back to Cornwallis. "They are at present quiet and peaceable. They say they will send deputies to enter into treaty," How reported. "They promise to take English commissions, instead of French, and receive His Majesty's presents."

Cornwallis decided that as soon as the British garrison finished repairing Louisbourg and arrived in Halifax, he would send two companies to Minas to build a barrack and then winter in it. Just to keep an eye on things. He sent an armed sloop to the Minas Basin as well, to show the French he was in town. He wanted to display his military prowess. It was up to the Acadians whether it was used to protect them or to slaughter them.

Inigo Bruce drew up plans to clear a wide area on the Halifax shore. A central clearing was called Parade Square and blueprints called for a church (St. Paul's), a parade square, courthouse, prison, storehouse, a governor's house and batteries. Cornwallis also planned to break a road to Minas and to Sandwich Point. One side of the town would open onto the beaches and the rest would be protected by a seven-sided town wall. The settlement of Halifax was underway.

3

War Erupts in a Restive Province

The first shots of the resumed war between the Mi'kmaq and British came in Canso soon after Cornwallis arrived at Chibookt. The hostilities were no surprise to the New Englanders who had lived in the area for years. The New Englanders had tangled with the Mi'kmaq for generations, and always assumed they would resist the British invasion with all of their strength. It was only the newly arrived Old Englishmen who imagined the land was unoccupied and could easily be taken. The war resumed in the summer of 1749, when a group of New Englanders arrived at Canso to revive the fishery. They came across a Mi'kmaq village. The men had gone away to hunt and fish, while the women and children stayed in the village. The New England fishermen killed twenty women and children.

The Mi'kmaq men returned to discover the massacre. The air was filled with the wails of their mourning. Then rage replaced grief. They planned their revenge. The Mi'kmaq were experienced on the water and had for centuries travelled Mi'kma'ki in canoes. When the Europeans arrived in their outsized canoes, the locals quickly adapted. The grieving Mi'kmaq men seized a passing fishing vessel from Boston, taking hostage the crew of twenty. They released the hostages, but kept the ship and used it to launch raids against the English.

In Shubenacadie River, leaders like Jean-Baptiste Cope struggled over how to respond to the invasion. The Catholic mission, which had set up at Shubenacadie in 1738, argued for withdrawing from the peninsula. The priest, Jean-Louis Le Loutre, was a passionate promoter of France's ambitions in Acadia, but was also an ally of the Mi'kmaq. Shortly after the English landing in 1749, he announced he was pulling out of the interior of the peninsula and moving his mission to the isthmus of Chignecto, closer to the French military. He hoped to attract soldiers, officers and sympathetic settlers to start a new community loyal to France. Le Loutre, who had lived many years with the Mi'kmaq, understood that some held their land very close to their heart and would see moving as treason to their ancestors and surrender to the British. But still he invited them to join him. Dozens accepted his offer and relocated from Shubenacadie to Chignecto. Those who were leaving with Le Loutre planned to travel slowly among their old allies, the Acadians, to invite them to leave the peninsula and form a new community closer to the French.

But more than ninety members of the Shubenacadie band said no – including Cope. They would not abandon the homes their ancestors had occupied from time immemorial. Cope was one of the most respected elders among those who stayed and soon became their leader. While Cornwallis claimed the land for Britain, a growing movement of Mi'kmaq formally declared their opposition to the new fortress, and to all European claims on their land. A branch of Mi'kmaq leaders declared themselves *"les sauvages"* and said the land belonged inalienably to their people. They issued a statement to that effect. A translation of it appeared in colonial newspapers.

"I am sprung from the land as doth the grass. I that am savage, am born there, and my fathers before me. This land is mine inheritance, I swear it is, the land which God has given me to be my country forever," the declaration of independence read.[19]

Another group of elders gathered at Port Toulouse, a French village later called St. Peter's, on Cape Breton in 1749 and composed a letter to Cornwallis rebutting his claim to their territory. They specifically referred to British works fortifying what Cornwallis called Pleasant Point, and what the Mi'kmaq called Amtoukati. The finger of land extending into Chebucto harbour was the site of the annual Spring Feast, when Mi'kmaq from all over the Seven Districts would gather under the first new moon of May. In later years, it was known as the Feast of St. Aspinquid of Agamenticus as some Mi'kmaq converted to Catholicism.

The elders claimed Kjepouktouk, what the English were now calling Halifax Harbour.

---

19 Plank, Geoffrey. Page 129.

"The place where you are, where you are building dwellings, where you are now building a fort, where you want, as it were, to enthrone yourself, this land of which you wish to make yourself now absolute master, this land belongs to me. I have come from it as certainly as the grass; it is the very place of my birth and of my dwelling, this land belongs to me, the Micmac, yes I swear, it is God who has given it to me to be my country forever," they wrote.

"Show me where I, the Micmac, will lodge? You drive me out; where do you want me to take refuge? You have taken almost all this land in all its extent. Nothing remains to me except Kjepouktouk. You envy me even this morsel ...

"Your residence at Port Royal does not cause me great anger because you see that I have left you there at peace for a long time, but now you force me to speak out by the great theft you have perpetrated against me."

The words fell on deaf ears. Mi'kmaq warriors began to plan their resistance to the occupation.

4

Cornwallis Sworn in as Governor

On July 12, Cornwallis was sworn in on board the *Beaufort* as governor of Nova Scotia. It was a hot, clear day. John Salusbury was with him and took notes in a diary that would eventually be published as *Expeditions of Honour*. Cornwallis's mission was unambiguous: he wanted to clear the peninsula and reserve its land solely for people of European descent. He was to establish the fortress city at Chebucto and then quickly expand out with other Protestant settlements. The Board of Trade instructed him to send some Protestant settlers to live in Acadian villages. The hope was that intermarriage and an upright example of the benefits of loyalty to the Protestant British Crown would soon assimilate the Catholic, French-speaking Acadians. Initially, he intended to send French Protestants to make the assimilation easier, but later London feared that strategy would backfire and leave them with a French, anti-British alliance dominating the Fundy coast. Germans would be sent instead. In the end, the assimilation strategy did not amount to much. The Acadians remained Acadians, struggling to balance neutrality. Some had loyalties to France, others liked the idea of trade with the British, and most shared relationships and relatives with the Mi'kmaq.

On Thursday, July 13, Cornwallis ordered gates built at the harbour mouth after a schooner was spotted lurking to take off some of the setlers. It was an ongoing problem. That same week, soldiers tracked down four deserters hiding out in the woods of Pleasant Point and plotting a trip to New England. They were dragged back to Halifax.

Cornwallis's first act as governor of Nova Scotia and Acadie was to summon his council to the *Beaufort*. It was agreed that council would meet on the ship until enough woods had been cleared to build a safe home for His Excellency and a meeting space for the council. On July 14, he addressed the new council. Despite his English bias, he was a practical man and saw that many of the dandies brought from home were not cut out to run this wasteland. Most of his council was local – New Englanders, displaced from Louisbourg, who knew how to operate in the New World.

"Having made choice of the following Gentlemen to be members of the Province of Nova Scotia, you must each take the follow order," he said, looking in turn at Paul Mascarene, Edward How, John Gorham, Benjamin Green, John Salusbury and Hugh Davidson, the men who would form Nova Scotia's new council government. Cornwallis administered the oath to each man, he reading and they repeating his words. All swore loyalty to the interests of the British Crown, the security of King George's person and government and the succession of the crown on the heir of the late princess Sophia being Protestant and extinguishing the hopes of the pretended Prince of Wales and his open and secret abettors. Each man also took the Declaration mentioned in the Act of Parliament from the twenty-fifth year of the reign of King Charles II, 1685, which specifically addressed dangers from Catholic people and lands.

One by one, each man swore his oath: "I do swear that as a member of this council I will always act faithfully and honestly and to the utmost of my skills and knowledge for the service of His Majesty and for the good of this province, so help me God."

That was followed by an oath for impartial administering of justice "I do swear that as a Member of this Supreme Court of Justice I will always give my judgment impartially and to the utmost of my skills and knowledge according to justice, right and equity, so help me God."

Duly sworn in, the new council then administered Cornwallis's oath as governor, the same taken by all New World plantation governors. He swore to do his utmost that the laws relating to the plantation be observed. Cornwallis opened and read the king's commission for them, focusing on the instructions relating to His Majesty's French subjects and the declaration to be upheld by His Majesty's order.

Mascarene read the oath the French inhabitants had historically taken and delivered a copy to Cornwallis. And that was when Cornwallis discovered his first problem. Mascarene explained that while the French inhabitants had taken the oath before, it was understood they had a military exemption. The Acadians swore they would never join the French, but would not swear to the section of the British oath stating they would have to take up arms against any enemy of the English king. Mascarene, who had long administered the qualified oath in his role as head of the Annapolis fort, asked if the tradition would continue. He himself had preferred that way, opting for "lenity and humanity" to secure their neutrality, if not loyalty.

Paul Mascarene had been born Jean-Paul Mascarene in France in 1684, but his parents fled with him to Geneva when he was an infant because of religious persecution against Protestants. He later moved to England and joined the military and was posted to Boston in 1711. As a bilingual Protestant, he was a valuable liaison between the British rulers and the French and First Nations inhabitants of the area. He specialized in peacefully resolving disputes and courteously collecting tributes from the Acadians of Nova Scotia. He played an important role in negotiating the 1725 peace treaty between the Mi'kmaq and the British in Nova Scotia. The army officer and engineer became the province's lieutenant-governor in 1740 and held the post until Cornwallis arrived. He was seen as a pragmatic diplomat able to provide a sharp analysis of complicated situations.

Mascarene's 1720 *Description of Nova Scotia*, written to the Board of Trade, laid out the province's situation. The Acadians would not swear an unqualified oath to the British Crown while the British were confined to a small military presence at Annapolis. The scattered Acadians could not be convinced that the small British fort could offer them protection, or that they must respect its authority. He recommended a stronger military force throughout the province to enforce an unqualified oath. Those who swore it could stay, but those who demurred would be relocated to French-held territory. He also urged the Board of Trade to settle the province with English-speaking Protestants. With the arrival of Cornwallis, he wondered if that day had come.

The council discussed the risks of insurrection, of French incursions, and the likelihood that the inhabitants would prove dangerous if given more slack. Cornwallis argued that the Acadians had been allowed religious freedom and possession of their land, but had not returned the favour with loyalty. He accused them of having "openly abetted or privately assisted His Majesty's enemies" by offering them shelter, provisions and intelligence.

Cornwallis decided a military exemption was too big a risk. "The clause appears in the oath of allegiance. The inhabitants either swear the oath, or they don't. They cannot pick and chose and delete passages not to their taste," he said. "Let the French know that they must take the oath without any conditional clauses understood or any reservations whatever."

Three French inhabitant deputies were waiting ashore for Cornwallis's ruling. They expected it would be a formality and that the old agreement would stand. The three were Jean Melanson from Canard River, Claude LeBlanc from Le Grand Pré and Philippe Melanson from Pisiquid. They were rowed to the *Beaufort* and summoned before Cornwallis. He assured them of the full protection of His Majesty, and that they would be assisted in any way necessary, but they would have to take the oath in full.

"It is the same rule of law for all," he said.

The three exchanged looks. Philippe Melanson explained they had come primarily to pay their respects to the new governor and to know their condition henceforth in Acadie. "Your Excellency, many of the inhabitants are especially eager to learn – will they be able to keep their priests?" he asked.

Cornwallis nodded. "You shall always have them – provided that no priest should officiate within the province without licence first obtained from myself," he said.

The three deputies were given copies of the oaths and declaration and told to issue them to the Acadians. Each person had to take the oath. "Return within a fortnight and report the resolutions of your several departments," Cornwallis said. "And instruct the other French settlements that I desire to see their deputies as soon as possible."

The deputies agreed and left the ship to carry out their mission.

Council next discussed the other major source of trouble – the Mi'kmaq. Cornwallis outlined his plan to drive them out of Nova Scotia and reserve the peninsula for Europeans. The difficult question of what to make of a child born to an Acadian and Mi'kmaq was not addressed. It would be important to isolate the Mi'kmaq from the Acadians and especially from the imperial French in Canada. It was feared they were working together to disrupt the British settlement.

"A little chicanery between the French and the Indians," John Salusbury wrote. "A little management with our force will bring 'em to reason."

July 15 saw a weekend council meeting assembled on Cornwallis's ship at ten a.m. Saturday. A soldier had been sent to the St. John River on the mainland of what the British considered to be Nova Scotia. It was the ancestral homeland and military headquarters for the local Mi'kmaq and Maliseet people. It was also close to the French settlement Saint Jean, or Saint John. The St. John River was a vital artery between Quebec and Nova Scotia. Both the French and English feared the other would use it to launch an invasion. The solider presented his urgent report to council.

"Indians have assembled in great numbers at Saint John," he said.

Cornwallis saw such a gathering as a prelude to a joint Mi'kmaq-French attack. It also indicated that the French believed the "Nova Scotia" ceded to Britain ended at the Isthmus of Chignecto. If the Mi'kmaq of the St. John River were allied with the French, it made him doubt the trustworthiness of the Mi'kmaq on the peninsula. He planned to keep a close eye on the situation.

"This is scarce to be reconciled with the peace Mr. Shirley is treating them with," Salusbury wrote, referring to the Massachusetts governor.

On Monday, July 17, a dry day after a weekend of torrential rain, Cornwallis summoned the council to swear in William Steele as its new member. The first order of business was to work out a way to discourage settlers from resettling themselves in the welcoming towns of New England. "I have composed a proclamation regarding settlers quitting the colony without my permission," Cornwallis said.

The proclamation warned that departing without permission was forbidden and there was no easy return for an errant settler. The council approved it and published the proclamation around the camp that evening. Next to it was a proclamation against the retailing of liquors without a licence, likewise read, approved and ordered posted within the camp. After the meeting, Salusbury left the ship to lounge on the shore. Sloops arrived daily in the harbour and work on the settlement proceeded at a good pace.

The next day Cornwallis swore in the settlement's first justices of the peace for the Township of Halifax: John Brause, Robert Ewer, John Collier and John Duport. "I swear that as Justice of the Peace on the Township of Halifax I will do equal and right to rich and poor to the utmost of my knowledge according to justice, right and equity, so help me God," the men said in turn.

Cornwallis issued another proclamation: the settlers should assemble in the morning into separate companies with their respective overseers, and each company should choose a constable. The threat of attack was on his mind and he wanted in part to frighten the settlers, but also to begin creating real defences for the new town.

On July 20, Salusbury spent the day fishing with a friend. He grumbled about his delayed commission. He had expected a swift rise in rank – it seemed one of the few comforts to offset the hardships of life in the colonies – but so far nothing was coming his way. "I've heard rumours, but nothing happens. It's very hard," he complained.

That Sunday, the colony had its first Christian service. It was an open-air affair on the sandy shore of the budding town. Cornwallis joined twenty-two others for the sermon. Salusbury then walked out to Pleasant Point, ostensibly to see if the *Diamond*, a schooner from Louisbourg and bearing Colonel Peregrine Thomas Hopson, had arrived. It hadn't, but he spent the day at the beach just in case. It arrived the next night, followed by three more ships the next day in heavy rains.

It rained all that day too. The late July weather was cooling and the settlers took to wearing coats in the evening. When the rain finally stopped at night, Salusbury strolled through the rough path cut in the woods to Pleasant Point and treated himself to a bath in the shallow water.

Administratively, life in the settlement ticked by in late August. Cornwallis swore in Hopson as governor-in-chief of Cape Breton and ordered a regiment of foot to be formed. Ten Acadian deputies arrived to pay their respects to the new governor, but the issue of the oath was unresolved. Salusbury joined Hopson and Cornwallis for dinner on the *Beaufort* amid an evening clogged with heavy fog.

Cornwallis met again with the Acadians the next day. The rain and fog still smothered the little hamlet. In weather like this, Halifax seemed a bleak parody of London. It had grand street names boasting of illustrious dukes, princes and kings, but they were just mud tracks still littered with tree stumps. People had addresses, but their residences were just bivouacs built of brushwood, old ship sails and with earthen floors. A fire was lit in the centre of each for warmth and cooking. That meant they all had a hole in the roof that let rain in better than it let smoke out. Men coughed incessantly and spat thick phlegm onto the dirt floor.

The wealthier settlers remained on the ships. Those living in the "town" were mostly men, mostly rough, and getting rougher. The few English gentlemen who had brought their families kept a close eye on them and forbade them setting foot on land.

The weather agitated Cornwallis's rheumatism and he complained of sore joints and cursed the weather. He composed himself before the deputies were brought in. "And what resolutions have the French inhabitants taken in consequence of His Majesty's declaration?" he asked.

Jean Melanson delivered a letter saying it contained their answers. It was read in French and English. The council retreated to discuss it and formed the opinion that with regard to their priests and religion, the French inhabitants could be assured of the free and public exercise of their religion and of being allowed a sufficient number of priests.

"Provided that no priest shall presume to officiate without licence first obtained from the governor. All priests must also take an oath of allegiance to King George," Cornwallis said.

Everyone around the table agreed. The deputies were brought back in to hear the response, which was read by Hugh Davidson. He cleared his throat before addressing the sticky subject of bearing arms.

"With regard to the second article in their letter demanding an exemption from bearing arms: it is the unanimous opinion of the council that no exception should be granted them, but that they should be told peremptorily that they must take the oath of allegiance as offered them, for that His Majesty would allow none to occupy lands in his territories whose allegiance and assurance in case of need could not be depended on, and that such as should behave as true subjects ought to do will be supported, encouraged and protected equally with the rest of His Majesty's subjects."

Davidson paused as the French translation was read. He resumed in English: "That His Excellency will send persons as soon as possible to the French districts at Annapolis River to the Grand Pré and to Chignecto to administer to the inhabitants the oath of allegiance and that all such as are willing to continue in the possession of their land and to be faithfully subject to His Majesty must appear and take the oath before the end of October, which will be the last day allowed them.

"His Excellency has appointed two of the council at Chebucto and at Annapolis Royal to administer the oath to such as shall choose to come to either of those places."

It was non-negotiable: the oath had to be taken. By the first of August, reports came in that the deputies had delivered Cornwallis's message. Religious freedom would be granted if the Acadians promised to be loyal subjects and acknowledged they lived in King George's domain. If they did not swear that oath, they would have to leave Nova Scotia. They would surrender their right to the land and gain nothing from handing it over and would not be permitted to take any but basic possessions before trudging off into the woods for French-held territory.

The Nova Scotia government was confident the inhabitants would sign the oath, and even more confident the military might of King George would fix the problem if they chose rebellion. While they were offered the option of leaving for French Canada, it was hoped the harsh conditions of expulsion would deter them from leaving. They worked the farmlands, one of the few true areas of European progress in Nova Scotia, and without them the farms would fall fallow and the colony would suffer a potentially fatal setback.

On August 8, the deputies were back in Halifax harbour. After a fretful few hours waiting on the shore, they were ferried out to the *Beaufort*. Each deputy was called in alone to have the oath read to him in front of Cornwallis and the council. Each had the same question.

"If we have a mind to evacuate our lands, would we have leave to sell our lands and effects?" they asked.

Cornwallis shook his head and spoke slowly. "By the Treaty of Utrecht [1713], there was one year allowed to you from the surrender of the province wherein the French inhabitants might have sold their effects, but at present those that should choose to leave rather than be a true subject to the King could not be allowed to sell or carry off anything," he replied.

The deputies spoke rapidly in French to each other before begging leave in English to return to their department to consult with the inhabitants. Cornwallis's face grew cold. He was getting tired of the constant delays.

"I warn you that whoever should not have taken the oath [by the end of October] should forfeit all their possessions and rights in this province [and] whoever should leave this province without taking the oath of allegiance should immediately forfeit all of their rights."

When the deputies left, the council suggested to Cornwallis that he order all of the Catholic priests into Chebucto as soon as possible. It might prove informative to hear from them directly to better gauge the mood of the Acadians. Cornwallis nodded and instructed Davidson to send the orders.

The tributaries of power kept flowing into Halifax. The Sunday after the deputies left, Cornwallis and the council prepared to meet with the other critical players in Nova Scotia – the Mi'kmaq. The representatives of the St. John River Indians had arrived and stood waiting on the shore.

"We have been sent by our tribes to pay our respects to his Excellency and agree upon articles of a lasting peace upon the same footings as the last made in 1726," a representative said. The message was relayed to Cornwallis. Council read the old treaty and agreed it would be prudent to renew it in this changed political landscape. 1726 was a long time ago in geopolitics. The Mi'kmaq were to be ferried aboard early the next morning.

Cornwallis got on with other business. He informed council that he was ready to announce the divisions of the lots. Each settler would be granted his own territory and could start to build his home.

"But I desire your opinion on this question. When the lots are given out tomorrow, should the settlers be given the land on the condition that they first be employed for a few days to throw a line of defence around the town?" he asked.

Perhaps it was the steady stream of blank-faced strangers professing a strained loyalty to his king, or perhaps it was his military training, but Cornwallis was feeling uneasy about the undefended colony. His own quarters were being constructed and life on shore would be significantly more dangerous than life on the *Beaufort*.

The council agreed with his plan. When the settlers assembled Monday morning in the cleared parade square at the centre of the cleared forest, the overseers told them they would get their land only after a few days' employment casting a line of defence about the town.

"Afterward, you must build your houses within its security," the proclamation went on. Each man was to be paid a decent sum per day of work. This angered Cornwallis. No one would pay a higher price for a lack of defence than the settlers, he reasoned, so why should the Crown pay them to save themselves? But the overseers pointed to the low character of so many of the settlers and argued on practical grounds that the money would provide motivation otherwise lacking. The critical thing was to get the defences up.

The settlers gathered tools needed to clear back the forest and the engineers guided efforts to turn the cut trees into sharpened pickets that could create a strong line of protection around the settlement.

5
First Meeting with the Mi'kmaq

On Tuesday, Cornwallis and the council invited the Mi'kmaq representatives from the St. John River on board the *Beaufort*. Cornwallis as yet had no ambitions to drive the Mi'kmaq from that area – the peninsula was his prime focus – but he remained suspicious of their suspected alliance with the French at the Saint John fort. He greeted them on his ship.

"Welcome to Chebucto," Cornwallis said. "What is your view in coming from Saint John?"

A representative of the deputies spoke. His words were translated into English, and Cornwallis's into Mi'kmaq.

"As your Excellency ordered us to come, so we came in obedience to your orders," the representative said. His European name was Andre, and he came from the Minas or New Minas Basin.

Cornwallis was pleased with the response. "I have instructions from His Majesty to maintain amity and friendship with the Indians and to grant to those in this province all manners of protection," he said.

"We have seen the last treaty with France and are glad of it," Andre said.

"I am willing to enter into Treaty with the Indian chiefs and with those of the St. John Indians in particular. Have you authority for that purpose?" Cornwallis asked.

The deputy replied, "We reckon ourselves included in the peace made by the Kings of Great Britain and France."

Cornwallis paused. "I ask if you are empowered from your chiefs to make a particular treaty with me."

After the translation, Andre nodded. "Yes. We come on purpose."

"From what tribes and from what chiefs are you delegates?"

They answered: Joannes Pedousaghtigh, chief of the tribe of Chignecto Indians, François Aurodowish, Simon Sactawino and Jean-Baptiste Maddouanhook, deputies from the chiefs of the St. John River Indians.

"Do you remember the treaty made with your tribes in 1726?"

"Yes. Some of us were present when it was made."

"Will you have it read to you?"

"We have a copy of it ourselves and we are come to renew it."

"Have you instructions from your tribes to renew the same treaty?"

"Yes."

"Then it is necessary that the treaty be read."

The treaty was read in English, French and Mi'kmaq.

"Do you agree to renew every article of the treaty now read to you?" Cornwallis asked.

"Yes," Andre said.

"Then I shall order a parchment to be ready for you to sign tomorrow and Captain How shall carry it to Saint John to be ratified," the governor said.

"Agreed," nodded Andre.

Cornwallis turned to other matters. He glanced at council member John Gorham before speaking to the Mi'kmaq. "Do you know what became of five of Captain Gorham's Indians that were taken at Goat Island?"

Gorham's Rangers were a mix of New Englanders, non-Mi'kmaq First Nations and what he called "half breeds" – people of mixed ancestry. Five of them had recently been taken captive at Goat Island in the Annapolis Basin.

Andre answered, "They carried them to Quebec."

"Where, exactly?"

"At the Trois Rivières near Quebec."

"Do you know who killed Captain Gorham's men at the St. John River?"

"Three of Passamaquady and one of the Penobscot Indians, who know nothing of the cessation of arms," Andre explained.

Satisfied, and certain that the deputies would make sure all of their tribes would know hostilities had ceased, Cornwallis dismissed them.

Andre and the others paddled back to shore and set out on foot and then canoe on the journey inland to inform their leaders.

Cornwallis turned to the third threat to the colony: unregulated booze. He issued a proclamation about "spurious liquors" and strengthend the penalty for selling alcohol without a licence. He also added a reward for any informer who tipped his government off to illegal distilleries.

Cornwallis also read from a letter just arrived from England containing King George's instructions for dealing with all persons in custody. The colonial government was to set up a general court without delay to try the accused. The court was to meet Thursday morning and start determining all civil and criminal cases. A jury would be drawn from the general population to hear the more serious offences.

6

The Birth of a City

On a warm late August afternoon, Cornwallis left his quarters with Hugh Davidson and walked through town. He had been laid up for a few weeks with work and rheumatism and wanted to get a sense of how the settlement was developing. The defences were taking shape and a few industrious individuals had completed their houses. Cornwallis's own quarters were nearly ready. It was a squat, plain house of two storeys, cannily positioned and carefully armed to protect the governor. Embankments surrounded it and guns were positioned on its four corners. Cornwallis would live there in high security, safe even if the town defences were overrun. It would also act as Halifax's first council chamber.

Cornwallis could see the harbour was busy, with more than a dozen ships at anchor and a steady stream of traffic in and out bringing supplies to and from New England. Walking down the thin, dirt roads to the waterfront beach, he sighed. He knew the settlers recognized him – he could tell by the way some stiffened and stared at him and the way others doubled down to the task at hand. But most continued to sit in the sun, perhaps taking the care to conceal the illegal alcohol that was helping ease their today into tomorrow.

There were a couple of thousand people in the settlement. Enough to start a small English village. Or a few blocks of London. But Cornwallis had a hard time convincing himself this lot was destined for greatness. Most of them still lived on the ships, ferrying ashore in the morning to work at building their homes. "The number of industrious, active men proper to undertake and carry on a new settlement is very small," he observed. "Of soldiers, there is only 100."

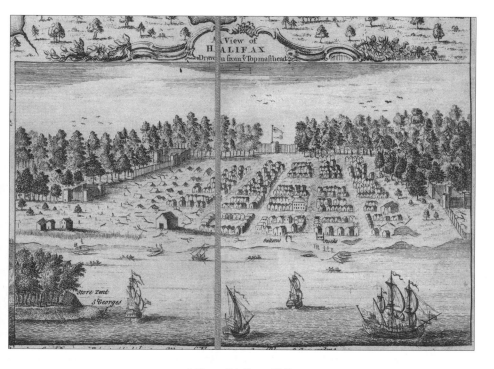

A View of Halifax c.1749.

Most were simply escaping the squalor of a poor person's England. In retrospect, Cornwallis thought the emphasis on free food for a year was not a wise one. Anyone who had built something with his life would not be lured to the unknown by a promise of what was already guaranteed. Only the desperate would ditch everything for nothing.

As they walked, Cornwallis counted out loud. He was tallying up the number of tradesmen willing and able to get to work. "One hundred," he concluded as they reached the water. "One hundred men willing and able to work. The rest are poor, idle vagabonds that embraced the opportunity to get provisions for one year without labour, or sailors that only wanted a passage to New England."

Yet the reluctant adventurers seemed to have avoided understanding that there would not be a fleet of servants sailing ahead to clear the land, plant the food and tend the wild stock.

Cornwallis mustered some good cheer. His health was strong, the weather was warm and the harbour stuffed with fish. He saw strange animals called moose peering through the woods – giant hunks of meat awaiting slaughter. He had been at work only a few months and already the rough seed of a town was sprouting green shoots. There were gardens – food for the coming winter. And he had established peace with the Indians and the French inhabitants. If that bubble of safety could be protected for a year, the town could take root.

But the colony bled settlers from the start. Many of the men were just after free passage to New England and scampered off to finish the trip. "Some have come like it's a hospital and they just want to be cured of venereal disorders, some of them incurable," Cornwallis griped.

In his experience, idle, abandoned fellows like them were the most troublesome and prone to mutiny. They preferred chaos to order and could manage to convince others that the unknown was better than the known. "But these men cost the government a great deal of money, so I'll do all I can to make them useful. I worry I'll be obliged to send many of them away," he noted.

He warned anyone who took to wandering it would not be tolerated. "Anyone absent two days together without permission will forfeit all of the rights and privileges of settlers," he admonished.

Eight men absconded to Canso to try their luck before returning to Chebucto. Cornwallis struck their names off the books and ordered them to vacate the province. They begged for mercy, but he sent them packing. It sent a clear message to the rest: however bad you find your lot inside the fort, it'll be worse outside the fort. And once you leave, you can't come back.

He returned to his quarters and composed a letter to his bosses back home. He asked them to send more industrious, easily governable men to him. "We need Germans," he concluded. "A proposal was made to me at Spithead that all Protestant tradesman and soldiers willing to come here should have the same rights in this province as His Majesty's subjects."

He reconsidered it on the shores of Nova Scotia and it seemed a much better idea. "These settlers don't even have shoes, stockings or shirts," he grumbled. "And I shall be obliged to furnish what is absolutely necessary."

*   *   *   *   *

Later that summer of 1749 Governor William Shirley of Massachusetts Bay confirmed the French were fortifying Saint John, a site very close to the growing encampment of Mi'kmaq. Cornwallis flew into a rage. "That is a direct violation of the treaty," he shouted to silent, stone-faced men on the council. They had seen their commander angry before and no one had any desire to be the lightning rod drawing his wrath out of the clouds. "St. John River is undoubtedly within the limits of Nova Scotia. A French fort there might be of dangerous consequences to this province and to the other British colonies in North America."

Apocalyptic scenes played out in his mind of the French capturing Nova Scotia and the whole of North America, leaving Britain's New World in tatters, and his career in ruins. He sent the armed sloop *Albany* to the St. John River to get a first-hand report of what work was being done. "Demand to know by what authority such forts are being erected," he instructed Edward How. "Prevent them from making further progress. Or even demolish what they've built, as you see fit. Do whatever it takes. I will give you a declaration to deliver to the commander of Saint John Fort – that is, if any one dares answer to that title. Assert in the name of the King of Great Britain that he must stop."

Dealing with the French incursions delayed work on the town, driving up bills as he had to pay labourers longer and feed the settlers. A hot summer and drought drove up the price of supplies brought in from Boston, further depleting the coffers.

Cornwallis glowered at the New Englanders price gouging him and sent an officer to Boston to negotiate a better deal for the greater good of King George. On the plus side, the town had been fully cleared and lots marked out for each settler to build his home. Many houses were started and in just a month, the untouched woods were becoming a recognizable settlement. A collection of little wood houses, huts, and big log houses stretched for half a mile on either side of the town.

The settlers were joined by many from the British evacuation of Louisbourg. A few adventurers from New England had reversed the usual flow and moved to Chebucto. Rumour was that another one thousand New Englanders planned to arrive before winter.

Cornwallis ordered all government ships travelling from New England to Halifax to give free passage to would-be immigrants.

Captain How returned from the St. John River with unexpected guests – deputy leaders from the Mi'kmaq. They renewed their submission to the British king and signed an article of agreement reinforcing the 1726 treaty. They left for home the same day, paddling across the harbour and vanishing into the woods. Cornwallis was in good spirits, though troubled by persistent reports that the French and Mi'kmaq were often seen together.

How said they had searched the river for the French, but found nothing. Eventually, a schooner arrived and its crew informed him the French were further up the country with the Mi'kmaq. Captain John Rous, a Boston man who first arrived in Nova Scotia to participate in the 1745 siege of Louisbourg, took possession of the schooner, promising to return it after the mission was completed, and went to the French. Rous, the senior naval officer in the colony, met with two French officers, thirty soldiers and about 150 Mi'kmaq. The French planted King Louis's colours on the shore within musket-shot of the *Albany*. When Cornwallis heard this report, his face darkened. The messenger faltered. "Go on," Cornwallis ordered.

"Well, we made them strike their colours directly, delivered your letter and received an answer. The French were only there to prevent the English from settling there, they said. They demanded also that French inhabitants be allowed to freely and publicly practice their religion."

"Prevent the English from settling? Did they not cede that land to our king?" Cornwallis asked. The messenger started to answer, but was silenced by Hugh Davidson. While France and England had agreed to cede Nova Scotia to England, they had not bothered to draw a boundary. The French extended their Canada claim right to the peninsula connecting the lobster-shaped land to the mainland. Of course they maintained the lobster's claws, too – Île Royale. But Cornwallis believed the Nova Scotia boundary pushed deep past the peninsula and to the edge of Quebec.

Cornwallis fumed. He sent Paul Mascarene back to Annapolis Royal to dispatch one hundred men to furnish Minas with a blockhouse fortification and provisions for the winter. "It is not easy to know the designs of these French inhabitants, but one may see what kind of subjects they are from their aversion to aver allegiance to His Majesty," he said, "and their willingness to consult the French governor."

"We need more Protestant French," he concluded.

7
The Threat of Winter War

Cornwallis surveyed the extent of the fortifications in early September. The walls were sturdy, and there was a good thirty feet of clear space between the pickets and the woods. The pickets ran from the harbour water up the citadel hill, crossed halfway up its slope, and then came back down the other side. The town settled at the bottom of the slope. More people made their final commitment to life in the New World, packing their belongings and leaving their nautical homes of several months in favour of their new homes on land. For many, especially the women and children, it was the first time they had stood on solid ground since leaving England. Ship legs had long replaced land legs on even the novice ocean travellers, and it took a few days for Halifax to stop wobbling under their feet.

Children too young for labour scampered about the encampment – the only ones thrilled by the adventure, it seemed. But hesitant, too, as more than a few had gone exploring in the woods and never come back. Most probably got lost in the vast, unfamiliar forests, others fell into holes and died, and a few likely were victims of predation by bears, wolves and other animals. But legends arose telling a different story – that the Mi'kmaq had captured and killed the children. The children were accustomed to terrifying stories about Jews and witches, both of whom were regularly attacked, expelled or killed in Europe and used to frighten English children into behaving properly. To many settlers, the little understood Mi'kmaq mainly existed as a primitive, semi-supernatural threat that could materialize out of the woods at any time. There was no record of Mi'kmaq ever targeting European children, but the powerful legends kept youngsters within the fort walls.

Conditions were bad inside the fort walls. Blackflies made people miserable by day and mosquitoes drove them mad at night. All the pale faces were scorched red as tender city skin cooked under the hot sun. Hands were chafed from wielding axes and settlers stooped, limping, as their city bodies buckled under the pain of frontier life. More than a few had been badly injured when they learned the hard way how a tree falls. A few terrifying blazes threatened to raze the settlement when attempts at clear-cutting on the cheap went awry. There was a manic energy to push the woods far away from the settlement. Clear ground would make it harder to sneak up on the town. "I think our town is as secure against Indians as it would be if it was regularly fortified," Cornwallis said admiringly.

"I have intelligence from Cape Breton and all parts of this province that the Micmac design to make some attempt against this settlement. They are joined by the St. John Indians and headed by one Le Loutre, the French priest."

A few weeks previously, Cornwallis had received information that the Mi'kmaq had taken twenty Englishmen prisoner at Canso in what the British saw as an unprovoked attack. It was said some Mi'kmaq were patrolling the Canso Strait in a pirated English ship. Five of the prisoners were settlers from Chebucto visiting in a schooner and the rest were from New England. Cornwallis immediately sent ships to their rescue, but with instructions to "avoid quarrel" with the Mi'kmaq. In the end, the Mi'kmaq took their prisoners to Louisbourg and sold them to France. The French sent them back to the British.

Cornwallis thought the French were behind the Mi'kmaq attacks on his settlers. In particular, he focused on the French priest Jean-Louis Le Loutre. Le Loutre had been born in France, but moved to Louisbourg in 1737. Now aged about forty, he had spent the last twelve years travelling the region in his canoe, doing missionary work with the Acadians and Mi'kmaq. He spoke French, Mi'kmaq and likely some English. His main base was the chapel in the Mi'kmaq village of Shubenacadie. He had good relations with the British until 1744, when France and England resumed fighting in the War of the Austrian Succession (1740-1748). Le Loutre effectively became a military leader operating with a great deal of autonomy between the French and Mi'kmaq and was a hated and feared opposition to British imperial ambitions in Acadia.

"The French are doing everything in their power to excite the Indians to molest us," Cornwallis wrote to London. "I heard from an officer – a settler – at Minas that they are all colleagued with Le Loutre. It is my opinion that if the Indians also begin, we ought never to make peace with them again. It will be very practicable with an addition of force by sea and land to root them out entirely."

Cornwallis still held hope for his plan to remove the Mi'kmaq from the peninsula of Nova Scotia. He did not want a fight with them to drag on and flare up over and over again; he wanted a final solution. With the Mi'kmaq gone, the French would be deprived of their ally. For the isolated Acadians who remained, Cornwallis could demand their fidelity. He felt confident that with no allies left, they would take the full oath to his king.

"Nova Scotia then would be the strongest colony His Majesty possesses," he wrote.

The new fortress city of Halifax had a satellite. Cornwallis had sent Gorham and his rangers deep into the basin to the far northeast corner where a river emptied into the harbour. Cornwallis called the river the Sackville and ordered Gorham to set up an outpost on a hill overlooking it. The Sackville also overlooked the traditional route the Acadians took to Chebucto from Pisiquid. Pisiquid, or Pisiguit as the Mi'kmaq pronounced it, was a key Acadian settlement about forty-five miles from Halifax. The name Pisiguit was a Mi'kmaq word meaning junction of waters; it was where the Avon and St. Croix rivers flowed into the Minas Basin. A Massachusetts expedition had attacked and razed it in 1704, but it was slowly, cautiously rebuilding. The settlement would be renamed Windsor when an influx of New England Planters arrived in 1764, following the expulsion of the Acadians.

Gorham's Rangers established themselves near the head of the Sackville River to guard communications with Minas and command the bay. Cornwallis sent a vessel to assist him and supplied materials to build barracks. Gorham built his fort near Mi'kmaq camps. It was a location that had drawn people for millennia, as the fish in the river were a vital component of their diet and it was a major transit artery to the interior. The rangers were armed with guns and regularly killed the Mi'kmaq they saw near their fort. The camps were ultimately abandoned and the Mi'kmaq were dislocated from their vital food resource.

On August 30, a ship from Liverpool, England, arrived with 116 fresh settlers. They quickly cleared a spot for their houses on two newly cut streets. Cornwallis observed, "Everything is going very well indeed, much better than could have been expected. The settlers of late behave very decently."

8
The First Murder and Execution

The summer of 1749 saw Nova Scotia's first official murder. Peter
Cartcel was the accused, and Abraham Goodsides the victim. Cartcel
was an oddity among the early settlers of Halifax. He was from France
and spoke little English. He'd sailed on the *Baltimore* with the original settlers. Goodsides had been a boatswain on the *Beaufort*, the ship that served
as Cornwallis's floating city hall. He was English and spoke very little
French. Still, on the afternoon of August 26, the two were talking on the
Beaufort in what common language they could manage when Goodsides
abruptly asked Cartcel why he "used him ill." Cartcel replied in French, so
none of the many onlookers understood what he said. It was never clear if
Goodsides did either, but he decided it was a further insult and challenged
Cartcel to a fight. In case the language prevented Cartcel from understand-
ing the challenge, Goodsides slapped him across the face. Witnesses reported Cartcel instantly produced his knife and thrust the four-inch blade into
Goodsides' chest. "I am gone," Goodsides said before dying. Other sailors
descended on Cartcel and he fought several off before being overpowered.
He was jailed and the case brought to Cornwallis.[20]

Cornwallis followed the model used at Annapolis Royal and named
himself and six councillors as a general court to hear the case. None of
them had legal training, but he thought establishing the rule of law was
more important than having training. It was essentially a civilian version
of the court he had served on after the Pacification of Scotland. Five days

20 Jobb, Dean. *Bluenose Justice*. Halifax, Nova Scotia: Pottersfield Press, 1993. Page 86.

after the killing, Cartcel stood trial in one of the few buildings completed on the shore – a warehouse. Four witnesses described the altercation and all pointed the finger at Cartcel. The Crown indictment stated that he, "not having the fear of God before his eyes, but moved and seduced by the instigation of the Devil, had most traitorously and voluntarily killed and murdered against the peace, crown and dignity of our sovereign the King."

Cartcel had no lawyer, barely spoke English, and mounted no defence. An interpreter translated his not guilty plea to the court. The case of King vs. Cartcel was held before a twelve-man jury appointed by Cornwallis. It had sailors, a surgeon, a schoolmaster, farmers and artisans. They were all English. The jury deliberated for thirty minutes before finding Cartcel guilty. Cornwallis sentenced him to hang. Cartcel asked for and was given access to a clergyman. Two days later, the settlers assembled on the shore to watch Cartcel led to the scaffolding and hanged until he was dead. Less than a week had passed since the killing.

"We endeavoured to follow as near as possible the English laws and customs," Cornwallis wrote to London. "We may have failed in form, but the substance and design of the law was certainly observed."

He posted his letter to London describing the colony's first legal effort. The eventual response praised the trial as "very regular and proper" and said it would "convince the settlers of the intention of conforming to the Laws and Constitution of the Mother Country in every point."

The hundreds of settlers watching the execution got a clear message – the long arm of England's law comfortably reached these rough shores.

*   *   *   *   *

Justice was patchy in Nova Scotia. There are no records of anyone being charged with murdering a Mi'kmaq during the century, but Mi'kmaq people were often collectively punished for the crimes of others. In July 1724, the court at Annapolis – the one which inspired Cornwallis – met to discuss the fate of nine Mi'kmaq held captive in the fort. The province's lieutenant-governor, John Doucett, met with his court-council in the garrison to discuss a problem. The Mi'kmaq had declined to recognize the British king as their sovereign and so were declared in rebellion. The Mi'kmaq warriors raided British outposts and attacked sentries in an attempt to drive the British out of their territory. In response, Doucett had nine

Mi'kmaq abducted from a village, brought to the fort and held. The British issued demands and said they would execute the hostages one by one until their demands were met. Doucett told the various Mi'kmaq chiefs they must submit to his government, promise to demean themselves peaceably, and to inform his government if any other Mi'kmaq were not planning to submit. "Upon which promise, the Indian prisoners here were treated with all humanity and kindness, till by some articles of peace with the savages in general they might with security be released," he wrote.

But if any British subjects were killed, or the garrison came under attack, he warned he would start killing prisoners.

On July 14, a Mi'kmaq warrior party fell on a British patrol, killed the sergeant of the garrison and attacked the garrison itself. Another soldier was killed in the attack and four injured. Two English houses were set on fire and two men, one woman and two children taken hostage; all were released unharmed.

Doucett gathered his court-council. "It is our opinion that since all the kind usages this barbarous people have received seems rather to render them more inhuman and treacherous, it will be for His Majesty's service, the security of this garrison, and the English subjects inhabiting about it, to make reprisals by the death of one of the savage prisoners in custody to deter them from any further outrage, when they will lay under the fear of losing eight more still left in our possession," Doucett ruled.

The guards picked a young Mi'kmaq chief from the cells and brought him to the scaffold. The man was not charged with any offence, and it was not suggested he had participated in any criminal activities. He stood on the gallows, had his ceremonial headdress removed, and the noose placed around his neck. The people of Annapolis gathered to watch as the trapdoor beneath his feet opened and he strangled to death.

* * * * *

Cornwallis sat in his room writing by candle. He pleaded with London to send more armed sloops, or it would be impossible to hinder the French ambitions. The settlement needed provisions and livestock, too. He explained his plan for the Mi'kmaq. He felt there could be no peace with them, so there must be fighting. But he explained to his bosses in London he did not want a war that would lead to a truce, only to be followed by more war. He wanted one final war that would drive the Mi'kmaq off the peninsula and conclude with no peace treaty, but with the end of the Mi'kmaq in Nova Scotia. He wrote to London that this would be "very practicable" and "no very difficult matter."

The damp fall weather afflicted his bones with rheumatism. It was going to be a long, hard winter. Ghosts of Duc D'Anville tormented his sleep. When the tide was low, the skeletons of the ill-fated ships rose above the water. Soldiers and rangers travelling from Halifax to Gorham's fort regularly discovered decomposed French soldiers. A few reported finding skeletons still in uniform, collapsed against a tree. These were presumably the last to die, when none were left to bury them. It was a chilling sight.

Good news came the next day. The French inhabitant deputies returned to Halifax with a letter signed by one thousand Acadians. Cornwallis was content that fire had been doused for the moment. But on September 18, bad news arrived. Two frantic messengers delivered two frantic letters from Minas. Captain John Handfield, who had spent his entire military career in Nova Scotia, wrote that two settlers had been attacked by the Mi'kmaq at Chignecto. In the ensuing melee, three Englishmen had been killed and seven Mi'kmaq slain before the rest escaped.

Handfield said Le Loutre had recently relocated to the isthmus with some Mi'kmaq, and it was highly probable he was there to incite them to war. Cornwallis called an urgent council meeting on the *Beaufort*. They resolved to send a letter to the French governor of Île Royale, or Cape Breton Island, asking him to recall Le Loutre. He also told the governor that if any French subject entered Nova Scotia without permission and joined the Mi'kmaq, it must be looked upon as a breach of faith and friendship of which the British king should be informed.

As the leaves turned an extraordinary firework of red, orange and yellow, and as the air cooled toward mid-fall, Cornwallis stood contemplating the fence that blocked the king's settlement from the "savages" in the woods beyond. Inside the fort, things were improving. Even the least industrious men had realized winter was coming – a winter unlike anything many of them had experienced before. The New Englanders painted a vivid picture of snow not just dusting the ground before melting away as it did in England, but falling and staying, stacking up in thick layers until it accumulated halfway up the trees, as deep as a man is tall. This would not be a damp, cool winter of England, but a deep freeze that could set in any time in late fall and stay into the spring. Those without warm houses would not be inconvenienced – they would be dead.

Outside the fort was another matter. Cornwallis worried about a winter attack from the Mi'kmaq. He had made peace with the St. John River Mi'kmaq, but not with many others. He particularly feared bands based in the south at Cape Sable and in the north at Cape Breton and from the island the Mi'kmaq called Epekwitk. In European eyes, the island was held by France and called Île Saint-Jean, or St. John's Island, renamed Prince Edward Island when the British seized it in 1758.

"Encouraged and set on by the French, they will give us trouble. All my accounts from Cape Breton denote it. They will attack the settlement. They'll come from the Cape Sable, the St. John Island and Cape Breton – from all over the peninsula. Le Loutre, the priest sent from France as a missionary to the Micmacs, is with them," he wrote.

Cornwallis spat at the man's name. "He's a good for nothing scoundrel as ever lived. So far, they have taken a vessel with sixteen or eighteen men at Canso. I sent four men after them. The men came back – but not the vessel. They've attacked at Chignecto and killed three men. Eight Indians boarded the vessel to traffic in a friendly manner – then tried to demolish the crew in a surprise attack. Luckily, seven out of the eight Indians were killed or desperately wounded and we had only three killed," he told London.

"Next, six men were sent out from Chignecto idly, without arms, to cut wood for the mill. The Indians lay in ambush and killed four men, carried off one. The other escaped and gave the alarm, upon which I sent a detachment. But they [the Mi'kmaq] soon made off – cut off – the heads of two and scalped one. I had a guard at the mill. They did not choose to attack. These scoundrels will be troublesome."

John Gorham was not fazed by the trouble; he had always taken it for granted. He urged Cornwallis to employ his rangers to clear the woods around Halifax. Otherwise, there would be no living in the settlement.

"The French are behind this," Cornwallis wrote to London. "I made known to the Micmac that His Majesty graciously intended friendship with them. I exhorted them to assemble their tribes, told them that I would deliver the presents the King, my master, had sent them. They seemed well inclined. Some even stayed trafficking amongst us, well pleased. No sooner was the evacuation of Louisbourg made and Le Loutre sent among them and they vanished and have not been with us since.

"The St. John [River] Indians I made peace with. They made submissions to the king. It was word for word the same treaty as made at Canso Bay. I intended to keep up a good correspondence with the St. John Indians, a warlike people."

Gorham said none of the Mi'kmaq could be trusted. Cornwallis agreed and said so to London. "The treaties with the Indians are nothing. Nothing but force will prevail. The French of this peninsula behave strangely, insisting upon the reserve of not carrying arms, or not taking the oaths and leaving the country. Leaving the country is bad, as it strengthens the enemy. But it would be better that happen than for us to yield to them. They are, I fear, a secret, inveterate army preying upon our bowels masked. At bottom, nothing can please them. Nothing but severity or greater power awe and bring them to their duty and allegiance. This settlement touches them to the quick. Believe me, they will leave no stone unturned to render it ineffectual. We cannot permit that to happen."

He wrote that on September 30 a body of savages fell upon some men cutting wood near the sawmill in Dartmouth and "barbarously" killed four and carried away one. Cornwallis pleaded for more resources so that he could get the job done. Without deep investment, the colony would come to ruin. But with a little watering, the garden would flower.

"Within four years, I will make Nova Scotia His Majesty's, to all intents and purposes great and more flourishing than any part of North America. At present it stands naked and exposed in its very infancy, yet it is more valuable than Cape Breton. Ten times more! Give it walls and forts and we will defy the power of France. And yet more, much more, might be done to make Halifax and Nova Scotia His Majesty's."

Cornwallis updated his paymasters on the settlement's progress. What had been woods on a hillside just months earlier was now a cleared settlement with three hundred houses built and more nearing completion. "This is not some airy project. We need not look further; in Halifax, the king is in possession of a valuable treasure that nothing but superior force can take from him."

Money was becoming a problem, but Cornwallis was convinced every penny spent in Nova Scotia would be returned tenfold. Nothing was idly thrown away, nothing unused. This province had to be protected for His Majesty at any cost.

9

The First Scalping Proclamation

On October 1, 1749, Cornwallis gathered his council to discuss the growing French and Mi'kmaq problem. After long hours of thought and conversation, he had decided it was time to implement his solution. The bright success of Culloden and the Scottish Pacification may have been illuminating his mind when the councillors met in his home on Parade Square. He outlined the options. One approach involved redeploying their limited military resources to push back the French and their Mi'kmaq allies. Another option was to arm the settlers, so that if the fort were attacked over the winter, at least they would be able to fight for their lives.

Council discussed both options, but decided there was no greater advantage to be had from repositioning the troops, who were already strongly arranged, and that arming all the settlers would potentially prove more dangerous than facing a full attack. Council resolved to arm the ordnance artificers (the men who kept the colony's weapons in good working order), the New Englanders who had fought in Louisbourg and other battles, and any settlers who had completed military service for the Crown. Therefore, Halifax would not be undefended, but neither would it be full of ordinary men packing firearms.

Council turned to the Mi'kmaq problem. The settlement was small, isolated from the empire it served and the settlers' appetite for battle was weak. They had crossed the ocean to escape the poverty and deprivation of the Old World for the supposed prosperity of the New World. They had little interest in laying down their lives for king and country. The council talked about the hostilities committed by the Mi'kmaq at Canso, Chignecto and, just the day before, the sawmill in Dartmouth. This last incident would become the *casus belli* for the coming war.

John Salusbury reported on the attack to council and later recorded his impressions in *Expeditions of Honour*. He wrote that the young settlement was battered by rough weather in the week leading up to the attack. Sunday, September 24, brought cold weather and a growing wind. The week that followed was tossed by misting rain, hard showers and "the hardest gale since we came."

"The rain continues with cold, but the cold always less in proportion as the wind abates. The wind comes to the south. The rain continues," he wrote. September 29 was Michaelmas Day and offered clear skies. On this day before the sawmill attack, he saw little threat from the natives, but worried about the loyalty of the Mi'kmaq based on St. John's Island (Prince Edward Island). "I know not what to think of the Indians. They cannot essentially hurt us, but their not appearing looks not well and those at St. John's Isle not coming as they promised is worse," he wrote. "Those under Le Loutre are certainly determined against us, and without French and Scotch knavery we may defy them all."

His bravado crumbled in the next entry when he recorded the attack on Major Guillman's men in Dartmouth Cove. To the English, the Dartmouth site across the harbour was a convenient place to station a sawmill so they could make use of Nova Scotia's ample supply of wood to build their own homes, rather than rely on expensive imports from New England. Dartmouth was chosen for convenience, and because the site had a strong enough river to power the mill. For the Mi'kmaq, the same site was the head of a crucial waterway used for fishing and travelling. As the British refused to enter into negotiations with them to discuss territorial claims, the Mi'kmaq had decided to take any expansions of Halifax as an act of war and to attack them.

Salusbury recorded the details in hurried, partial sentences: "Major Guillman attacked at his sawmill. Six of his people clearing the river but two hundred yards from his fort shot at. One escaped, the five butchered. He is supported. The murderers fled." It was a day free of fog, so reinforcements easily paddled across the harbour. A detachment of rangers pursued the assailants into the woods. Three Mi'kmaq were caught. The rangers beheaded two and scalped the third.

This bloody raid so close to Halifax shook everybody, though Salusbury claimed the settlers were "in high spirits."

Council sat grim-faced as he delivered his report. "Should we declare war against the Indians?" asked Hugh Davidson.

Cornwallis said no. "I am of the opinion that to declare war against them would be in some sort to own them a free and independent people, whereas they ought to be looked on as rebels to His Majesty's government or as so many bandit ruffians and treated accordingly," he said. "If there was to be a 'war,' it will not be a war that ends with a peace agreement. That will only delay the final battle for another time. No, it would be better to root the Micmac out of the peninsula decisively and forever. In order to secure the province from further attempts of the Indians, some effectual methods should be taken to pursue them to their haunts and show them that because of such actions, they shall not be secure within the province.

"I give orders to the commanding officers at Annapolis Royal, Minas and all others within the province to annoy, distress and destroy the Indians everywhere."

After further discussion, council settled upon its course of action. Not war, but destruction. The government of Nova Scotia would encourage and pay for the murder of all Mi'kmaq of any age or gender. A company of fifty men was raised in the settlement to scour the woods around the town and kill or disperse any Mi'kmaq. A further one hundred men were to join John Gorham over the winter and hunt Mi'kmaq people across the entire province. To collect their pay, they were to cut part of the scalps off of their victims and bring them to a government post. Anyone who tried to help a Mi'kmaq would be subject to being harassed or killed.

Cornwallis stood at the table to read the final text, which was to be issued in a proclamation the next day and read and posted across Nova Scotia.

"Whereas, notwithstanding the gracious offers of friendship and protection made in His Majesty's Name by us to the Indians inhabiting this Province, the Micmacs have of late in a most treacherous manner taken 20 of His Majesty's Subjects prisoners at Canso, and carried off a sloop belonging to Boston, and a boat from this Settlement and at Chignecto basely and under pretence of friendship and commerce; attempted to seize two English Sloops and murder their crews and actually killed several, and on Saturday the 30th of September, a body of these savages fell upon some men cutting wood and without arms near the sawmill and barbarously killed four and carried one away.

"For those causes we by, and with the advice and consent of His Majesty's Council, do hereby authorize and command all Officers Civil and Military, and all His Majesty's Subjects or others to annoy, distress, take or destroy the Savage commonly called Micmac, wherever they are found, and all as such as aiding and assisting them, give further by and with the consent and advice of His Majesty's Council, do promise a reward of ten Guineas for every Indian Micmac taken or killed, to be paid upon producing such Savage taken or his scalp (as in the custom of America) if killed to the Officer Commanding."

When he said, "as in the custom of America," he was not referring to Mi'kmaq custom, but to the custom of British colonial governments. Massachusetts had pioneered the practice in 1696 and revived its bounty in 1744, offering cash for the scalps of Mi'kmaq men, women or children. Cornwallis extended that decree to Nova Scotia. The French offered their own scalp bounty, paying for the scalps of British soldiers, and urging Mi'kmaq warriors to ply that grim trade. There is no record of any Mi'kmaq leader issuing a similar proclamation.

While waging destruction with his right hand, Cornwallis thought it prudent to hold an olive branch in his left and sent one thousand bushels of corn and five hundred bushels of wheat to the St. John River Mi'kmaq.

Salusbury picked up his diary. "Council held. Orders prepared to pursue the Indians and war declared," he said. This indicates that while Cornwallis declined to officially declare war, at least some of his council understood they were at war with the Mi'kmaq. "God almighty prosper us. What for the St. John [River] Indians now? Proposals of wheat to retain them perhaps now too late. We have no intelligence of any kind. Rangers necessary and immediately."

Salusbury pivoted mid-entry to personal concerns. The mail had arrived from England. "Letters for everybody but me. Surely nobody would detain my letters and it is almost impossible that everybody should neglect me. Hetty [his wife] must have wrote. Why should not Tom [his brother]? We cannot expect any account now till spring. This with everything almost breaks my heart, but this more than anything."

The proclamation was signed by Cornwallis and the council. The rangers and civilian volunteers were ordered to clear the Mi'kmaq off the peninsula of Nova Scotia. Major Guillman left for New England, where he would raise a company of rangers and bring them back to Halifax to further the clearance. Volunteer units were raised from the settlers and patrolled the woods near the settlement. Cornwallis, perhaps suffering another bout of rheumatism, retreated to his home. He would spend almost half his time in Nova Scotia confined to his bed with rheumatism.

Salusbury found himself at a loose end. He had hoped for promotion, or at least promotion to improved living quarters, but was disappointed. "I am left in my old hole on board the *Beaufort*. Davidson takes possession of the cabin. I care not," he wrote.

Throughout the winter the rangers, volunteers and adventurers combed the woods of Nova Scotia in the hopes of finding small groups of undefended Mi'kmaq. While no accurate records were kept for how many bounties were paid, some individual accounts give a sense of the scale of the raids. In one incident, a party of Gorham's Rangers brought in twenty-five scalps, claiming a bounty totalling £250. The paymaster protested some of the scalps were likely Acadians, but he was ordered to pay the full amount.

This was a recurring problem. What exactly constituted a Mi'kmaq person? What if someone was mixed race, with a Mi'kmaq mother and an Acadian father? What if the Mi'kmaq blood was a grandparent? Cornwallis did not spell it out in his bounty. Previous bounties from the Massachusetts government had decided that if someone was mixed race and living in an Acadian village, they were exempt from the bounty, but that was not addressed in Nova Scotia.

Nor was the question of personal loyalty. If a Mi'kmaq village, family or individual supported the British Crown, or wished to remain neutral, they could not. The scalping bounty effectively removed all people classified as Mi'kmaq from the law. This was also true if a person was in fact from another First Nation. Anyone coming under the broad category of "Indian" was not protected by the British state and could be killed. Countless Acadians died and in some cases it is reported that rangers turned on each other, or made the most of Mi'kmaq attacks, and sold the scalps of dead rangers to the British government.

10

Dawn Raid for Scalps

Following the bounty proclamation, soldiers, settlers and mercenaries roamed Nova Scotia hunting Mi'kmaq families. Few records were kept, but a 1759 raid illustrates the methods used to cash in on the reward.[21]

Colonel Scott and Major Samuel Rogers hunted Mi'kmaq around Digby. They recruited a "much respected" Trout Cove man called Richard Robert Annabury and he recorded one raid in the autumn of 1759. Locals were troubled by rumours of a Mi'kmaq village near Crowley's Point. Rogers rounded up some rangers and went after them. The group marched overland toward Bear River, crossed the river and travelled through woods following the river and the Annapolis Basin. From there they passed to Baxter's Point and finally, by using a spyglass, were able to see their enemies in the distance. It was a normal village comprised of elders, women, children and men.

Rogers wanted to surprise them to maximize his return on the money he had invested in the rangers, so he ordered his men to sleep in the woods that night. While they relaxed, Rogers crept to the Mi'kmaq village for a moonlight reconnaissance. The families were celebrating a festival of some kind. They took turns singing, dancing and joking. The British soldier watched, observing the location of the tents and who slept where. Annabury noted that none of them knew anything about this particular

---

21 Wilson, Isaiah. *Geography and History of the County of Digby, Nova Scotia*. Halifax, Nova Scotia: Holloway Bros., 1900. Page 25.

village, but Rogers declared his intent to kill them all "in retribution for former acts of violence committed by their race."

Rogers went back to his men and explained the plan: the rangers would attack at dawn. Surprise was crucial, because there was no money for escaped villagers. The rangers slipped softly through the woods and closed the remaining distance. Silently, they entered the village. Rogers indicated the chief's home and the men broke into it and killed him while he slept. They managed to kill several more people before the alarm was raised and the villagers fought back or fled. Deprived of any weapons, they ran in disorder, mothers grabbing children, fathers protecting families, and the rangers hacking at everyone with their sharp axes and knives and firing muskets at those who escaped immediate bloodshed.

The rangers chased the fleeing villagers along the shore and trapped them on a point of land. The rangers opened fire and killed most as they scrambled down the bank. Those who escaped into the water were prevented from returning to land and drowned. Only a few escaped the killers and ran into the woods. The village was razed. The site of the massacre was renamed Rogers Point.

Isaiah Wilson, the author of *The Geography and History of the County of Digby, Nova Scotia*, the book recording the massacre more than a century later, described the Mi'kmaq as the "primeval inhabitants of our country" and wondered why they resisted British rule. He speculated that they held the materialism and social hierarchy of Europeans in contempt. "They believe all men equal," he wrote. "Their principal abhorrence of a civilized way of life seems to arise from what they observe among people who style them barbarians, whose corruptions and false ideas of things they affect to despise, and none more so than the respect paid to riches, which are, they remark, frequently possessed by the most worthless of mankind."

Wilson explained away the massacre with a brief note that the "Indians, however, often harassed the English settlements in various parts of the province." He then notes that the Mi'kmaq "race is rapidly decreasing" at the time of his writing, a decrease he blames on their lifestyle exposed to the elements.

II

Winter Takes a Toll

The council gathered in Cornwallis's house on October 14. The governor's home was a rough affair, made out of hewn lumber and surrounded by dirt embankments with guns at each corner. The new quarters hosted their meeting about minor issues besetting the province. Cornwallis issued a proclamation that a £10 reward was on offer for tips leading to the detainment of whoever had assaulted one of his officers.

It was brought to his attention that the settlement faced a rather grim problem. People were dying and those without family were being left to rot in their homes, or even on the street where they fell. Cornwallis summoned the justices of the peace. He gave them power to compel up to twelve people from the area of a dead person to carry the corpse to the grave and attend the burial. "If they decline without good reason, he will have his name erased out of the Register of Settlers as unworthy of His Majesty's bounty," he said. This meant they would no longer receive rations from the government.

Hugh Davidson drew up another proclamation and Cornwallis signed it. Rheumatism was setting in with the winter; his hand shook, and the letters sprawled on the page. Council decided they would attempt to keep ships coming and going to New England all winter. Those who knew the area said the harbour would remain passable. There would be no ships from England, so it was vital to keep ships going to the other colonies. "I think it quite proper, in case of any accidents," wrote Salusbury. "Besides, it will give us a better figure to the enemy and Indians who might be prompted, if the shipping left us, to be troublesome."

Cornwallis's own ship, the *Sphinx*, left Halifax for Madeira. Salusbury sailed with her as far as Sambro Head and then made his way back to Halifax. Salusbury went to Cornwallis's house that night and slept on the ground in Richard Bulkeley's room. "The first time I lay on shore since I left Portsmith," he noted.

In early November, John Gorham rode back into town stinking of the wilderness. Cornwallis heard him bellowing ungratefully from the beach as soon as he hopped out of his schooner. "Where's my money?" he shouted to the settlement at large. Cornwallis, cooped up in his quarters, made no move to provide a response. Gorham revelled in his role as the lone wolf patrolling the outermost reaches of Nova Scotia to keep it safe from savages while the city slickers toiled in Halifax, but when it came to wanting money from the Crown, he had a lot of company. There was an orderly queue wanting cash from Cornwallis and he saw no reason to let Gorham jump ahead.

Gorham treated Cornwallis with thinly veiled contempt, and as a member of the council, he could not be ignored. He laid out his claim in a notice read out at the next meeting.

"I am here to present you with a memorial regarding the hardships I lay under by not being regularly paid either upon account of my company or for my vessels that had been hired into the service by Governor Shirley and desiring that you, your most excellent Excellency, and the council would advise me what method I should take to be reimbursed for considerable sums expended in the province in Our Majesty's service," he wrote.

Cornwallis read it with a stone face. He knew Gorham was right – he was owed money – but it was not a priority. Cornwallis recommended Gorham take his case "to the grace of the Duke of Bedford" in England. Council voted in favour of his plan. Another financial problem booted down the road. More problems were coming. While the latest batch of Haligonians showed little energy for clearing the woods around town or starting work on their plots in the surrounding forests, they had pursued the extinction of trees within the settlement with the avarice of sinners. It was mostly done to feed the fires in their homes, as it was already bitterly cold at night and few wanted to venture into the greater woods for fuel.

104 – Jon Tattrie

Cornwallis issued a proclamation forbidding the cutting down or barking of any more trees within the fort and barricades, and ordered settlers to preserve those that remained as an "ornament" and shelter to the town.

More problems arrived in the form of stolen livestock. Cornwallis read his proclamation for the council's approval: "We shall issue a proclamation requiring that all persons convicted of stealing or destroying oxen, cows, sheep [or] goats shall be punished according to the utmost rigor of the law of England," he declared.

He also had to deal with an angry man who appeared shaking before council and had to be continually told to lower his voice while speaking in the presence of His Excellency. The man laid out his case: he had travelled from England with every intention of settling in Nova Scotia. He received his lot and then left the province, with Cornwallis's permission, to attend to business in New England. But when he returned, he found a stranger had settled on his lot and built a home. The man explained that the squatter was present. The man came forward. Cornwallis interviewed both then ordered the squatter to leave the land to its rightful owner.

The next petition was from inmates of the new public jail. Several settlers languished there. With no trial, they couldn't be convicted and penalized, or declared innocent and return to the settlement. Cornwallis agreed to call a general court at the end of the month. It would be held twice a year from now on, in April and October.

Council agreed. "Ed. Cornwallis" affixed his scribble to it and excused himself. Snow had not fallen, but the temperatures had. It seemed none of his English clothes could keep out the chill. The walls of his quarters seemed more holes than wood, and the wind always found a way in. He dreaded the dark winter to come, when communications with England would slow, and even exchanges to New England or Annapolis would dwindle almost to a standstill. But he knew the Mi'kmaq had lived in this winter season for generations. His enemies would not likely find themselves slowed.

*　*　*　*　*

On December 6, Cornwallis decided to better fortify the settlement for the winter. Accustomed as he was to building military forts and barracks, the slim line of pointed sticks protecting this civilian settlement from deep dark woods and the Mi'kmaq and French beyond seemed precarious. He asked council who among the settlers could be trusted to bear arms and form a militia. He wanted one from each quarter of the town. People had to understand that if the settlement were attacked, no winter help would arrive from England, not even from New England, and it was more likely that Halifax would have to trek across the frozen land to save Annapolis, rather than Annapolis would ride to the rescue of Halifax.

"To form the settlers into a militia will be of the greatest consequence to this settlement," he said.

Another proclamation: Cornwallis ordered all male settlers aged from sixteen to sixty to assemble on the parade square Sunday after church and form into militias. He affixed his shaky signature in smeared ink. After the militias were organized, he turned back to the courts. He laid out scrupulous rules to ensure justice for his settlers.

"Whereas we are above all things desirous that all our subjects may enjoy their legal rights and properties, you are to take especial care that if any person be committed for any criminal matters, he have free liberty to petition for himself or otherwise for a writ of *habeas corpus* which upon such application shall be granted and served on the provost marshal, gaoler [jailer] or other officer having the custody of such prisoners," he dictated to Davidson. "Said provost marshal or other officer shall within three days after such service make return of the work and prisoner before the judge who granted out the said writ and there certify the true cause of the imprisonment."

Cornwallis was satisfied. King George's just hand would reach firmly into Nova Scotia. Even prisoners accused of treason and felony would have liberty to petition in open court for their trials and to present their claimed innocence. There would be no rough justice for settlers in this rough land.

12

Hundreds Die and Fears Mount of a French/Mi'kmaq Attack

December had started with a spell of fine, clear weather, but on December 16, the settlers awoke to a shock of thick frost covering everything. It was a bright, clear morning, and they were amazed to see their own breath hang before them. By the afternoon, the skies had filled with grey, fluffy clouds. It began to snow at three p.m. Two inches would fall – not a lot by Nova Scotian standards, but more at once than many of the settlers had ever seen.

Cornwallis sat in his study rereading the intelligence report he had received that morning. The gloomy skies necessitated the lighting of candle lamps and the fire roared in the fireplace. It was still cold and dark and he strained to read. The governor of French Canada was preparing a winter expedition. He was coming in force to Halifax. The French had recruited every Mi'kmaq warrior they could find, all of whom willingly took up arms against King George. It was said the French alone numbered six hundred soldiers. The Mi'kmaq probably doubled their ranks. That brought them roughly equal to the total population of Halifax – one soldier or warrior for every man, woman and child under Cornwallis's custody. France and England were officially at peace, but it was always an unstable detente.

"I cannot think that the French in open violation of faith and treaty would march against any of the forts made since our arrival," he muttered aloud as he wrote to update London. Davidson sat in the corner wearing his heavy coat and preparing paperwork for the next council meeting. He looked up when Cornwallis spoke as he wrote.

"But notwithstanding, I am of the opinion that it is best to act so as to be secure against all events and therefore I will assemble the council to consult with them if they could think of anything that could be done for the further security of the town," Cornwallis said, looking out his one window. There was little activity that day – the first deep cold of the year had stunned the settlers into hibernation. He would have to rouse them. "I can think of nothing that could be done. Unless the settlers would join together and fell down all the trees around the town ..."

He sat up alert and turned to Davidson. "Let us go look for ourselves," he said. He pulled on his heavy coat, hat and boots and stormed outside. Davidson jogged to keep up. Cornwallis crunched through the vacant streets, the light snow settling on his shoulders and head, his breath pumping in front of him like smoke from a discharged cannon. They followed the streets to the gates, nodded to the guards, and stepped outside. Davidson was nervous – he spent little time unaccompanied in the great wildness of Nova Scotia. Cornwallis pointed to the dark line of evergreen trees some yards from the town's picket defences. The snow draped on the trees like white dresses. The firs seemed to deliberately offset each other, so that even at the forest edge your eyes could penetrate only a few feet. After that, the dark conspiracy of branches confused everything.

The woods were too close, Cornwallis decided.

Davidson stomped his cold feet and agreed.

"We must order the settlers to cut them back further. They must do it tomorrow – it can be left no later. Otherwise, the Indians will use it as shelter to attack. Send out the order – the settlers are to gather on the parade first thing tomorrow. Tell them to bring their axes, saws – any tools that will be handy. This is to be preferred over all other work. By sunset tomorrow, I want to gaze at a vast, empty plain before the wild forest resumes."

Davidson nodded again, shivering.

The next day after church, it happened as ordered: hundreds of men launched a Highland Charge on the woods, hacking back the trees until all useful hiding spaces were gone. Cornwallis inspected the work at sunset and nodded his approval. He slept soundly that night.

*   *   *   *   *

Christmas passed with humble services. Prayers for salvation were as sensitive as charred skin as the settlers faced the reality of winter in the New World wilds. But European poverty burned deeper in their memories, and they redoubled their efforts to make their lives successful here. The problem of corpses persisted. Bodies were less often left on the streets, but loners were now posthumously concealed in their huts. Cornwallis issued a proclamation requiring all housekeepers to inform a clergyman of a death in their home within twenty-four hours, or be fined or jailed.

The rations most subsisted on were salted meat and people ate little that was fresh. It had been weeks since fruit or vegetables were available. Cornwallis had posted a guard on the little river flowing down the citadel hill – the only source of fresh drinking water in the settlement – but it was impossible to keep clean. Thousands of people living, bathing, defecating, and urinating in such a small area turned the water bad. Settlers became even more lethargic than usual. A general malaise fogged the rough town. Skin grew spotted, and people's gums became spongy and bloody. As winter whitened the land, settlers grew paler, more depressed and found the prospect of any movement unappealing. Scurvy had arrived. A typhoid fever epidemic also broke out.

A few died, then a few dozen, then a few hundred. Some counted one thousand dead settlers that first winter. Cornwallis ordered people to put out their dead the day after death – no more wakes, no more home burials. Sections of the town were commanded to organize men to carry and bury the dead at the new cemetery south of the main settlement. The graveyard, eventually known as the Old Burying Ground [now at the corner of Barrington Street and Spring Garden Road], was an acre of land outside of the palisades. Vernon the Carpenter was told to mark the initials of the deceased on the coffin to keep some semblance of order.

Not surprisingly, given the bad health, the long, dark, cold nights and constant fear of attack, liquor flourished. Cornwallis and his council fought a running battle as illegal taverns popped up in private homes one night, before disappearing and rematerializing in another house just before his soldiers could move in. The soldiers had little motivation to stop the flow of booze – who liked a cheap drink more than they? William Croft was stripped of his liquor license for letting soldiers get drunk at his house. It made little difference – the soldiers soon found other places to drink.

Cornwallis finished the council business and adjourned. The others rose and left his quarters for their own. Cornwallis stayed inside, his rheumatism paralyzing his will. He sat at the window and watched the snow blow from trees and roofs, creating a blizzard all by itself. The wooden fence protecting the settlement had snow drifted halfway up the pikes. Cornwallis had a mind to order men to clear the ground, until John Gorham pointed out that a clean surrounding of snow meant any spies would be detected by footprints. That soothed Cornwallis – he began to see the snow as an informant and frequently scanned it for footprints.

Life had slowed in the settlement. Few ventured outside. Trips into the woods were done quickly, in groups big enough to ward off attack. The Mi'kmaq seemed entirely unaffected by the winter but were rarely seen around the settlement as most had departed to winter hunting grounds in the interior. Their clothes and their homes kept them warm. The provisions gathered in finer weather together with the meat hunted in the winter formed a rich diet. They appeared in summer health while the settlers languished in winter sickness. Unlike the stranded Europeans, Mi'kmaq travel through the land was not slowed by the snow and ice. They seemed able to travel without leaving a trace. To counter the fear, and to earn some spare cash, idle men joined Gorham's Rangers in patrolling the province. Many bolstered their incomes by bringing a bagful of scalps to Halifax or Annapolis. Many preferred to target women and children, as they could offer less resistance and posed a lower risk than men.

Cornwallis received reports daily in January. He rarely left his home, for the cold exacerbated his condition and made even holding a quill impossible. Sunlight lit the days only briefly, before the land returned to its natural darkness. The settlement made deeper raids on the woods to turn trees into heat and light.

Cornwallis grew frustrated. The settlement was always on the edge of collapse. Despite 150 years of European presence, Nova Scotia was essentially still a colonial infant. It needed nurturing from Mother England to grow – but grow it would. He knew it would stand alone and prosper, but it needed help first. His bosses in London, those men who had King George's ear and controlled the money, did not see the value of Nova Scotia. They evidently did not see much value in Cornwallis, either, as France and England had resolved Nova Scotia's border dispute without his opinion, and without informing him until after the matter had been completed. France would keep the land on the mainland; Nova Scotia would be

confined to the peninsula. Cornwallis felt disconnected. That felt dangerous. He paced, airing his thoughts to Davidson as he prepared to write to
London.

"I am thoroughly convinced we shall not be able to support the just
claims we have, nor answer the expectations of London when they sent
me here, without an additional force," he said. "I didn't even know until
Bedford wrote me that the two Crowns had agreed upon setting the limits
of Acadia. London will see how unjustifiably the French act even in this.
If the boundaries are to be set, then surely neither nation should possess
any port or place in dispute until the limits were settled to the satisfaction
of the two Crowns."

Despite the paper truce, the French kept trying their luck near Chignecto, the bridge of land that connected peninsular Nova Scotia to the rest
of North America. For France the isthmus and mainland was now officially part of Acadie; for the Mi'kmaq it remained Siknikt and Kespek. Cornwallis reluctantly accepted it as the new border of Nova Scotia, but he did
not believe France would stop at the new border. He believed they were
biding their time to develop an army with the Mi'kmaq before attacking the peninsula. "The Indians are now assembled there. I am ashamed
to admit the first advice I had of it was from Monsieur Jonquiere himself. [Jacques-Pierre de Taffanel de La Jonquière was the governor general
of New France.] It's impossible to get intelligence from those parts," he
complained.

Cornwallis believed the Acadians were secretly working with France.
The Mi'kmaq were massing everywhere, and harassing his settlers. He felt
trapped by snow and thick ice, unable to send orders by land or by water.
There were routes overland, but if he sent enough soldiers to clear a path
and protect itself from Mi'kmaq attack, it would leave Halifax unguarded.
In particular he worried about France taking Chippodie, an Acadian settlement near the disputed border region.

"If the French attempt to take Chippodie I shall be obliged, in honour
of the king I serve, and to the Kingdom of Great Britain, to make use of
all the strength I have to prevent it, to frustrate their perfidious designs.
They are stirring up the Indians from all parts. I have reason to believe
the St. John Indians, notwithstanding the solemn treaty we entered into
with them and that they acknowledged King George, will break off and
the other Indians will join them," he wrote.

He feared England's enemies would join France and overrun the settlement. The Acadian loyalty leaned toward France and some had even married Mi'kmaq, meaning their children had Mi'kmaq blood in them. The worst would take up arms, but even the best would help the rebels. "Upon my word, the settling of this province, preserving our rights and making this country what it is intended to be – a frontier to the other colonies – depends upon more force," he said, pounding his fist into his palm.

It would be expensive to defend Chignecto, but cheaper than trying to reclaim a lost province. And the more they invested in Nova Scotia, the sooner it would stand on its own feet and start contributing to the greater empire. "If people can be protected, they will flock to it," he predicted. "When the country is settled, small will be the force to maintain it in peace or war."

"Write this to London, Davidson," he said. His secretary raised the quill. Cornwallis dictated:

"As it is impossible to say how long the peace may last, add strength to the infant settlement while you may effect it and prevent the French from possessing a country they have long sought, with much expenditure of blood and treasure. If attained, it will be to them of more value than the mines of Peru or Mexico."

*　*　*　*　*

Cornwallis went over the books again. There were provisions for three thousand people for nine months, but the bread and flour supply was only good for six months. He hoped winter would break before his supplies did. He imagined the settlers huddled in their houses and decided to be hopeful. They would be able to fend for themselves after a year – apart from the aged, the sick and the helpless children. If hard times fell, London would have to send more food for everyone anyway. It would be cheaper to invest now and stave off disaster, than to neglect Nova Scotia, provoke a disaster and then be faced with a costly bailout. Or lose the province forever.

He drew up a wish list of things he'd like to see on an English ship sailing into Halifax harbour. Salted beef, pork, bread, flour, and rice. He would put it in the King's storehouses to be used in an emergency. He knew the settlement would not starve in its first winter, but he saw no harm in raising the spectre of empty storehouses to his masters in London and to his charges in the province. Better the settlers thought food was low, rather than inexhaustible. Otherwise, too many men would still prefer to make a living by idly collecting handouts than to work for themselves.

* * * * *

In early January 1750, Cornwallis sent John Gorham to Pisiquid to root out the Mi'kmaq villages. Even as he departed, other reports reached Halifax: a number of the Penobscot Mi'kmaq had joined with the Mi'kmaqs at Minas to attack the fort there. While many Acadians were viewed as allies of the Mi'kmaq, others presented themselves as loyal to the British Crown and terrified of Mi'kmaq raids. One group of Acadians in Halifax petitioned Cornwallis to declare martial law until the danger passed. Council debated whether the Acadians were genuinely loyal and afraid of the Mi'kmaq, or orchestrating a ruse to cover collaboration. Should council declare martial law?

"I do not perceive the danger to be sufficient, or the attack certain enough, for such drastic measures," Davidson offered, "though it is certain the Indians design to attack us."

Cornwallis interrupted him. "Yet if the settlers would only work a few days to throw up some necessary works and keep a guard every night in a quarter, the town would be secure against any number of Indians," he argued.

The others concurred. Council said it would be pleased if Cornwallis would appoint officers to the militia of each quarter to improve their readiness to fight. He also gave the militia captains the power to send to jail anyone who disobeyed his orders, including declining guard duty when it was his turn, or declining to work at any task necessary for the defence of the town.

A supply ship from the Duke of Bedford had arrived from England and tied up in the harbour. It was a welcome site, but it was vulnerable to Mi'kmaq attack as it lay fatly at anchor. The vessel's cables and anchors were in poor condition and could not support the ship anchoring in the winter harbour, so it was decided to moor it on the far shore, near the Dartmouth sawmill, where it would be more protected from the elements – but more exposed to attack. Cornwallis sent an armed sloop to investigate the ship when it anchored near Dartmouth. He decided to leave the supply ship where it was. It was within range of the small fort at the saw-mill, he argued, and so safe from Mi'kmaq attack.

"The only danger I see is if the water freezes and the Indians attack over the ice," he said. "I have instructed the crews to constantly break the ice up to prevent that passage."

But council still feared attack and wanted the ships ordered closer to the main settlement. Cornwallis compromised and agreed to send the port captain over to make an inspection in the next days. Council would act on his advice.

13

Rough Justice on the Frontier of an Empire

The frozen settlement crackled in the cold morning as February 1750 dawned. White snow sparkled like diamonds as the distant sun sent cool rays to play atop it. Ice floated in the harbour. Seals bobbed in the water, lying back and observing the new busyness on the formerly quiet shore. Moose and deer had been hunted out of the woods near the embryonic city and retreated further into the province's interior.

Cornwallis blew on his hands and reported the captain's findings about the supply ship anchoring near Dartmouth. "He sailed to the cove by the sawmill and inspected the sloops. He confirmed my thoughts – the ice is cut clear of the ship every night and it is perfectly safe. We shall leave it where it is," he told council.

The new month brought new problems. The settlement had always been populated with layabouts chasing the dream of a free handout from the state, but now it was being inundated with profligates fleeing debts in Europe. "If we do not act to discourage this, Nova Scotia will become known as a refuge for debtors. We have enough scoundrels as it is. They don't need further encouragement," Cornwallis said.

After much discussion, council agreed that if a debtor fled to Nova Scotia, his land in the province could not be used to repay his debts in England or elsewhere, but all of his personal possessions were open to the collection of debt contracted anywhere. It was hoped this would discourage the idea of the province as a destination to escape British debt law, while at the same time preventing the settlement from turning into a vacant lot of absentee landlords who had won Nova Scotian land in London courts, but had no desire to emigrate.

Liquor continued to be a problem as the settlers drank the winter away. Illegal ale houses opened and closed every night, moving around like the winter stars, ducking below the horizon by morning light. Close one, and it rose again down the street. Already, the jury had investigated forty dens. An increase in duty on alcohol would only harm the settlement's legitimate establishments, so the council increased the financial penalty for the illegal sites and boosted rewards for informants.

"But it still seldom to never has the desired effect," Cornwallis sighed. "Let's add corporal punishment. Enough to render the retailer infamous."

The council warmed to his proposal. A first offence would land the offender in the stocks. The guilty party would have their hands and head locked into the wooden contraption in the Grand Parade. A second offence would earn the offender twenty lashes in the parade. Shame and physical pain would perhaps work where sanctions and economic punishments were failing.

Council ground through its business. The long winter of idleness had generated bickering among the militias. One corporal had even drawn his sword on an officer after a perceived insult. Another soldier threw snow at his commanding officer before dragging him into a snowbank during a fight. Cornwallis called the soldiers before him and each pleaded his case. After they left, he decided that while the sword-drawing corporal had indeed been insulted, the bigger point was respect for authority. He sent word to the corporal that he must either publicly beg for forgiveness from the offending officer, or go to jail. The snowball thrower was to be held in the stocks and whipped twenty times.

The snowballer's punishment was carried out the next day. Word had spread quickly through the little village and hundreds turned out to the Grand Parade at noon to ensure a good view. The offender was led out by two burly soldiers and jammed into the stocks. His head was shoved into the bottom of the yoke and his arms hauled into place beside his head. The top was brought down quickly so it drove the man's throat into the bottom, forcing a yelp from him to the delight of the crowd. The soldiers adjusted his position and locked him in. He was left to his audience. They knew what to do: fruit was scarce in a Nova Scotia winter, but a few mouldy scraps were found and hurled in his face. Rotten fish was more plentiful and provided most of the projectiles.

Cornwallis, listening from his quarters, had no doubt that many of the loudest jeerers had egged the man on to attack his superior.

A roar rose at the back of the crowd, which swiftly parted to allow a grinning butcher through with his steaming delivery: pig guts. He carefully arranged them on the snowballer's neck like jewelry. He was swiftly bettered by a stable boy. Usually at the bottom of Halifax's social pile, he revelled in his temporary elevation and threw a fresh horse patty directly into the face of the stocked prisoner.

When the citizens had had their fun, the soldiers returned and pulled the man's shirt off. It was three degrees below zero, but the cold was the least of his worries. To a rising cheer, the elder soldier brandished his cat, a short wooden handle to which nine waxed cords were attached. It was usually at home on the *Beaufort*, but had been brought ashore to mete out justice on land.

He held it theatrically in the air before slicing it down onto the snowball thrower's back with a snap. The first blow raised five welts – and a whimper from the braced prisoner. The punisher ran the cords through his fingers to strain the clotted blot and bits of flesh. He came down less ferociously for the second strike, as the lashes were to be moderate. Cornwallis wanted a show of public pain and humiliation, not an execution.

But the next eighteen lashes still left the man looking like cougars had mauled him. After thirty minutes of theatre, the stocks were raised and the broken prisoner dragged through the crowd. The offal necklace and fecal face paint ensured him a wide berth. He was returned to his barracks. The satisfied crowd dispersed.

14

Cobb's Not-So-Secret Mission to Attack Chignecto

Hot rumours flared in the cold winter. The Mi'kmaq would capital-ize on their natural advantage and attack. The Acadians who lived in Halifax were certain the invasion would come in February. When the month arrived, they melted away like spring snow. Cornwallis thought of rats deserting ships.

"The attack is imminent," he muttered. Reports reached him that an army of thousands of Mi'kmaq was preparing to attack. "If the Indi-ans keep together at Chignecto, they either have designs to attack or take one of the outposts," he reasoned. "Or maybe it's just a blind to cover the French attack."

But winter blinded him. He could not send a small expedition to sur-vey the situation first-hand for fear they would be captured or killed by the Mi'kmaq. He could not send a large expedition, for fear the Mi'kmaq would slip past them and attack a weakened Halifax. He had no facts – only rumours that swirled like a blizzard. Cornwallis stewed. His temper bubbled.

He decided to send a sea militia to the basin at Chignecto. He turned to a Halifax man called Captain Silvanus Cobb, who knew the area well and was a man "fit for bold enterprises" – and this would be very bold indeed. Cornwallis met with Cobb and laid out the plan. Cobb would take his sloops *York* and *Halifax* and sail the winter waters to New Eng-land to find reinforcements in the form of mercenaries up for adventure. 'I propose you raise about one hundred men at Boston and sail directly to Chignecto, land the men and surprise as many old Indians, women and children as you can," Cornwallis said. "You have been there often – you know every house. I promise you a considerable reward if you can take Le Loutre, too."

"Sir, it is hardly possible that I could fail," Cobb replied.

"I like this enterprise," Cornwallis wrote to London as the man departed. It could solve the intelligence problem, thwart the Mi'kmaq, and not leave Halifax underdefended. He dispatched Cobb to Boston with letters recommending him to the British commander there. He would raise a mercenary expedition force to carry out Cornwallis's secret mission. No Acadian or Mi'kmaq spies would spot troop movement from Halifax, so no alarm would be raised. Cobb's crew would catch them unawares. That surprise would be key to the mission's success.

A few weeks later, word trickled back to Halifax that Cobb had landed in Boston and that his bold enterprise was the talk of New England. Cobb had even taken out an advertisement in the newspaper seeking fellow adventurers for his "cruise" up the Bay of Fundy.

Cornwallis lowered his head into his hands. "How it could enter into a man's head to publish such a loose and unguarded advertisement I cannot conceive," he groaned. The French and their First Nation allies had eyes and ears everywhere. If he in distant Halifax had heard about the advertisement, he was sure his enemies had too. So much for the surprise attack. Cornwallis sighed heavily. These were not Cumberland's crack troops clearing the Highlands.

"I need to put a stop to this voyage. It's the only prudent thing to do," he said. "Order Cobb not to proceed."

The mission was aborted. Cornwallis was back in the dark about what was happening almost everywhere in Nova Scotia, apart from what happened inside the fortress walls. Desperate for intelligence, he sent a letter to the priest at Cobequid, reminding him he had a duty to present himself to Cornwallis. But the priest sensed the weak hand behind the letter. The courier was stopped and detained. The priest did not reply.

Also in February 1750, he received word from the Board of Trade offering support for his bounty on the Mi'kmaq. "As to the measures you have already taken for reducing the Indians, we entirely approve them and wish you may have success. But it has been found by experience in other parts of America that the gentler methods and offers of peace have more frequently prevailed with Indians than the sword," they wrote.

"If at the same time that the sword is held over their heads, offers of peace and friendship were tendered to them, then one might be the means of inducing them to accept the other. But as you have had the experience of the disposition and sentiments of these Savages, you will be better able to judge whether measures of peace will be effectual or not. If you should find that they will not, we do not in the least doubt your vigour and activity in endeavouring to reduce them by force."

Cornwallis would stick to the force method for two years, before finally accepting the wisdom of the board. In June, he had the council raise the bounty to £50 per head. John Gorham, who voted for the original rate, also backed the increase. His rangers were among the chief beneficiaries of the increase.

15

Father Le Loutre's War

A rainstorm in late March erased much of the thick snow surrounding the town. Inside the fort, banks that had been amassing alongside cleared paths slowly diminished. The woods remained impenetrable. But the bright sun shone longer, waking and warming the settlement out of its deep-freeze. Frequent fog added a new level of difficulty to communication and weeks went by without word from Annapolis and the outlying barracks.

"Thank God it is now over," muttered John Salusbury as he took his place at the council table. "Those in Annapolis and Minas call this a long winter, with more snow than is common."

Cornwallis opened the meeting and got directly to its purpose. Like the season, it was time for the settlement to spring out into the rest of the province. They were not here to plant one fortress city and shiver inside; the mission was to start with Halifax and to spread out with other settlements, and to convert the Acadians to a Protestant, British way of life. Cornwallis saw the Chignecto isthmus as the key to victory. It was a bridge of land connecting the lobster of Nova Scotia to the rest of British North America. If France took control of the isthmus, her troops in Canada would take over Nova Scotia and throttle the peninsula. He wanted to seize control of the isthmus and push France back deep into Canada. The land invasion would press out from Halifax. A sea attack would bolster it. Facing an amphibious assault, the Isthmus of Chignecto would rapidly fall completely under British rule.

"In my own opinion, it is absolutely necessary to secure the isthmus immediately if a sufficient force can possibly be spared for that purpose," Cornwallis told the council. "This seems to be the critical moment. The French inhabitants are in suspense, the Indians assembled there with the French company and missionaries who stop at nothing to prevail on the French inhabitants to leave the province. There is intelligence that the French officers have actually erected some kind of fort in those parts."

Cornwallis had thought about it long on the deep winter nights. He feared the Acadians would leave, taking with them their livestock, farming ability and industriousness. That would leave Nova Scotia a barren land. There were not yet enough Protestant settlers to work the lands and he could not yet make them safe to do so. Bringing in new livestock would cost an enormous amount of money and attract negative attention from Whitehall. If his resources were so diverted into repopulating with human workers and animal livestock, the core duty of holding the province would be weakened. He feared the Mi'kmaq would mount a full assault. He worried the French would molest Nova Scotia from Canada, in spite of official peace between France and Britain.

He saw a common solution to these multiple problems: take the isthmus between Nova Scotia and Canada. That would keep the Acadians in, the French out, and deter either from further pestilent alliances with the Mi'kmaq. In the meantime, the scalp bounty would distract and weaken the Mi'kmaq, driving them out of his realm. Those remaining would face a stark choice: allegiance to King George or extinction. He proposed sending a detachment of four hundred men to the isthmus. It should be enough to secure Chignecto, without exposing Halifax. "That will not weaken the force necessary to protect this settlement," he concluded.

The expedition would include men from the rangers working for Gorham, Clappham and Guillman, several light armed sloops and other supply boats. Salusbury would join them. Major Charles Lawrence would command. Council unanimously approved his motion. Cornwallis smiled tightly as he dismissed the council.

Salusbury shared his excitement in a letter to his wife back in England. "I shall now see whether the French have had intelligence of this and satisfy all suspicions, but whether they have had intelligence or no, please God we are strong enough to bring them to reason," he wrote. "And grant O God that in the whole of this transaction I may behave so as to give me self-satisfaction that I may be the more worthy to embrace thee, my dear wife. God bless thee and the poor little girl [his daughter], and grant that we may once more meet – never more to part."

Cornwallis was in the thick of Father Le Loutre's War, though he likely never called it by that name. On March 30, 1750, he directed Major Lawrence of the 40th Regiment to take three hundred regulars, rangers and volunteers to Chignecto and to build a blockhouse there. Lawrence would march his troops overland to Minas Basin, where they would link up with the sea militia under Captain John Rous's command. Rous's ships would transport the army into Chignecto Bay and land the infantry at the mouth of the Rivière Missaquash. The amphibious assault would offer surprise and security – a straight land march to Cobequid would have cost many men to guerrilla attacks from the Mi'kmaq.

On April 5, 1750, Lawrence gathered his forces at Fort Sackville near Halifax and marched to Pisiquid.[22] Gorham's Rangers formed the advance guard and slipped quietly through the woods to detect and disrupt any ambushes. Lawrence kept a tight order on the main body of soldiers.

"They never went out of our ranks, lest the enemy might have taken advantage. Truly in millions of places, twenty men might have annoyed us greatly," Salusbury noted in his journal. In fact, they travelled unmolested and arrived in Pisiquid April 8. John Handfield's company marched from Grand Pré to join forces. The advancing forces all noticed one strange thing: the Acadian villages were empty. Not abandoned – the homes were well kept and the dikes in good shape – but the people were gone. Lawrence understood that to mean the French and Mikmaq forces were at hand and ready to pounce. He waited for Captain Rous's fleet.

Rous had sailed from Halifax with the sloops *Albany*, *York* and *Halifax*, plus six transport ships, on the same day as Lawrence. But it took them ten full days to reach Minas Basin and collect the infantry. Further delays slowed progress and they weren't able to depart until April 18. The heavy ships sailed past Cape Split on the outgoing tide, but the shifting waters of the Bay of Fundy stalled the fleet and it could not get past Cape Chignecto. The tides eventually drove them into Apple River. Rous forced his will over nature and the convoy crawled along the coast toward the Missaquash, where it finally landed the infantry. But the slow, land-hugging progress had been seen by many. Warning fires dotted the landscape, sending word of their progress to the waiting French. As the

22 Grenier, John. *The Far Reaches of Empire*. Norman, Oklahoma: The University of Oklahoma Press, 2008. Page 155.

infantry marched to the French fort at Beaubassin, more smoke belched into the sky. This was bigger than warning fires.

Bartello's Rangers went ahead to gather intelligence. Bartello, who had fought with Cornwallis in Flanders, saw Beaubassin was in flames. The rangers entered the town cautiously and inched through the burning buildings. There was not a person in sight. Father Le Loutre and the Mi'kmaqs had burned the Acadian homes to prevent any more Acadians from living on British soil. They had relocated west into strongly held French territory.

On April 22, Lawrence met the French commander, La Corne. They faced each other under a white flag of truce – La Corne on the French side of the Missaquash, Lawrence on the British bank.

"You have reached the border. Proceed no further," La Corne told Lawrence. He indicated the massive dike, behind which his men and Acadian allies were entrenched.

"We found the enemy ready to receive us in all forms," wrote Salusbury. Ghosts slipped through the woods; Lawrence had no doubt the Mi'kmaq lurked, waiting for the moment to attack. The British detachment that had passed through Grand Pré had confiscated firearms from the local Acadians, which had angered them. That likely led the Acadians to set the fires that tipped the French off to the British attack. French troops had then burned Beaubassin.

Lawrence considered his options. He knew France was standing on English territory and had no right to it. And yet to attack would be an act of war against France, which he had no authority to order. He decided to withdraw. By four p.m., he was marching his troops through ruined Beaubassin. The treachery of the French inhabitants was proved. "The inhabitants are certainly irreconcilable, to burn all," noted Salusbury. "In this fury, I hope they will not join the enemy."

Lawrence held a war council the following day. They voted to return to Halifax. Worried a sea voyage to Halifax would look like a retreat, Lawrence marched hundreds of well-armed men right down the middle of Nova Scotia to make a show of British power. En route, he built Fort Edward blockhouse at Pisiquid. He left a detachment to operate the blockhouse and keep a tenuous British hold on the land.

The peace of winter seemed an illusion. It was only the inhalation of a long fight. War was now roaring back over the land.

Cornwallis met the retreat with barely contained rage. His enemies were plotting his destruction. Without a strong British fort at the Isthmus of Chignecto, France ruled every part of his territory except Halifax and Annapolis. He considered sending a reliable officer in an armed sloop to Chignecto, but worried the time it took to travel and return with intelligence could prove fatal. He reassured himself that the French couldn't have done much over the winter, apart from fortifying themselves where they stood. That would make it harder to dislodge them, but surely not give them the ability to dislodge him. But what if France sent more force, more money? He could be driven into the ocean. His subjects were terrified of the French, and even more of the Mi'kmaq. Everyone knew of someone caught by the Mi'kmaq and sent to an unspeakable fate. The nerve of his settlers was wavering.

Cornwallis sat in silence as he heard the report. His men had found Beaubassin reduced to ashes. They had encountered Le Loutre at the head of the French regulars, Canadian fighters, rebel inhabitants and the Mi'kmaq. The French flags were planted on the dikes. The boastful priest vowed to defend the ground as French "until the last extremity." And Cornwallis's men had been compelled to retreat because England and France were technically at peace. Cornwallis could not let the insult stand. He wrote to London, pleading with them for more money. They had invested so much in Nova Scotia – to abandon it now would be to lose everything. Without paying for more soldiers, more forts and more scalps, it would be taken by the French.

"Every man that goes will be an inveterate and dangerous enemy. If the French settle them all over what they impudently call their territory – the north side of the Bay of Fundy – it will be no easy matter to oblige them to remove," he wrote.

London must send more money, and use more force. The fate of Nova Scotia and the entire northern colonies depended on it.

16

The Cost of War Threatens to Bankrupt the Colony

Cornwallis's mood darkened with the arrival of a ship bearing a letter from Whitehall. He had opened it in good cheer, expecting praise and support from the Board of Trade, but found only complaints. The president of the board, George Montagu-Dunk, Lord Halifax, an early supporter of both Cornwallis and the colonial expansion, worried now that Nova Scotia was costing too much and returning too little.

"We laid before you in our last [letter] the very great uneasiness which had arisen to this from not having your accounts transmitted to us. Then receiving them since in the manner we have done, without any vouchers for many of the most considerable articles, created further difficulties," J. Greenville wrote on behalf of the board. "But we have the pleasure to inform you that we were able from your accounts themselves to give such reasons in justifications of the past expenses as were satisfactory to the House of Commons."

There was praise for Cornwallis, too, and "the astonishing progress which you have by your active leadership and wise conduct made in so short a time toward perfecting the great national work you are engaged in."

But there was a darker tone. He was warned not to get sloppy with his records. "More arrears would disgust Parliament; there is no other method of avoiding to incur them, but the keeping steady to a plan of expenses," Greenville added. "We told you of this mistake both in the most early and friendly manner we could."

Greenville also asked if he could trim yet more of the budget. Cornwallis had been racking up big bills by importing limestone. Couldn't he explore local materials? A former Nova Scotian now in London had told them there was plenty of suitable stone in the province. The board issued veiled threats to cut his core funding if he asked for too many "extraordinary" works. What was extraordinary and what was ordinary was not clarified.

London reminded him that it was not relations with the Acadians or Mi'kmaq, or thwarting French ambitions, or expanding the settlement without exposing the settlers to starvation or invasion that was most critical to the colony's success. The most important people were those who controlled the purse strings. Cornwallis's ability "to preserve the good opinion and affection of Parliament towards it" was paramount to preserving the funding. He had their support – for now at least. "You are mistaken in imagining that any bill was protested," Greenville assured him.

As to his request for extra money: "It is impossible to express our astonishment at so large a demand coming so early and so unexpected and our uneasiness is the greater as it comes without any letter from you that might explain to us on what account or for what service the bills have been drawn," Greenville chastised him. "This new account of bills opens so very disagreeable and unexpected a scene to us that until we receive fresh information relative to the affair, it is not profitable for us to write to you with that degree of precision which it would be our duty to do if we were masters of the whole.

"We can do little more than express our uneasiness upon the present occasion that either you or your successor or whatever may be the exigencies of government will not have a single shilling to provide for them, or that if you do we shall be reduced to the sad necessity of applying another year to Parliament for exceeding, which we have great reason to apprehend will never be allowed."

On the topic of Acadians and Mi'kmaq, the board noted that an earlier letter from Cornwallis had given "a very satisfactory prospect" of peace with the Mi'kmaq and a decline in hostilities with the French. "Should these two great counts be brought about, they will not only be the best justification of the past measures and exceeding and greatly mend your own personal honour, but to the likeliest means of [reducing] future expenses," Greenville noted.

With regard to the money Cornwallis had paid so that the French would release some of his English prisoners, he wrote, "We can have no objection to the humanity of the action …. but the sum paid to the French seems to us a little unreasonable when we consider what was the number and the rank of the persons ransomed."

His masters reminded him what they thought his priority should be. "The whole thought of government will be turned toward the clearing of the ground, the cultivating of friendship with the Indians, the incorporating of the neutral French among the other settlers, the encouragement of the fishery and the raising of produce within the settlement for the support of the people and the relief of the public."

The board noted his request to postpone the arrival of more settlers to allow those present to expand into their unclaimed land grants outside of Halifax, but it couldn't be helped. More settlers were already on the way and it would be impossible to alter their makeup or delay them for the next spring. Whitehall noted his complaints about the last batch of useless settlers and promised to send better people, and to send them earlier in the year. He had complained of their sending him settlers in the fall, when it was impossible to establish them independently before the harsh winter froze any seeds of ambition they may have brought. The next batch would be there by May and they would be three hundred strong and loyal Swiss Protestants. They would arrive owing him one year's labour at a shilling a day to recover the cost of their passage.

Cornwallis had previously written to London that Catholic settlers were to be avoided. It was proving hard enough to convert any of the Catholic Acadians to Protestantism. The province did not need more. Whitehall agreed and apologized to Cornwallis for accidentally sending him forty German settlers who turned out to be Catholic. "We look upon Roman Catholics as not entitled to the privileges granted to the settlers and if any such be found among them, we don't doubt but you will think it necessary to the peace and security of the province to send them away again," it added.

A militia was to be the colony's next task, but that might fall to the next governor. Cornwallis could prepare the ground by winning the hearts and minds of the Mi'kmaq.

"As it will be impossible for you to make any great progress in a work of so much necessity before the time of your return, it is unnecessary to enter in this letter into the particulars of such an establishment.

Should it be in your power before your return by any opportunities of friendly intercourse to gain over the minds and disposition of the Indians with your province to the interest of Great Britain, such a reconciliation will be a great additional strength to the settlement, an effectual discouragement to the French and the best provision which the province can have for its future peace and security."

Friendship was cheaper than war and with a little encouragement Halifax might even start to trade with the Mi'kmaq and thus advance its commercial prospects, and those of all of Britain. "It should always be remembered that the best defence which any province in America can have against every other enemy is the hearty alliances of those Indians who border upon it," the board wrote.

Well done, they said, for getting the settlers to work for their provisions. It was a good saving. Avoid conflict with the Mi'kmaq – it was too expensive. Instead, develop trade with them to bring in extra income for the colony.

Whitehall told him it was not a priority to expand the colony now, but to reinforce the Chignecto area. Their sources told them the lands around Minas were fruitful and ready to be cleared. "The German Protestants are by disposition and habit of life more inclined to husbandry than fishery," London said. "It will be proper to send as many of these as you can spare from Halifax to inhabit and cultivate such parts of the peninsula that they can dwell in with security."

The problem, Cornwallis reflected, was that if the board did not send sufficient force, "such parts of the peninsula that they can dwell in with security" would of course be limited to Halifax.

London's letter was a long, messy tract weaving up and down the page, full of ink blots, crossed-out words and shrinking print as the end drew near. London's financial worries kept rising, as though the letter writer was constantly interrupted by messengers bearing new suggestions for saving cash. "What checks do you keep upon the store keeper and what is the proportion of waste?" they asked.

It finished in a blurry smear that Cornwallis strained his eyes to decipher. It was praise for his work so far. "There is nothing remains under this head but to commend, as we do with the utmost satisfaction, the spirit and great ability with which you have resisted to the utmost extent of your force the perfidious and unwarrantable attempts of the French upon His Majesty's rights," Greenville wrote.

"... we have made the strongest representations to His Majesty to have an additional naval force sent this year for the protection of the fishery and the security of the province. But above all things, we earnestly recommend it to you as an essential point, without which all other schemes for the final success of your undertaking are as nothing, kindly and invariably to keep within their grant of Parliament.

"We bid you heartily farewell and are your very loving friends and humble servants."

A short letter followed the first, chastising him for his behaviour toward the Mi'kmaq. Peace was favoured over persecution. War was too expensive. Cornwallis was flummoxed.

"It was never in my thoughts to exercise any cruelties upon the Indians," he said to Davidson. "All I meant was that I should never think of making peace with them when they offer it, as hitherto has been done, without their giving any kind of security that they will observe their agreements and treaties. We have already seen how little the best of them, those of St. John River, regard the most solemn treaty. By all accounts I can learn, they never miss an opportunity of doing any mischief attended with gain, be it war or peace."

He suspected London did not understand the scale of the Mi'kmaq problem. A force of Mi'kmaq warriors had assaulted the fort at Minas. The attack was thwarted and the fort was reinforced by an officer and thirty men and the commander sent John Gorham after the retreating warriors. Gorham's Rangers chased the Mi'kmaq deep into the woods. They captured none of the warriors, but did come across three local lads left for them. The Acadian boys had spent some time with the Mi'kmaq – only because they feared death if they left, the boys hastily assured Gorham.

He brought them overland to Halifax and presented them to Cornwallis in his chambers.

"I wish you had taken some of the old rebels so I could have made an example of them," Cornwallis complained.

He probed them for intelligence, but found little of use. The boys were sequestered to a British fort for their own protection. Cornwallis ended the meeting in high anger. How could London constantly urge him to cut costs and make peace with the Mi'kmaq, who were so keen to continue waging war? How could he fight them on their own turf when every musket shot needed a receipt?

He needed to solve this problem. Nova Scotia required a firm fort at Chignecto. He found more funds for the scalping proclamation. He was certain that if he kept up the pressure, and continued hunting and harassing the Mi'kmaq by sea and by land, they would either abandon the peninsula or make peace on any terms the English imposed.

Rumours again swirled that French Canada was preparing a full invasion of Nova Scotia, backed by Mi'kmaq allies and Acadians. The prospect terrified the settlers. Cornwallis pretended to be unaffected by the talk and continued building his town. He grabbed every spare man and extended the barricade right down to the water. It was normally impossible to get them to work without great wages, so he used their instinct of self-preservation. He sent more axmen to the surrounding woods and cut the trees back one hundred yards further all around the town. The woods were still filled with savage shadows. The wind still whispered a war cry. Falling rain still beat a war drum.

Another petition landed on his desk, signed by a great many of the residents of the settlement, asking him to declare martial law while the alarm continued. He consulted with the council, but they decided against such drastic action – for now. Instead, he formed all of the settlers he could find into ten armed companies. The farmers and fishers marched each evening on the rough, uneven Parade Square until he was confident they understood the seriousness of the threat. Any man who neglected his duty or outright refused it was imprisoned for twenty-four hours and fined five shillings.

Halifax had soon raised a rough militia of 840 men. The officers were high quality, but the foot soldiers were weak. It amazed Cornwallis that they could be so terrified of a Mi'kmaq attack, and yet so cavalier about defending themselves. Who did they think was going to protect them?

Acadians drifted into the settlement for jobs on the public works. They also brought trickles of information. There had indeed been a Mi'kmaq party at Cobequid all winter – a grand total of thirty people. Cornwallis sent a detachment to dislodge them and bring the local priest back to him. Gorham, back at council, advised it was not practical to go to Cobequid then, but Cornwallis ignored him.

The patrol left and returned without having met the Mi'kmaq, but they did bring the priest. Council called him before them and questioned him, but he said little of use. Each question produced an answer that was long and tedious and entirely devoid of truth or useful information, as far as Cornwallis could tell.

Cornwallis asked, "Why did you not answer my letter? Why did your deputies not come to make submissions?"

The priest answered both questions with one answer: "We were afraid of the savages."

The melting snow left woods filled with footprints. Intelligence was often contradictory, but Cornwallis built up a picture of what was happening. He thought the Acadians at Chignecto had been made to swear an oath of allegiance to the French king and Cornwallis believed Le Loutre was behind it. The priest had spent a week at Cobequid in January. Cornwallis believed he paid the inhabitants for damages caused by Mi'kmaq attacks and had travelled with Mi'kmaqs. Le Loutre was building an army to join the massive French force. Cornwallis feared England was preparing to return Nova Scotia to the French, just as it had done with Louisbourg.

Cornwallis kept the Cobequid priest by his side as another patrol went out to retrieve the courier. The priest had sent a letter to La Loutre requesting the English messenger be freed. Cornwallis treated the Cobequid priest like royalty, as if they were two European gentlemen in a primitive land. He hoped, plied with liquor, the priest would slip up and reveal the true state of affairs.

The priest soaked his tongue with rum, but did not slip.

A reply came back from Le Loutre demanding ransom for the captured courier.

Cornwallis hurled the letter to the floor. "We have spent much blood and treasure to gain this province and now they would have us purchase part of it at the expense of public faith and national honour!" he roared.

He summoned his council and demanded all Acadians take the oath of allegiance. "This matter is of the utmost importance," he said.

17

The New Town Flowers in the Spring

By mid-April 1750, Halifax was starting to look like a proper town. Nightmares of the D'Anville disaster ebbed from the collective mind. Fears of starvation and mass death eased. Fears of Mi'kmaq invasion and Acadian insurrection increased. Halifax was stable and growing, and Annapolis had not changed in decades, but the rest of the province remained claimed in name only. It needed bodies – loyal, Protestant bodies – to turn the paper empire into a physical reality.

Cornwallis felt the rheumatism ebb from his bones and so took himself on a tour of the town. The snow had melted and the scrubland between the wall and the woods was regularly cleared, leaving a wide-open no man's land buffering the settlement. The streets cut up the hill were more than just technical drawings on the land – houses occupied the sides of many of them. A few had started gardens. Stacks of firewood sat neatly beside most.

Communal works had grown up too. There was now a common land for grazing livestock and a public garden for growing food. A church frame had been ordered from New England and was on its way. It was based on the new Marylebone Chapel in London and promised to bring the elegance of England to the New World. A small hospital had replaced the floating hospital aboard one of the ships, adding to the sense of permanence. The tough winter had killed many, but had bound the survivors closer together. A small public school was operating to educate the children and to care for the orphans. Many young ones had lost both parents, either on the voyage over or during the brutal winter. Halifax could now raise the boys until they were old enough to apprentice as fishermen. The girls relied on the hope of a good marriage.

Cornwallis walked to the waterfront beaches. It was a fine, clear day. A few sloops sat at anchor, and fishing boats came and went. Rough docks had been established to ease transit from water to land and a few men stood on those, angling for lunch. Though the winter had been difficult, the harbour had not frozen solid. That allowed ships to continue to come and go, keeping Halifax connected to the rest of the colonies and England at home. Nova Scotia's governor gazed across the harbour. He spotted a few dark heads floating above the water – the ever-curious harbour seals. And beyond them, woods. The stalled sawmill was invisible among the trees on the far shore.

Cornwallis turned his eyes south to the long mouth of the harbour he had sailed down upon arriving the previous summer. He had studied the land well as he sought the ideal location for Halifax and had kept meticulous records of his observations. He remained content with his choice, but saw a lack of defence, should the French decide to invade by sea. He looked back across the harbour to the hidden sawmill. Perhaps it was time to really commit to a second settlement on the far shore. It would boost Halifax's defensive ability with a well-armed twin. It would also help the fishery, one of the few bright spots of success for the colony, as it would operate under the watchful eye of the garrison. The proximity to the Shubenacadie waterway inland could prove doubly useful. A well-armed settlement would keep it out of the hands of the Mi'kmaq and open the route to British trade.

"Easily helped, easily supplied and protected," he surmised of the new town. "While there is any danger from the Indians, the more compact we are the better."

Another solid British presence would mean more settlers, more hands to help with the work, more children to continue the presence, and above all, safety in numbers. And it wouldn't be some distance down the coast, where in winter a cry for help might never be heard. No – it would be right here, where he and his soldiers could keep constant watch. It would also discourage attack on Halifax, as a retreat and reinforcements would be permanently on hand.

"When once this harbour is secure, well peopled, a certain fishery established, people will come from all ports without any expense to the public and it will be easy to expand to other parts of the province," he wrote to London. "Nothing will give me greater pleasure than to hear that their Lordships have fallen upon some means of sending over Germans and other foreign Protestants."

Cornwallis's rheumatism soon returned and he was once more confined to his chambers as the spring progressed. The damp air locked up his joints and made movement painful. He called council together and Davidson ran through the latest business. Three Acadian deputies had come pleading for permission to evacuate the province and carry off their possessions. The French were offering enticements if they relocated to Canada, and threats of what would happen if they stayed. If Cornwallis let them leave, the issue of oaths and religion would be solved. But Nova Scotia would be left uninhabited. With barely enough Protestant bodies to populate Halifax and Annapolis, Cornwallis would not allow the hardworking Acadians to leave with the tools that fed Nova Scotia. Until more settlers arrived, the Acadians were stuck.

Cornwallis dictated a long reply to Davidson, which crunched down to one word: No. Cornwallis affixed his shaky signature to the letter and sent it.

Council then turned to finances. The winter had frozen productivity and the constant danger of Mi'kmaq attack meant Halifax could barely send patrols of soldiers and rangers out of the fort, let alone farmers to plant seeds that could grow to feed the settlement. Most of the settlers technically owned acres and acres of land, but it was buried under thick woods and surrounded by shadowy hostility. As the snow melted, so did the food reserves.

Cornwallis resolved to write to the Board of Trade and assure them that while he was being as frugal as possible, and not wasting a single pound, he still needed funding. But London was easily distracted, dealing as it was with dozens of such letters from local commanders all over North America, the West Indies, East India and Africa. All the while, King George was occupied by the endless conflicts in Europe. Cornwallis defended Nova Scotia in terms everyone could understand: money. It was a vast and wealthy province, he wrote, and needed only wise investment to pay off in abundance.

"But without money, they would have no town, no settlement and indeed no settlers," Cornwallis muttered as he prepared to answer their letter. "Who else can say not a pound was misspent on a governor's summer mansion? Every pence has gone to clearing the ground, building the town and keeping soldiers and settlers from starving or deserting. Lots in Halifax are now worth 50 Guineas. If there was no public money circulating, lots would be given for a gallon of rum."

He scoured his books looking for ways to cut the budget. "We'll have to let go the apothecaries, Merry and Reeves, and discharge some of the surgeons," he said. "We have to start saving money."

Inflaming matters, one of his subordinates had slipped off to New England with £900 out of the communal coffers, without permission. Cornwallis fired him and prayed he would return to Halifax so he could be made an example of on the beach gallows. Cash was in short supply and many of his usual lenders in New England had started balking at offering more credit to Nova Scotia.

"If London sends sufficient force, and my credit is restored, I will answer for it that the province will soon be as valuable as ever it was proposed. Whether the French inhabitants stay or go, but without force and without money, nothing can be done," he said to Davidson. "And London is complaining about how much rum and molasses we go through. It's not a penny more or less than what Louisbourg got. Besides, the King's Brewhouse is ready. What we should do is let some private citizen make beer and sell it to the settlement and rent the brewhouse from the public for £40 a year."

New reports reached him of trouble approaching. The intelligence now said Le Loutre had amassed 2,500 men in Chignecto and was planning to take the forts at Chignecto and Minas. "It will be a general massacre," Cornwallis concluded. And if they fell, Halifax could follow, and the entire colonial enterprise would collapse.

He wrote alarmed letters to his counterparts in Massachusetts and New Hampshire, warning of dire consequences for everyone if Nova Scotia fell.

Around the same time that Cornwallis's attention was focused on defence and protection, he founded a Freemason Lodge in Halifax. He became the initial Master Mason of what was known as First Lodge, later called St. Andrews Lodge No. 1. It would continue for centuries as the oldest Freemason centre in the British overseas empire. A Masonic lodge founded in Halifax in 1786 and closed in 1810 was named in his honour. One founded in Dartmouth in 1926 would again take Cornwallis's name.

18

Unrest in Acadia

On the first day of May, 1750, Cornwallis sat at his desk composing a letter to the Board of Trade. He was distracted: he dated it May 1, 1850, before crossing out his mistake. He was agitated. He had to sell London on the success of Nova Scotia, but his rheumatism so often confined him to his bed that he had seen no more of the province's progress than had the Earl of Halifax in London. He scribbled out the letter as best he could and had a courier carry it to the *Taggart*, then anchored in the harbour.

"Put in at the first port and send my letter to His Majesty without delay," he commanded of the ship's captain. The ship directly lifted anchor and caught a strong wind out of Chebucto harbour.

The French had taken possession of Nova Scotia on the opposite side of the Bay of Fundy, from Chignecto to the St. John River. They claimed the "Acadia" ceded to England in 1720 referred only to the land on the peninsula, not that beyond the isthmus. They argued that even the settlement of the border between France and England left all of that territory in French hands. This meant it was not an act of war when they attacked and burned down Beaubassin, carrying all of the inhabitants and their effects beyond the river and out of Cornwallis's reach. It was not an act of war when those inhabitants, now armed by France, formed into companies and joined Le Loutre's forces of regulars, Canadians, rebels and First Nations in an army 2,500 strong. Messengers chased each other to Chebucto bearing letters from Le Loutre. French scouts roamed northern

Nova Scotia, telling British settlers they must evacuate, or forfeit their lives. They put a stark choice before the Acadians: rivers of milk and honey flowed in New France; in New Scotland, it would be rivers of blood. Join France or face terrible consequences.

It was not a difficult conversion for many. Nova Scotia's northern Acadians drifted across the conceptual borders to Canada. Cornwallis saw a developing disaster that could cost him the province. The more obedient settlers sent him letters, asking permission to leave Nova Scotia. Many added they would not be planting that season, as they did not intend to be there to reap in the fall. "It's entirely against their inclination," Cornwallis said. "Le Loutre threatens them with a general massacre by the savages if they remain in the province."

His temper rose and he shouted scorn down on the French – always promising one thing with one side of their face and threatening the opposite with the other.

"There may be official peace in Europe, but they continue the war here by all open and secret means of violence and treason," he wrote to London. "They openly support and protect the savages, our declared enemies; they fight under the French standard; they keep the King's subjects, his officers and soldiers their prisoners; they spirit His Majesty's French subjects to rebellion and threaten those that remain faithful with destruction. They send their slaves, the savages, through the whole province to perpetrate every villainy; they set fire to a town they themselves allow to be the King's."

And yet he knew what the French clearly knew: he could not stop them.

"It is my unhappiness to be obliged to see these monstrous proceedings and not have it in my power to redress or revenge them," he said.

"If rigorous actions are not taken at home and sufficient force sent to drive both French and Indians out of the Province, we must rest contented to possess and defend the spot of ground Halifax stands on. No other settlement can be made. The Province will be forever a state of perpetual war, the scene of French and Indian treachery and villainy."

By May, a problem was apparent in the town. Mostly the roads were cut in simple grids across, up and down the slopes of the citadel hill. The beach was still a beach, but looking more and more like a port. The swamp was mostly covered with infill. The tents that had populated the shantytown the summer before were gradually being replaced with some form of more permanent housing. Frames were even arriving from New England and it was hoped the Dartmouth sawmill would soon be able to produce materials to build houses and other permanent structures. But now and then, the orderly streets yielded to disorderly vacant lots. They had been assigned to settlers, but some were idle. Cornwallis could not tolerate that – use them or lose them, he warned. Some would-be settlers had vanished into the woods and seas bound for New England, while some had just avoided doing any of the required work.

More ambitious settlers would often slip into the void and build a house on abandoned lots, but then the legal owners would return and demand the house be taken down.

"But he had not done the least thing on his lot in the eight months he had it," Cornwallis seethed about one particular absent landowner. The governor used his state powers and retroactively transferred ownership. Contrary to the earlier case, this time the new owner – the one who had built the house – got to keep it. It set a precedent. If it wasn't obvious that you were developing your lot, the Crown could take it back.

While some scrambled to get back into Nova Scotia, others begged to leave. Cornwallis received another letter from the French inhabitants of Annapolis Royal requesting permission to exit the province. They said they never considered themselves subjects to the King of New England. Surely an error or a mistranslation. Not a direct insult.

Cornwallis sent urgently for the deputies. They arrived and pleaded befuddlement, saying they did not understand the petition themselves.

"Well, then, who wrote it? And when? Where?" he demanded.

The French deputies made no answer.

Cornwallis switched tactics. It had not escaped his notice that this was his first meeting with deputies from the Annapolis Acadians.

"So, sirs, please tell me why the deputies chosen for the year and approved by myself did not present the petition themselves?" he said, mustering up every ounce of imperial disdain in his being.

The deputies demurred. They did not know.

"Please leave," he told them.

They did – but not the province. The thousands of solid, Protestant settlers swarming Halifax and en route from Europe were a good start, but they did not have enough bodies to occupy the farms and dikes of the Annapolis Valley. And he did not have the military power to protect them away from the forts. The Acadians would have to stay for now.

As a sop, Cornwallis and the council agreed to the appointment of a new Catholic priest for the inhabitants. He was required to take the oath of allegiance to King George and swear to not leave Nova Scotia without express permission from Cornwallis.

Meanwhile, council legislated the shantytown into a proper capital. They established a farmers' market on what was grandly titled Water Street and regulated it to handle the cattle and sheep brought to the settlement. Another new law required residents of Halifax to keep the street clear in front of their homes. Piles of snow had stalled the city all winter, and now debris, trash and excrement fouled the lanes. Each owner was to diligently keep the pathways clear to let the settlement's veins flow freely.

*   *   *   *   *

In July 1750, Cornwallis received news from England that made him very happy. He called in the council and told them with a thin smile that King George had seen his vision for Nova Scotia as warden of the North American colonies and agreed to pay for the construction of a fort on the Isthmus of Chignecto, near the burned Beaubassin.

"What do you think is the best method to effect it?" he asked his colleagues.

After much discussion, they resolved to consult with Captain Edward How and inquire how many ships he thought he would need to do the work.

But London's largess did not go beyond the basic fort. Letter after letter demanded tighter financial accountability from Cornwallis. At one point, he was directly accused of neglect. When he read the letter, he fumed. He sputtered out his thoughts ahead of preparing a formal response.

"It's true, I did not acquaint them with every skirmish that happened between the forces at Chignecto and the Indians, backed by the French," he said, pacing his office. "I thought it unnecessary, as I had so fully and repeatedly informed their Lordships of what was to be expected from the behaviour of the French and their missionaries. But I think I may venture to affirm I have never omitted writing to the board upon anything essential or new.

"The hostilities of the French and Indians I can't call 'new.' As to the essential part of it, they have not wanted information. On the first of January I wrote to them concerning the sloop *Wren* that was missing with cannon. Did they care? No! They just wanted less money spent.

"The Indians have certainly harassed us much, but his Lordship can be no stranger to it nor at all surprised if he will have recourse to my letters. Had reinforcement of 500 Canadians been sent, you might have depended upon being instantly informed of it."

He felt he had warned them amply of the hostilities he was likely to face – and told them when the inevitable happened.

"Have I not said the French will act in that open and audacious manner? Have I not repeated the necessity of force, by sea and land? Did I not last fall represent the sea force the French had at Louisbourg? And did I not say that I had little reason to expect a less force this year? And has not what I said been verified?" he asked rhetorically.

He sat down with his quill. "Did I not acquaint your Lordships of the attack made last fall upon the *Albany* by a ship that was supplying arms and ammunitions to the Indians? Did I not tell you sending for priests would be necessary and that no good could be expected from French Missionaries?"

And with scant funds coming across the ocean, how could he know what was happening when he could barely keep Halifax running, let alone the vast network of soldiers and spies required for better intelligence? At times it seemed his full-time job was following every pound as it travelled from hand to hand in his frontier outpost. Who was paid, how much, and for what? What greater good was accomplished with each expenditure?

As other troubles and excitement flared up in Europe and other corners of the growing empire, Nova Scotia sank from the king's view. Peace with France was bad news for a colony founded to thwart the French threat at Louisbourg. Cornwallis lay awake at night, rubbing his rheumatic hands and dreading the day Halifax became nothing more than an expensive mistake, a high-salaried warden guarding worthless forests.

Cornwallis requested permission to travel home. He wanted to go to London in person and stand before his former colleagues in the House of Parliament and shame them with a careful and full accounting of the colony's expenses – and to illustrate to them directly the current and future value of Nova Scotia. He hated to act like a beggar, but he would do it for Halifax. And to protect his name.

"I hope I shall be pardoned," he scrawled. "I shall exculpate myself from any charge of neglect or disrespect toward their Lordships."

He signed off the letter and then added a postscript: "I have ordered a committee of council to examine the public accounts."

19

Slave Trade Comes to Halifax

Cornwallis walked along the waterfront on a late summer day. The harbour was busy with trade ships from New England bringing supplies and taking his settlers. The outflow had slowed, at least. Surviving the first winter had stiffened the settlers' resolve. It had also strongly illustrated the importance of planning ahead, of building solid, heat-holding homes, of chopping enough wood for the winter and working hard while it was warm and clear outside. It fortified the fear of attack. The winter had killed many and weakened many more. It was not hard to imagine that if the town was attacked in January, and the homes razed in a fire, that few would see another spring.

Cornwallis spent his days scrimping on money, bargaining for better prices for goods, and compelling the settlers to start developing their own capacities to sustain themselves. He wrote to London in page after page of great detail about the minutiae of his financial maneuvering in the hopes that they would finally understand that he would no sooner waste a penny of the King's than he would eat his own fingers. But at the end, he could not alter the math: he was going to exceed the grant. He needed more money. Fortifications, blockhouses, soldiers and ships – the war with the Mi'kmaq and the French and the hostilities with the Acadians were very expensive.

He sat at his desk and composed a letter to Lord Halifax, George Montagu-Dunk. "My Lord, I am sorry to see the absolute impossibility of not exceeding the grant for this year. I heartily wish I could have made

such savings as to be able to keep within the sum limited, so earnestly recommended to me by your Lordships," he wrote.

"But I know you will not approve of my putting a stop to all works
going on here. And if I did, how shall I carry into execution the important plan laid out by your Lordships and approved by the King for this
summer?"

His tone was sharp, but it emphasized that he could not follow their
instructions without their resources. He couldn't reclaim Chignecto and
drive the French back without an army. The settlement could not survive
without provisions. Nova Scotia would stand on its own one day, but it
needed to be fledged yet. Throw a baby bird out of the nest too soon and
it has no choice but to fall to its death. Feed and nurture it a while and
it will spread its wings and fly. Nova Scotia was a baby bird on the edge
of the nest. The lots promised in London that had lured so many reluctant adventurers were still occupied by thick packs of pines and firs. Only
deer and squirrels drew sustenance from them. He could not send settlers
to farm their rightful land without more money, and more muscle.

"And worse, those parts will be so infested with Indians that without guards it will be dangerous to go into the woods for materials or firewood," he added.

But if he could pull it off – if he could establish a mighty fort at
Chignecto, it would be the greatest thing done or imagined in this province. The intelligence from that part of the province had lately been positive. Spies reported that the French detachment in Chignecto was to be
retired back to Canada. He wasn't the only one whose tightening purse
strings from Europe were restricting his ability to operate in the Americas.
That was doubly good news, because even if he could march on Chignecto
with the same army Cumberland and he had used to clear the Highlands,
he could not directly attack the French. They were officially friends.

While he was confident Chignecto could be held with a fort, the
question of establishing a permanent settlement there was for now beyond
his means to protect. He was already barely keeping the wolves at bay in
Halifax and Annapolis. A third, distant site could stretch his resources too
thin. More settlers were due to arrive any day. Meanwhile, he had soldiers
begin to clear George's Island. The little rock in the harbour would be
called into double service – to act as a fortress protecting the harbour and
to house any freshly arrived settlers who required a period of quarantine.
The trees were cut and turned into blockhouses and a battery.

The settlement's rough pike wall had weathered the winter and was being repaired. Lumber, so expensive to have shipped in from New England, regularly melted away to unscrupulous settlers. He had sent sorties exploring for limestone, but so far had found nothing. Bricks were of a decent quality, and some solid buildings took shape: the courthouse, a prison, and a powder magazine.

Cornwallis turned uphill for home. A short walk brought him to the centre of Halifax, the rough Grand Parade that had been smoothed to function as a marching ground. The church frame had arrived and was being erected at one end. The plans called for a court to be built at the opposite end. Eventually, his meagre house would be replaced with a grander home for future governors.

A big crowd packed the parade, haggling with a man on a stage. Thomas Bloss, a Royal Navy officer, had just arrived with sixteen people he held as slaves and was auctioning them off. He touted them as being great for housework, chores, or fieldwork. Perhaps sensing that the thin soil of Nova Scotia was unlikely to sprout plantations, he changed tack and boosted the values of the slaves as seamen. The skeptical crowd was told the African men tied up on the stage could crew vessels involved in maritime commerce.

Cornwallis spotted Joshua Mauger at the front. Mauger owned ships and was involved in trade. Cornwallis suspected he was slicing off part of legitimate trade into his own storehouses for illegal sale, but had no strong evidence. Mauger haggled with Bloss over the price of a young black man who was well built and appeared healthy, despite the heavy bruising on his face. Halifax had 3,000 inhabitants, including about 400 slaves, or about 7.5 percent of the population. Many worked as personal servants and others did the hard work of building Halifax: cutting out the streets, reshaping the hill and developing the waterfront. The settlement had a population of seventeen free black people. They lived mostly together in a shadow settlement just north of Halifax. In later years that group of free blacks would be pushed down to the land by Bedford Basin as the city grew. Their community was dismissively called Africa-ville, a name that eventually became a source of pride for many Nova Scotians.

Cornwallis paused. He admired the way Bloss handled himself. After the auction was concluded and the black people sold, the governor walked over to Bloss and introduced himself. Cornwallis was impressed, as he shared in a letter to London. It had occurred to him that he would be a step closer to getting back to England if he could first convince the board that able men abounded in Nova Scotia and would handily carry on his work.

Perhaps he could return to England the next year. "If the province is upon a good footing and Colonel [Charles] Lawrence, who I can confide in, is made Lieut. Governor, I may be of more use at home than here. Captain Bloss, a half-pay captain of the Man of War, is come here. [He] has brought with him sixteen Negroes, has built a very good house at his own expense, is a reliable, worthy man; he is going home to pass some accounts that is necessary for being abroad many years. When he returns I must beg your Lordships to appoint him of the council. He will be of service here and as proper a man as you can appoint," Cornwallis wrote of the slave trader.

In years to come, Halifax's slave trade would flourish. Mauger would play an increasingly important role. He had a few advertisements posted about town. A typical one read:

"Just imported and to be sold by Joshua Mauger and Major Lockman's store in Halifax. Several Negro Slaves, viz. a very likely Negro Wench, of about thirty five years of age, a Creole born, has been brought up in a gentleman's family and capable of doing all sorts of work belonging thereto, as Needlework of all sorts, and in the best manner, also washing, ironing, cookery and everything that can be expected from such a slave.

"Also 2 Negro boys of about 12 or 13 years old, likely, healthy and well shaped, and understand some English.

"Likewise 2 healthy Negro slaves of about 18 years of age, of agreeable tempers, and fit for any kind of business.

"And also a healthy Negro Man of about 30 years of age."

Slave ads would prove a crucial source of revenue for the first newspaper when it opened in a couple of years. It was also not uncommon to see signs for runaway slaves, offering rewards for their capture and threatening punishment for anyone not turning them in.

Slaves weren't the only people fleeing Halifax. At least fifteen soldiers had deserted in the summer. They had been sent out to patrol the woods around the settlement and encountered French and Mi'kmaq soldiers on a patrol of their own. The French promised money and easy lives. The British patrol defected.

Cornwallis sent an elite group of soldiers after the defectors. They caught nine of the fifteen. Two more were shot dead in a fight. Cornwallis held them briefly in prison before finding them guilty of treason. They were hanged from the beach gallows. The French agent suspected to be behind the desertions was also captured, along with two spies from Chignecto and a rogue British soldier from Cobequid. The value of the agent was confirmed when Cornwallis received a letter from Le Loutre offering a large ransom for his release. Cornwallis rejected the offer and ordered more executions.

Despite the progress in the province, he dealt with endless petitions from Acadians wanting permission to leave. These were mixed with letters from Acadians who had left in the first year and now wanted to return. Their letters blamed their own bigotry and the suspicions raised by Le Loutre for their hasty departure.

"Only that could so blind them to their sure interest and happiness," Cornwallis agreed as he read their correspondence.

A letter from Whitehall arrived confirming that another three hundred settlers "of the better sort," Germans and French Protestants, were heading down the Thames and crossing the Atlantic to Halifax. Cornwallis again eyed the potential settlement across the harbour for the Germans, but considered sending the Protestant French out among the Catholic Acadians to remove some of that bigotry and suspicion. The example of Frenchmen fleeing the oppression of the French king and living happy and fruitful lives abroad under the English flag could better inspire the Catholics to pledge allegiance to King George.

And every day, there were more houses, more gardens, and a growing fishery.

20

The Alderney Arrives

As the summer cooked the land in August, and the blackflies gorged themselves on red human meat, Cornwallis began sending letters back to Whitehall every few weeks. Over and over, he detailed the tiniest transactions, sealed the letter, and sent it to the piers to catch a ride on the next ship heading for England.

On an August day so hot he had to open his house fully to get any motion of air going, he batted away hordes of blackflies, sat down at his desk and wrote a long, terse letter to London. Rumours of Mi'kmaq attacks across the colony came to him as thick and as irritatingly as the flies. He dated it – August 18, 1750 – and started writing his complaints. The scarce supplies were always low. Replenishments from England, old or new, were never enough. He was running into credit troubles with the agents he dealt with in Boston. His regiments were not paid as much as their counterparts in the more established colonies, and so the temptation to slip into the woods or waters was constant. Why live in rough huts eating salted meat and sea biscuits for less pay, when an ambitious man could eat like a European king on a greater salary just down the coast in Boston? The same king's face graced all the coins.

"My Lords, as it is absolutely necessary that my regiment be paid in the same amount as Colonel Warburton's and Colonel Laserelles'," Cornwallis wrote, "I beg your Lordships will give directions to Mr. Killy to pay the agent for my regiment the four pence per diem stopped for provision."

He took a breath – and inhaled a blackfly. He spat it out and continued. He scratched his name to the bottom of the paper, sealed it, and sent it. His missive crossed paths with an incoming letter aboard the *Fair Lady*, one of the ships that had sailed in the initial voyage the summer before. It now plied its familiar trade back and forth between motherland and infant town. The letter was dated June 1. It reminded Cornwallis of the urgent and pressing need for detailed financial records. He began making notes for his own reply.

Better news arrived a few days later, spotted by soldiers relaxing in the water off Point Pleasant. They raced each other back to the fort to share it. The town's residents flocked to the waterfront, where Cornwallis and many members of the council joined them. It was first a dot on the watery horizon; then the rough outline of a sail; then a body; then a tiny ship; finally, the big transport vessel hove fully into view.

The *Alderney*, carrying 353 Protestant Europeans, tacked gracefully into the harbour and dropped anchor off the Halifax shore. The beaches were filled with settlers happy for a chance to celebrate, and for a chance to pause the hard work of clearing land and building a town.

Cornwallis watched, relieved it had come at all, but angry that it had come so late in the year. He had repeatedly told London settlers needed to arrive at the very start of spring to give them any chance at establishing themselves. With May, June, July, August, September and October to work with before November froze the land and ambition, the newcomers would have a shot at breaking open the Dartmouth land and building themselves some homes capable of withstanding a Nova Scotia winter. But arriving in late August, with the good days mostly gone, they would have to be strong men and women indeed to be weaned of the state's provisions in the first year. They had departed from Gravesend, England, and Cornwallis hoped that was not a foreshadowing of their fate.

Cornwallis wrote of the arrival and detailed every penny spent since his last letter, and fired the news back across the ocean.

Council met August 23 to decide what to do with the *Alderney*'s colonists. The decision was largely already made, but they went over the options again. They could add the settlers to Halifax, but the town was filling up nicely and there seemed no great advantage to be had in increasing its population. They could send them further into the province, inland or along the coast, to break ground on a new settlement, but Cornwallis's military resources were spread dangerously thin as it was. Reports of

Mi'kmaq hostility buzzed in on the summer heat wave. The settlers might as well try to establish a colony in the basin, for all the chances they would have defending themselves far from Halifax's garrison.

So it was decided: what had until now housed a small, slow-growing clearing that was supposed to become a sawmill would become a new town. A twin sister for Halifax – they could keep an eye on each other across the water. Sound travelled well – any attack on the little sister would carry across the harbour and help would be swiftly at hand. Cornwallis ordered a surveyor to pick the best spot. In the meantime, the *Alderney*'s settlers bobbed on the tides in the harbour. Little boats and dories ferried some into Halifax to meet the land, but most remained on board, peering over the ship's side to watch the curious seals bob alongside them. They learned they were going across the harbour. They looked at the dark, dangerous woods.

The new settlement was called Dartmouth, due to the low, green hills and proximity to water reminding some of Dartmouth in Devon. The little river flowing into the Chebucto harbour was named for its match over the ocean – the Dart.

The surveyor selected a spot. A grid plan was formed. The *Alderney* lifted anchor and crossed the harbour. The new settlers slowly unpacked themselves from their home of many long weeks and began the hard work of turning what seemed to be empty woods into a new world.

*   *   *   *   *

On September 13, 1750, Cornwallis received another piece of good news. The *Ann* had been spotted entering the outer mouth of the harbour, bearing three hundred German Protestant settlers. Halifax was turning into a strange, miniature mishmash of displaced Europe. So far, the French settlers had largely stuck with the French, the Swiss with the Swiss, and so on, but they were all united in Protestant loyalty to King George and Cornwallis was confident that as the generations went by, the differences in their origins would fade.

Cornwallis summoned the council to discuss the placement of the Germans. The options were familiar: add them to Halifax or Dartmouth, or risk sending them to start up a new settlement. Cornwallis favoured using them to settle on Chignecto, but despite the late warmth of heat, he knew summer was over and deadly winter could come at any time. The risk of Mi'kmaq and French attack would be high enough so far along the road toward Canada – he couldn't risk losing three hundred bodies to nature. But the province could also not afford to feed and clothe three hundred idle people for the many months of winter. Council decided to set the Germans to work for the colony. At the same time, council decided to discontinue free provisions for all but the most recently arrived settlers. The rest would have to stand on their own feet – to eat what they pulled from the water, the woods, or their own labour.

By September 25, the shortage of cash and the emptying food stores led Cornwallis to start discharging government debts not in money, but in labourer notes and certificates that could be redeemed in the spring. The men toiling on the fortifications, brick magazine and other public works were going unpaid. It was increasingly difficult to feed the thousands of settlers. Issuing certificates instead of cash was not a popular move, and still the migration to New England tempted many away.

But travelling to Boston was not easy for all. Those in poor health, with no money, and with families were stuck. Halifax formed an open-air prison for them. Especially the families – few could afford transportation to Boston and fewer still had the wherewithal and ambition to strike out into a fresh unknown, so recently after leaving everything their families had known for generations for a gamble on the New World. And the promise of those big plantation lots still fired the imagination. Many were increasingly skeptical that the government would provide those lands – and skeptical that Nova Scotia even possessed so much bountiful land – but everyone knew the Acadians lived on rich soil that yielded as good a crop as any in Europe. Settlers discussed among themselves the possibility the British Red Coats would drive the Acadians back into French Canada and turn the farmland over to them.

Alongside its grand plans for conquering the province completely for King George, Cornwallis and the council spent much of their days overseeing the basics of town life. It was brought to their attention that those ambitious enough to go out and catch dinner, and those who slaughtered their livestock, were just leaving the rotting carcasses where they fell. Cows and sheep that died of hunger, disease or misadventure were left decomposing inside the fortress walls. The soldiers constantly guarding the thin brook that supplied drinking water to the settlement could not protect it from this plague of dead creatures. Pine-scented Halifax was starting to smell like a London abattoir. Cornwallis issued a proclamation that everyone had to bury the carcasses of animals belonging to them when they died, or face a severe penalty.

He also issued a proclamation against selling goods for more than their value, to avoid profiteering, and a proclamation forbidding anyone from buying hogs, sheep or cattle outside of the market. Everything had to go through the farmers' market first.

He wrote to Whitehall again, once more accidentally writing 1850, and striking it out for 1750. He laid out his financial woes. His New England agents were not advancing him the money he needed to prepare the settlement for winter. His original budget of £40,000 was gone. He would eventually spend more than three times that amount to get through the first year.

"I have been in great distress for want of dollars the merchants in Boston would advance me. Nobody would purchase my bills there. I have had no answer," he told the board.

He had nightmares of another Jamestown, the first British colony in the U.S. Founded in 1607, the Virginia colony's "starving time" began in 1608 and eased only with the arrival of a ship with supplies in the spring of 1610. He imagined the Mi'kmaq and French finally launching their raid in January, only to find all of the settlers dead from starvation.

A letter arrived from London. His masters instructed him to settle the Germans in Chignecto upon arrival. Several days' march on the other side of the province. Right in the centre of the cold war between France and England on the isthmus. "Now? With winter pressing in? Impossible!" he shouted.

"It would be attended with infinite danger and very great charge. We can't send them without provisions for the winter. We barely have enough provisions in the stores for one month in this settlement alone, let alone a second town," he wrote in response.

But as short as supplies were, he decided to ensure the Germans had ample food and drink. They had just arrived in Nova Scotia. To relocate them a little further down the coast to more hospitable environs would be no burden for them. If they toiled on public works for their food, it would save him spending money on labourers.

This was barely decided when, on September 16, he got another letter from London chastising him for running up the bills. In a foul mood, he sat down and answered their letter paragraph by paragraph. He knew how they lived in London – to keep one of the lord's houses running for a year would keep half his settlement alive for the winter. After many, many pages of terse response (he must have feared London would now rebuke him for using so much ink and paper) he concluded: "The only uneasiness your letter has created in me is that any person under me should have given even suspicion of malpractice to your Lordships."

21

The Battle for Chignecto

Cornwallis found himself stooped over his writing table again on September 24. Rain pounded on the settlement, dropping straight down like cannonballs on his roof and slicing in like arrows on his windows. Fog and thick rain clouds had smothered the settlement for much of the month. It was not the cold he had been bracing for, but a saturation of air and body that created a chill deep inside no amount of clothing or fire could dislodge. It aggravated his rheumatism so that even holding the pen was painful. He rarely left his home. Council met under his roof, and all reports were delivered to him. The days grew shorter, but the work grew longer. His mind flickered frequently to his warm, bright, bustling London home. Here was only silence – the menacing silence of hidden eyes watching from hostile woods.

The settlement was sick. Coughs, sneezes and runny noses ran from person to person. It wasn't killing people – at least, not many – but it was incapacitating them so that public works slowed.

The land was sealing up for the year and the meagre harvest would offer little food. All of those fifty-acre plantations that had made Nova Scotia appear like Utopia from a London dock remained unbroken, tree-covered and soon to be buried under six feet of snow. The seas were always well stocked, but the wild weather made harvesting them more difficult. Several fishermen had died on the rolling seas in recent days.

He had paid a steep price to provision the settlement for winter. He had bought supplies without London's permission because the provisions promised from London did not arrive. The men stared down the harbour's mists with diminishing hopes. Cornwallis looked at his dwindling food stores, his shrinking balance sheet, and wondered how he could get through another long Nova Scotia winter. He even suggested London stamp a special coin for use only in Nova Scotia to secure the local economy.

He lifted his pen. He tried a familiar approach, since London did not seem to care for the health of her settlers. She cared always for the health of her empire.

"I cannot omit to mention again to their Lordships the great necessity I imagine there is that a naval force should be stationed here sufficient to check and frustrate any designs of our jealous neighbours against us. I have certain information that there have been seventy-gun ships and frigates at Louisbourg," he wrote.

"They might very suddenly put in execution any order from their court respecting us and I presume we have no reason to be less apprehensive of them another year. We must hope that they will not be permitted again to send a force to Louisbourg so much superior to what has been usual for the protection of their trade."

He put down his pen.

* * * * *

Cornwallis had planned another mission to establish a forward base of operation in Chignecto. Lord Halifax in London agreed and sent his protégé reinforcements in the form of the 47th Regiment from Ireland. On August 19, John Rous helmed the sea militia to Minas Basin while Charles Lawrence, now a lieutenant colonel, marched with seven hundred soldiers and several pieces of small artillery to Pisiquid and then Grand Pré. The amphibious invasion force met and the fleet sailed for Chignecto.

Gorham's Rangers once again acted as scouts, with Rous and Lawrence following. The rangers would supplement their official wages with scalps; at least two dozen people were killed for cash during the expedition. The troops landed east of burned Beaubassin on September 3. This time, word of their coming had not advanced before them in the form of hilltop fires and messengers. While the French did not oppose them, they ran into a stiff fight from Mi'kmaq warriors, their Acadian allies and Le Loutre. The Mi'kmaq and their allies had built breastworks, big mounds of earth built up to chest height to provide fortifications. The Mi'kmaq could fire over the top at the British, but the British return fire couldn't get through the breastworks.

A short, fierce firefight erupted and twenty British troops died before they could establish a beachhead. Once there, the highly trained and heavily armed imperial forces launched a barrage that drove the Mi'kmaq back, killing several of them. The rangers quickly scalped the dead warriors to take back to Halifax for cash. The Mi'kmaq withdrew, with the Acadians burning their fields as they went so their labour would not go to feed the advancing enemy. The Mi'kmaq and their allies retreated across the Missaquash River. Lawrence did not follow.

Instead, he had his troops erect a prefabricated blockhouse and barrack frames amid the ruins of Beaubassin. The post would eventually be called Fort Lawrence in his honour. It stood at the edge of peninsular Nova Scotia and came to be the *de facto* border between French and English land claims.

Cornwallis got word of the expedition's success. Lawrence wrote that his forces had met entrenched opposition from a number of Mi'kmaq and Acadians. Lawrence suspected some of the "neutral" inhabitants were in fact disguised Frenchmen from Canada. The English were outmanned six to one, he reported, but through gallantry and intrepid spirit drove the enemy out of its position. It had cost them a schooner and brought Lawrence's army down to 111 men. They lost more in attacking the breastworks as their enemies opened fire on them.

Lawrence had commanded his men to hold their fire until they were at the foot of the breastworks, to save ammunition, causing many to die without firing a shot. Once they reached the trench's edge, the English troops opened fire and the Mi'kmaq retreated. Lawrence could not tell if any Mi'kmaq warriors had died, but six of his men were gone, along with twelve wounded.

They drove on to the river and found the French on the opposite bank, fortified and waving the French flag. Lawrence claimed the land on the near side for King George and planted his flag. The French and the English shouted obscenities and threats at each other across the water, while the Mi'kmaq retreated and observed from the woods.

It was agreed that the two European sides would meet on the river, so the first meeting took place in a boat. It was a stalemate, or a victory, depending on how you saw it. Lawrence saw it as a victory. Cornwallis agreed to see it as a victory, but knew it was at least a partial defeat. The French stood on what he felt was English land.

He sent Hugh Davidson back to London on the next ship. The blame for the expensive, struggling colony went with him. Cornwallis probably felt a twinge of envy when he saw his colleague packing up and heading home, even though he knew Davidson would likely return and that surely London would soon grant his own request for at least a short visit to England. A sloop had recently been lost in action off Canso, and Davidson took the blame for that too.

Meanwhile Paul Mascarene, the long-time leader at Annapolis, offered his resignation. He wrote to Cornwallis, saying he was worn out and wanted to go home before he died. Cornwallis accepted his resignation and looked for a new leader with strong military experience. "Force will be necessary for some time," he reasoned.

He wanted Charles Lawrence to become his second-in-command, so wrote long letters to London praising his "victory" at the river. "He is a man of great honour and veracity and I am sure he would not do a dirty thing," he wrote.

Cornwallis figured they could work with Lawrence's enthusiasm for a higher role with a new title. There was no need to increase Lawrence's salary just now. That way, Cornwallis argued to Whitehall, if he had to take over for Cornwallis while the governor travelled back to England, they would only have to pay Lawrence half Cornwallis's salary for filling in. As a last note, he begged London to boost the colony's flagging credit in New England, or it would be ruined. Another £12,000 should do it.

"If the Province is next year in good shape, maybe I can go home," he whispered to the flickering candles as he sealed the letter. "Maybe London will give me a discretionary leave. If not next year, by 1752 at the latest."

He could taste London. He longed for its busy streets, for the power of living so close to the king. He knew good work in the colonies would bode well for his career back in London, but he worried that being too far from the centre of power for too long would terminally injure his chance for advancement. But, he knew, an even worse blow would come if he left the colony in ruin.

"I may be of more use at home than here," he allowed himself to write. He couldn't be seen to be too eager to leave.

He signed the letter and folded it carefully. A messenger raced down to the waiting ship.

Cornwallis suddenly had second thoughts. Perhaps he hadn't emphasized the expenditure of the money clearly enough. He shouted for the messenger to return. The governor took another sheet of paper and wrote a second letter, laying out line by line where every pound had gone – salary, food, weapons. He put the two letters together and the ship set sail for England.

Cornwallis managed to wait two more days before writing again.

*   *   *   *   *

Fort Lawrence was a strong British post in a restive area, but it was soon to be tested. Guerrilla warfare broke out as the French assisted the Mi'kmaq in their quest to push back English occupation of their land. And then disaster struck: Captain Edward How was killed.

A messenger brought the terrible news to Cornwallis in Halifax. At Chignecto on October 4, How sailed across the river to meet his French counterparts for a prisoner exchange. "He fancied he knew the French settlers and personally [that] villain Le Loutre," the messenger said. "He says his whole aim and study was to try at peace with the Indians and to get our prisoners out of their hands. He had often conferences with Le Loutre and the French officers under a flag of truce."

After the meeting, he had turned for the English fort, but was attacked by a volley fired from the French camp. How was struck through the heart and died. A Métis named Etienne Batard was blamed.

Cornwallis was seized with rage. He stormed his room, swearing he would don his old military uniform from the Pacification of the Highlands and attack Chignecto himself. "An instance of such treachery and barbarity has no parallel in history!" he yelled. "It is a violation of a flag of truce, which has ever been held sacred and without which all faith is at an end."

His men watched in astonished silence. They had seen their leader angry, but not out of control.

How was one of his most valuable allies. Born in Ireland, he moved to Massachusetts as a young man. He entered Nova Scotia sometime before 1722 and set up for the fishery in Canso. He married, had a child, and moved to Annapolis. His wife died and he married again in 1744. He fought when called upon, and worked when not needed in battle. Cornwallis had greatly relied on his knowledge of the land and his ability to find ground with the Mi'kmaq. He spoke French and some Mi'kmaq. In a memorial, Cornwallis would later write, "How always behaved with the greatest of fidelity and care in everything I required of him."

The loss of such an able man was a heavy blow. A despondent Cornwallis wrote to his masters in London. "The difficulties I have had this year in establishing at Chignecto ... I almost despair of surmounting," he lamented.

French and Mi'kmaq forces constantly annoyed English ships. Cattle were driven away. Fuel was impossible to find – the woods were too dangerous to harvest. Halifax could barely defend itself. But it did, Cornwallis reflected. The French did not conquer Nova Scotia. Mi'kmaq people were being killed and driven off the peninsula.

"By the indefatigable labour of Colonel Lawrence and poor How, it is accomplished. Their fort is finished, the barracks up, and I hope furnished with everything, for a long winter is coming," Cornwallis wrote. "I can furnish them with nothing, nor hear from them for four months to come."

But Lawrence wrote of hope. It was fine, fertile land and would make a noble settlement, if they survived the winter. "I shall send a number there in the spring," Cornwallis vowed. "When we are well established there, the business will be done."

Cobequid would follow. He would send for more trustworthy priests to serve the Acadians. Without reliable priests, the French missionaries would always step into the void and have cover for mischief.

"The expense of this year frightened me," he confessed. "I feel it as much as any man concerned for the public and should be very happy to contribute to the lessening of it. But in circumstances as we are in, it is impossible at present to set about that great and desirable work until the peninsula is secured."

Cornwallis turned to John Gorham for revenge. Rangers were recruited from across Nova Scotia and ads in Boston newspapers promised cash for each Mi'kmaq scalp or prisoner brought in. The Mi'kmaq and their Acadian allies fought back hard, killing Bartello, who had regularly scalped their warriors, as well as their women and children. He was ambushed by thirty-five Mi'kmaq and Acadians. Though he outnumbered them with his sixty rangers, he died along with six of his men. Another seven were captured alive. The Mi'kmaq warriors found a safe spot near the English troops and tortured their captives deep into the night. The howling of Bartello's Rangers echoed through the dark. The disturbed English troops had no choice but to listen, until death brought silence.

Gorham launched a counter-raid with thirty rangers into French territory and attempted to sack an Acadian village on the Rivière Petitcodiac, but the Mi'kmaq and Acadians fought them off. As autumn turned Nova Scotia's trees blood-red, the Mi'kmaq and Acadian allies turned the rivers red with the blood of British soldiers. Raids, ambushes and skirmishes haunted the troops every time they left the small fort. On September 28, the Acadian vessel *Jacob* brought thirty-seven British prisoners to Port Toulouse (St. Peter's) on Île Royale. At the end of the month, the Mi'kmaq and Acadian allies raided Dartmouth again and killed five settlers before slipping into the woods and escaping along the Shubenacadie waterway.

Peace only came to the settlement with winter. The Mi'kmaq warriors were not professional soldiers, but ordinary men who had to also care for their families. No Crown footed the bill for their campaigns. The fighting season was spring through autumn. Winter meant peace, as the Mi'kmaq broke into small family groups who travelled to winter hunting lands. Despite entreaties from France to participate in a year-long campaign against the English, the Mi'kmaq continued to refuse. Family came first and hunting took priority over fighting.

The rebels among the Acadians, deprived of their ally for the season, had problems of their own. They too had no formal Crown backing, so time spent at arms was time not spent at harvest. The scorched-earth policy that razed Beaubassin and so many Acadian fields created a refugee population of more than 1,100 inhabitants. Many fled to the French side of the Missaquash River, but those not involved in the fighting – those who had tried to remain neutral – were stuck with little food, and a long winter approaching. Those neutrals were equally terrified of the Mi'kmaq warriors, as well as the French and English soldiers. Neutrality was their only hope – but neutrality was no longer an option.

The late autumn of 1750 and the winter of 1751 saw peace falling with the snow. The Mi'kmaq left the battlefield. The British secured their gains. The imperial soldiers regularly patrolled the land around Fort Lawrence, but the Mi'kmaq ghost army had dissipated and frustrated soldiers griped they might as well be hunting clouds.

The Acadians fled, or tried to coax food from the soil.

* * * * *

November started with a ferocious rainstorm blasting in on a southeast wind. The sea was raucous, the tides ripping up the beach and lapping the huts that plied their trade along the shore. By November 11, the temperature had plunged. Two days of deep-freeze left the ground – and many of the settlers – frostbitten. Rain followed by sub-zero temperatures turned the settlement into an ice rink. As the town was built on a slope, the hospital was busy with people who had lost their footing and broken arms, ankles, wrists and badly bruised themselves.

Little snow had fallen, but it seemed only a matter of time before the white shroud buried the land for its winter death. A few flurries stirred at night, melting in the day's sunshine. It felt unnatural to the Europeans to see the sun shine so bright, yet to offer so little warmth.

The Germans had hunkered down and kept mostly to themselves. Few spoke any English, and instead each quarter appointed the person with the best skills in King George's language to speak for all. Many of them were sickly from the long journey and from poor adaptation to the rougher life in the colonies. Some had died already, before the winter reaped its deadly harvest.

"Old, miserable wretches. Those that have died will be a loss," Cornwallis muttered as he composed an update to London. "And they complain about their passage not being paid as the Swiss were."

Those who were healthy were indentured to do public work to repay their debt for passage.

Cornwallis was more impressed with the Swiss. "They are in general good, industrious people," he observed. He sent a dozen to Pisiquid to see the country. They returned well pleased with what they had seen and were eager to break the ground come spring. They had to be deterred from staying in the area and starting work straight away. Memories of alpine winters finally convinced them of the wisdom of wintering in Halifax. "The more of them we have, the better," Cornwallis wrote.

And they must come in May, not August, he reminded London. Swiss, or West Country English. The crew from Dartmouth had done a superb job of clearing the ground and starting a fishery. If they settled that fertile land, the colony would soon feed itself and Cornwallis would be saved the indignity of constantly pleading with London for more money.

As the fall wore on, reports of Indian attacks slowed. "I flatter myself they will grow tired or come to a peace. It is what I have attempted by all the ways I could think of, but their demands – or rather their priests' demands – are so preposterous and ridiculous that they can't be in earnest," he said.

Those "ridiculous" Mi'kmaq demands were comprehensive. The English settlers must leave Chignecto. The fortification must come down. The Mi'kmaq sought half of the land the English called Nova Scotia and to have no communication with the English. In return, the English should leave them in peace, not attack them, not occupy more land, not issue bounties for the scalps of their men, women and children.

Cornwallis scoffed. From his perspective, they were lucky to have their lives, let alone King George's land.

Lawrence sent word from Chignecto that the fort was established and safe. All expected to be attacked in the winter, but the officers were confident they could repel anything short of a full French invasion. The fort would serve as a benefit in addition to keeping the French and Mi'kmaq out – it would keep the soldiers in. Desertion was a routine problem. Soldiers would go into the forests to gather wood and never return. Some likely were killed by roving Mi'kmaq warriors or by other misadventure, but a number continued to abandon Nova Scotia for New England. Some even began living with Mi'kmaq communities, preferring their way of life to that of the English frontier. The fort walls would make that trickier to do unnoticed.

Cornwallis picked up his pen to update London on the latest chicanery from the French. They were "perfidious and unaccountable" and the peace signed in Europe meant little in the frontier. It was war in all but name. Gorham's Rangers roamed up and down the province, hunting Mi'kmaq families and bringing their scalps to Annapolis and Halifax. Their numbers were clearly falling as the pile of scalps rose, and the warrior retaliation became more brutal. The Acadians wrote saying they feared for their lives.

Captain Rous sailed the *Albany* to the Bay of Fundy, but met with a French brigantine and a schooner off Cape Sable. The French vessels were laden with provisions and ammunition that likely came from Quebec. The English ships fired at them to stop, but they kept going. Rous fired again and again, and the French returned fire. The *Albany* ran alongside the brigantine and took several rounds from its small arms. A British midshipman and two sailors were killed. Five French died in retaliation before the brigantine was captured. It was the second vessel the British had spotted loaded with weapons, ammunition and provisions from the governor of Canada in Quebec. Rous was certain they were bound for the St. John River Mi'kmaq.

Cornwallis received word in his quarters. His eyes narrowed. His lips tightened. When the messenger had relayed the news, the governor stood up angrily. "They are so bold and daring in direct violation of express treaties that I am astonished," he shouted.

The soldiers must protect the settlers, but their salaries and supplies cost so much that there was precious little left for the settlers to survive on. The Chignecto expedition was expensive, but Cornwallis could see no other way to secure the colony. Fortifying George's Island was likewise expensive, but nearly complete. The little harbour island was almost fully bald now, and bristling with enough guns to see off any sea invader. A strong palisade made from those same trees formed a formidable barrier to thwart a land invasion. Slowly, the British grip on the land was tightening.

22

The Mi'kmaq Return to the Battlefield

The year 1750 ended with a burst of good weather. Little snow had fallen in December and it was consistently warmer than the first winter. Clear sunshine cast sharp shadows as the Earth's star slid low over the southern sky from east to west, causing men to squint each time they turned in that direction. As New Year's Eve approached, a violent gale ripped off the Atlantic and pushed heavy rain onto the settlement for twelve unrelenting hours. People dared not go outside lest they be blown away, and the damage to the palisades and the houses inside them was significant.

The biting winds and rambunctious seas caused more problems. Cornwallis had ordered a sloop loaded with fourteen four-pound cannons and fifteen six-pounders to relocate from Annapolis to Halifax. It would greatly strengthen the settlement's defensive capability and allow swift and decisive response to any further attacks from the Mi'kmaq and their allies on Dartmouth. But the sloop never arrived. Its fate was never known, but it was presumed to have sunk. A small voice in Cornwallis's head worried that the Mi'kmaq, who were known to be accomplished sailors even on the open ocean, had taken it. The site of an English sloop manned by Mi'kmaq warriors bearing down on infant Halifax would be enough to break even the strongest settler's nerves.

Confined to his quarters by his disease and by weather, Cornwallis spent much of the winter counting money and carefully spooning out thin gruel to keep the colony alive physically – and politically. He kept rigorous financial records to avoid any further aspersions being cast on his command.

In early February 1751, English ships began reporting more Mi'kmaq pirate attacks. English sailors would be navigating along the coast when war canoes would materialize and open fire, capturing ships and booty before the sailors even realized what was happening. So far, mainly commercial ships had been taken and the Mi'kmaq showed more interest in the contents than the ships themselves.

In March, Cornwallis swore in new council members, new justices, and new clerks. The changeover revived him. It was a cold, snow-filled spring. It seemed as though Nova Scotia had a healthy ration of miserable weather – and it would be handed out each year. There was no cause to celebrate an unusually light December because you would only find yourself paying for it with a brutal March. Cornwallis felt better to have the worst of winter behind him and allowed himself to hope that it would be his last in the colony.

By March 28, the weather had warmed, but the news chilled the settlers' blood. The British were weakened after a long winter vigil, and the Acadians were fatigued from merely staying alive, but the Mi'kmaq closed their hunting season and returned to the battlefield well fed and ready to fight. On March 26, warriors sailed down the Shubenacadie waterway and saw the new English fortification at the crucial head was growing. The warriors attacked Dartmouth at nine a.m., coming up through the brush and opening fire. They killed fifteen settlers and soldiers and wounded another seven, three of whom would die in Halifax's frontier hospital. The warriors took six captives and faded into the woods.

The British garrison ran after the warriors. They caught three stragglers, more youths than men, and killed and scalped them. One British patrol chased the warriors deep into the forest, but found they had fallen into a trap. A sergeant was killed before they could escape.

The Mi'kmaq warriors returned two days later and launched another raid, abducting three settlers. Two weeks later, Mi'kmaq forces mustered in the woods outside of Halifax and launched a raid on the outskirts of the settlement. They killed two English soldiers, but were unable to attack the main fortification.

Salusbury, confident behind the strong fort, dismissed the attacks as trifles. Cornwallis wasn't so cocky. The governor's fear was justified. On May 13, a force of sixty Mi'kmaq and Acadian warriors invaded Dartmouth. As settlers fought back or fled for their lives, the warriors opened fire with the few firearms they had and with vicious hand-to-hand fighting with shorter weapons. Halifax heard the alarm and sent troops across the harbour. They passed fleeing settlers. The Mi'kmaq had vanished before the English reinforcements arrived. When the dust cleared, twenty-two settlers and soldiers were dead. More were missing as prisoners. The remaining settlers were devastated. The remaining soldiers were drunk; shaken by the power of the attack, many of Dartmouth's guardians took to alcohol to wash away their fears. Sitting in the blockhouses maximized the sense of being trapped; Salusbury noted the Mi'kmaq would "never cram themselves" into such a tiny fort and await attack, but instead actively chased their enemies.

As the summer of 1751 started in Nova Scotia, Mi'kma'ki and Acadia, the fate of the land was in the balance. The English used their "Flanders discipline" approach by building and maintaining a string of strong fortress outposts dotting the land. The Mi'kmaq had control over most of the territory and struck their enemies when they were ready and at locations of their choosing.

From all over Nova Scotia, letters poured into Halifax pleading for help. Mi'kmaq warriors terrorized the English everywhere they settled. Cornwallis received letters from neutral Acadians asking for help to defend against Mi'kmaq forces, but the governor said the Acadians would first have to pledge loyalty to King George and agree to take up arms against any British enemies. Caught in the middle of a brutal guerrilla war, most stuck to neutrality. Cornwallis sent one hundred regular soldiers and rangers to reinforce the small garrisons at Fort Edward and Fort Sackville. The soldiers were told to be vigilant - the Mi'kmaq might attack from the outside, or the Acadians could merely be luring them into a trap and turn on them from within.

Settlers fled Dartmouth in the days after the May attack. The settlement was heading toward extinction. Cornwallis wanted to show that he would not abandon anyone who stayed with him. To that end, he dug into the colony's limited purse and paid a group of Mi'kmaq £886 to release some of the captives taken from Dartmouth. They were returned unharmed. The long summer was spent repairing Halifax from winter damage, sending Gorham's Rangers on endless marches to Pisiquid and back, and growing the Halifax settlement to the point it was pressed against the fort walls. The Mi'kmaq, seeing the British stalled everywhere outside of Halifax, slowed hostilities and resumed their normal lives.

23
Cost of War Mounts and Parliament Questions Spending

The winter passed quietly, too. The Mi'kmaq withdrew from fighting to hunt with their families. Halifax withdrew into itself, tending to the endless problems of a new society comprised of thousands of people from all over Europe.

Word reached council that a man claiming to be a priest was performing illegal weddings. He was called before council and said he was indeed a priest and had been marrying people, but that he was legitimate. Only, he had lost his papers. Either way, he had not secured Cornwallis's permission to work as a priest in the province, so he was handed a stiff £100 fine and tossed in jail until he could pay.

All along the coast, ships sailed from Boston to Nova Scotia, from Annapolis to Halifax, from French Louisbourg to all other points. Mi'kmaq and Acadian pirates routinely hijacked them and stole the goods. Sometimes they took the crew, too, and ransomed them off. On occasion, they even took the entire ship and added it to their rebel army.

February's dreariness was interrupted by a few public whippings. The case that drew the biggest crowd was Stephen Adams and Thomas Greys. Both had been convicted of spreading false news to the prejudice of the settlement and scandalous lies about His Excellency, Edward Cornwallis. What exactly they had said about Cornwallis was kept under wraps. Several hundred people turned out to watch the two shivering, shirtless men receive twenty hard stripes each. Deprived of any details about the slander, the settlers made them up. The accusations grew more ribald as the rum flowed.

The business of running a settlement consumed much of Cornwallis's time. He was made aware of a growing nuisance in the form of foxes. The merchants of Nova Scotia requested a bounty be placed on the pests, and Cornwallis obliged. "There shall be paid out of the public treasury of the province a bounty of six pence per quintal [100 kilograms or 200 pounds]," he declared.

He also reset the prices for a barrel of pickled fish, for whale, seal or any other big sea creature. He was having problems with settlers charging exorbitant prices for fresh fish. "I have thought fit with the advice of His Majesty's council to issue this proclamation hereby forbidding all persons to demand or receive for any fresh fish by them to sell within this settlement any greater than six pence for every fresh fish of thirty inches long and with the same proportion for any larger catch," he stated.

It was signed and posted around the settlement.

A March letter from the Board of Trade had some good news. Parliament had renewed his operating grant. But the lords were unhappy that Cornwallis had exceeded his budget and would likely need more again for the year ahead.

"It was with some concern we again found ourselves this year obliged to go into Parliament with exceedings," the board said. They agreed with Cornwallis that it was unavoidable, yet it should have been avoided, as it turned Parliament against the undertaking. The board would have been able to better defend him if he had provided better accounts of where the money had gone. London and Parliament worried about big pots of money being spent under generic headings, the board told Cornwallis. A source in New England had informed them that people in Boston were buying cheap goods that could be traced to provisions for Halifax. Clearly, the Halifax settlers were getting enough food – so much so they could sell the extra.

"We should be unkind to you as well as unjust to the public if we did not without delay inform you of these matters coming before us as they do with good authority; we mention them as faults in your subordinate officers, which should be inquired into and prevented, and not with any view to complain of your conduct or as supposing you are not as desirous to see the above remedies as we ourselves are," they explained.

"We must observe on our own part that a large sum is charged in your accounts for rum, beer and bread, which we cannot account for, as all the persons victualled by the public must come within one of the two contracts. We should be glad to have information on this article."

The letter went on bristling with indignation at the latest sums Cornwallis had sent, and upbraided him for failing to keep Whitehall informed of events in Nova Scotia. Referring to his last letter defending the intelligence he had provided London, the board wrote, "You say in this letter you are equally surprised and concerned at a charge of neglect from our board and ask if you have not from time to time acquainted us with the general state of the province, to which we can only make this answer: That at the time that our letter of the 14 of June was written, we had been six months without any intelligence."

They had heard many, many rumours from traders and officers crisscrossing the ocean. The rumours made them uneasy with his silence. "In such a situation, it was natural of us, as well as our duty, to give you notice of the reports we heard and the uncertainty we stood in," they wrote.

The board told Cornwallis he would not retain the good opinion of Parliament unless he refrained from overspending in the future.

Summer saw the deportation of various unwanted people from the settlement, mostly Roman Catholics. Cornwallis feared their latent sympathy with the Acadians and Mi'kmaq – most of whom were fellow Catholics – rather than to him and the Crown. In Scotland, the Jacobites toasted their "king over the water." Here in Nova Scotia, he feared the Papists were secretly sipping blood-red wine to their high priest across the ocean. Council met to discuss the problem and agreed the best way to prevent future concerns was to block Catholics from landing in Nova Scotia altogether.

An inspection of the city's wood walls revealed them to be in poor condition. Cornwallis was again baffled that people could take their own security so lightly. He pressed settlers into action and upgraded Halifax's defences. He toured the town and took note of all undeveloped lots within the walls and reminded the owners they had to develop them, or lose them.

He was less concerned with the hardy souls who had dug out streets outside the walls. The Protestant Germans – who called themselves Deutsche and whom everyone else called Dutch – settled along dirt tracks cut out of the woods and named grandly for places back home:

Brunswick and Gottingen. They eventually spread out to the narrow land bridge connecting peninsular Halifax to mainland Nova Scotia into a sub-colony called Dutch Village. Halifax's black population, mostly trapped there as slaves, did most of the hard work of carving a city out of the woods. Cornwallis supported the expansion; it was after all part of his core mission in Nova Scotia to establish Halifax and rapidly build new settlements. He and his council decided the "Dutch" would be allowed to settle west of the main settlement. That would be near enough that he felt he could protect them against Mi'kmaq attacks, and allow them enough space to develop farmlands.

"Given the advanced season of the year and the circumstances of the province in regard to the Indians, it will be most convenient in many re-spects to place them for the present between the head of the northwest arm of this harbour and the mouth of the Bedford bay and to employ those who are to work picketing the area," he wrote.

Cornwallis erected three blockhouses between Bedford Basin and the Northwest Arm to protect them. The forts were connected by a rough military road that he had troops patrol regularly. The southern blockhouse stood at Chebucto Road and Armdale Road, the central at what would be-come Bayers Road and Connaught Avenue, and the northern at the far end of Windsor Street. In the decades to come, all would vanish – though a section of the Windsor Street military road would be turned into the driveway of a cemetery in Fairview, which was itself built on the site of the northern blockhouse.

He watched as the cost of all that work added up. He knew he had blown his budget – he had spent at least twice as much as he had been allotted. Anticipating complaints from London, he sat down and wrote a letter explaining the need to exceed his budget once more. "Not a pound shall be expended by me unnecessarily, but without money you could have had no town, no settlement, and indeed no settlers," he told the board plainly. "Tis very certain that the public money cleared the ground, built the town, secured it, kept both soldiers and settlers from starving with cold, and has brought down 1,000 settlers from the other colonies. Lots in Halifax are now worth 50 guineas. If there was no public money circulating, lots would be given for a gallon of rum. The money is laid out in building forts, barracks, storehouses, hospitals, churches, wharves, etc. Public works all that seem necessary."

He sealed the letter and dispatched it on a ship bound for England. Detailed financial reports were attached.

*   *   *   *   *

Cornwallis prepared to disperse the next shipload of settlers promised from London. "It would be most convenient to land them at Dartmouth and employ them in developing the back of the town," suggested Hugh Davidson, who had recently returned from London.

The new settlement was still shaken, still sparsely populated, but somewhat calmed by the late peace. The peace steadied Cornwallis's nerves, too. The vast guerrilla war he had been waging had bankrupted the colony. Parliament had authorized him to spend £39,000 for Nova Scotia in 1750. He had spent £174,000. Seven percent of that budget went to the rangers who, for all their bravado, had barely slowed the Mi'kmaq. Hubristic talk of rooting them out of their homeland permanently faded. The Mi'kmaq weren't going anywhere.

Cornwallis faced constant pressure from London to cut his costs, and he in turn looked at the rangers. Expensive and largely ineffective, they had waged two years of guerrilla war on the Acadians and Mi'kmaq and reaped a small fortune in the process. But for every dead Acadian and Mi'kmaq, there were a dozen potentially loyal – or at least neutral – subjects who were forever turned against Britain. Cornwallis suspected the fires that lighted the advance of Charles Lawrence's first expedition, and that resulted in Beaubassin being burned, had been started by Acadians in Nova Scotia fed up with ranger harassment. There was no bounty for Acadian scalps, but everyone knew it was hard to tell one scalp from another. Plenty of Acadians had been killed so the rangers could fatten their pocketbooks.

John Gorham perhaps saw the writing on the wall. He requested permission to return to England to put his financial affairs in order. He was fed up with Cornwallis, and Cornwallis was sick of him. During King George's War (1744-1748), Gorham had paid out of pocket to transform the schooners *Anson* and *Warren* into military ships for his rangers. The monthly rent he charged – £185, plus £90 for the use of his whaleboats – was constantly in arrears. Cornwallis declared the cost to be "most extravagant" and was reluctant to settle the account. Gorham was tired of defending himself to Cornwallis and of having to pull every penny out of him. He went to London officially to deal with personal financial matters, but also to take his case directly to the Board of Trade. He sailed home on his own, taking his wife and children with him. He would never return to North America. In September 1751, word reached Halifax that Gorham had died of smallpox.

The town continued to grow during the *de facto* truce with the Mi'kmaq and their Acadian allies. The Mi'kmaq war councils met and saw that they had profited handsomely from the conflict. The scalps of British soldiers and ransom for prisoners had turned into cash at Louisbourg. They had largely contained the British to the old settlement in Annapolis and the new outpost in Chebucto. The Dartmouth settlement was perhaps fatally weakened. The British troops in the rest of the province – at Fort Edward, at Fort Lawrence – were confined to their blockhouses. France had built a strong presence across the river from Fort Lawrence at Fort Beausejour, capable of holding thirty-two cannons, one mortar and a garrison of seventy men. A second satellite fort at Baie Verte, called Fort Gaspereaux, solidified the French presence at the frontier border between the empires. The Mi'kmaq always found a warm reception at the French forts. France was eager for peace and trade with the Mi'kmaq and watched in amusement as Britain broke its bank fighting them.

For the Mi'kmaq, the increasing French presence also put a stop to British expansion into their hunting grounds. The Mi'kmaq war councils decided there was little to be gained from continued fighting and kept their warriors from returning to the warpath in the spring of 1751. Le Loutre left Nova Scotia for Quebec, and then Paris, to seek support for the refugees who found themselves forced out of Nova Scotia into French territory. He gave goods due to the Mi'kmaq to the Acadian refugees instead. The Mi'kmaq leaders largely broke off relations with him after this snub.

The British were unable to find the Mi'kmaq, but eventually the Mi'kmaq found them. The Shubenacadie Mi'kmaq paddled down the waterway, passed Dartmouth and approached Halifax directly. Under the leadership of Jean-Baptiste Cope, they offered their terms for peace. Cope was suspected of ultimately being behind the killing of Edward How but the British had few options. Rather than signing a new treaty, the two sides renewed their friendship as outlined in Mascarene's Treaty and reconfirmed the 1749 articles.

"All transactions during the late war shall on both sides be buried in oblivion with the hatchet, and that the said Indians shall have all favour, friendship and protection shewn them from this His Majesty's government," the agreement stated. The British paid Cope's band in flour, tobacco and other trade goods and he agreed to stop killing and harassing the British soldiers and settlers. He also vowed to try to bring the other Mi'kmaq and Maliseet bands to the peace table.

Salusbury dismissed the whole show as a "foolish piece of formality." But the little peace held.

24

European Refugees Enticed to Halifax

While Cornwallis struggled to keep his settlement alive, British agents swept across Europe touting the virtues of the good life in the New World. The large plots of land that had lured the first settlers, and which largely remained forests used by the Mi'kmaq, continued to entice downtrodden Europeans in France, Germany, Switzerland and the Netherlands. British agents met with Protestant activists all over the tumultuous continent and sold them the same old dream. The contrast between the vision extolled by the agents of empty land waiting for hardworking settlers and the reality of a province fought over by three nations continued unchecked by reality. New Scotland remained the land where Plenty sat queen in the "age of gold," as the satirical ballads had it.

The promise of the New World may have been a joke to the upper classes, but to the poor and powerless, it had a potent allure. British agents brave enough to venture into wartorn France found an eager reception. France had a Catholic king, and was mostly a Catholic country. It also had a Protestant minority it was eager to convert or drive out. The possibility of a new start free from religious persecution drew crowds to hear the agents' promises.

Rumours of a Protestant colony with good farming land reached the ear of the refugee French farmer Jean-George D'Attrey, his family and friends in Montbeliard. They had fled their ancestral home land when the Lutheran church had been handed over to Catholics at gunpoint. D'Attrey, who had married a local woman named Elizabeth Vuillemenot just before fleeing Chagey, still walked with a limp from the shot he had taken in the thigh. For D'Attrey, sick of war, sick of famine, sick of disease, the promise of Nova Scotia sounded like heaven itself.

D'Attrey, Pierre Mailliard and the other refugees encountered an itinerant Protestant preacher spreading the word that the British were looking for foreign Protestants. The agent soon had a crowd around him. The preacher explained that the British had reclaimed Nova Scotia in the Americas and, having secured it, were inviting loyal men and women to settle it. Settlers would be transported to Halifax at no charge and would build the new city to repay their debt. Britain would provide everything from tools to build the city, implements to work the land and even linens to dress their beds. The fleeing Protestants would create a better life for their children than the centuries of starvation and warfare they had experienced.

The French refugees made their way down the Rhine River to Amsterdam. D'Attrey and Mailliard, both war veterans, prepared for the expedition. They put what few goods their families carried onto rafts and drifted down the Rhine toward Rotterdam. The three-week journey was tense because the lands they travelled through were under constant threat of war. Unrest in Europe dislocated hundreds of thousands of poor people. The voyage was expensive and the Protestants exhausted all of their savings just getting to Amsterdam.

In Holland, they located a British agent. He wanted German and Swiss Protestant settlers to go to Nova Scotia, but was persuaded to accept some French refugees when D'Attrey told him of their battle with Catholic soldiers. The agent offered what seemed to D'Attrey an unbeatable deal: free passage and free food for him, his wife and his sister for one year, plus land. It would do more to improve the family's fortunes in one move than had been accomplished in generations of battle in France. He would owe the Crown one year's labour to pay for his trip once he arrived in Halifax. "And you'll only be building the forts and fields to protect and feed yourself," the agent added.

D'Attrey booked his family passage on the *Sally*, scheduled to depart in the spring of 1752. The others did the same. A ship brought the refugees to London and they travelled on to the docks at Portsmouth. Here they discovered the first false promise from the British. There were no supplies waiting for them. Having exhausted their savings getting this far, the families spent an impoverished winter waiting for the *Sally* to depart. The crowd of foreigners around the docks grew and eventually the pressure forced the government to commission four ships to the New World: two would sail for South Carolina and two for Halifax.

25

The Lights Come On

L ife in Halifax was literally brightening. A trade mission to Boston
brought back four hundred lanterns for the landing places and rough
streets and lanes of the settlement. The lanterns were hung on posts standing eight feet high. When they weren't stolen or smashed, they did a passable job of lighting the town.

St. Paul's still had no pews, but it was the first Church of England
sanctuary in North America and had a strong congregation who flocked to
three-hour services led by Rev. William Tutty. Other Protestants were also
allowed to use it for prayer meetings on Sunday afternoons. The Dissenters, as they were known, had asked Cornwallis for permission to build a
church of their own. In December of 1749, the council granted the group
a church site on Hollis and Prince streets. Four lots sat there unused by
the four bachelors who had won them in the initial lottery. That land was
turned over to the Dissenters, but the church itself was not built until 1753
as the group raised money.

The city walls fell into disrepair again as the settlers expanded beyond their boundaries. The walls were no longer a defensive priority,
because the blockhouses built to guard the Germans in Dutch Village provided enough protection for everyone. The farmers began to produce crops,
although not enough to feed the city. Everyone looked with greedy eyes to
the fertile land of the Annapolis Valley, held by Acadian farmers reluctant
to feed Halifax. If only they could be removed and the land turned over to
royal Protestant farmers, many mused.

Joshua Mauger's influence grew. The suspected smuggler was becoming a major player in Halifax. He controlled part of the slave trade and established a fishery station at Mauger's Beach on Cornwallis Island (McNab's). He also set up a rum distillery near the Halifax dockyard, a large warehouse and a shop in town, plus a chain of trading posts deeper in the province to trade with the Mi'kmaq. He was contracted as victualler to King George's fleet in Nova Scotia, an account that made him prosperous.

Each ship from London brought word that the Board of Trade wanted more financial accounting. Cornwallis turned to his accountant, Commissary Little, and threatened to throw him into the woods if the numbers didn't start to add up. Little, a scrawny man who had nightmares that trees turned into Mi'kmaq and surrounded Halifax, begged for mercy. He was saved by the fact that whatever his shortcomings, he was the best accountant in Halifax. In fact, he may have been the only accountant in Halifax. Cornwallis made him double-check each expenditure.

While the pressure from London kept up, the letters dwindled. The whole of British North America was facing vast problems. Cornwallis wrote asking for more engineers to develop the public works. He had been promised three, but only one – Inigo Bruce – had come with him in 1749, and that lone engineer was charged with developing the entire colony. Bruce was about to leave without a replacement to take over.

After the quiet winter, the French resumed their meddlesome ways. The British fort at Chignecto was harassed. Soldiers who ventured into the woods for fuel were picked off by hostile French and occasionally Mi'kmaq warriors who had not heard of any truce. Cornwallis seized two French vessels in his territory and received an angry letter from the French commander demanding their return.

"I told him he should declare war against me," Cornwallis wrote to the Duke of Bedford. "Commence hostilities!"

War was not declared, but the French at Louisbourg seized four New England vessels and sent hostile Mi'kmaq from Canada to the Nova Scotia border. The warriors raided British outposts.

"In the night they attacked it and did some mischief by killing some of the inhabitants. I think four, and took six soldiers prisoner," Cornwallis wrote. "They weren't on guard, but off duty. The soldiers killed three Indians."

The British stayed in their strongholds and France slid agents across the border to warn the neutral Acadians that anyone helping the British by selling them food or acting as couriers would be killed. The neutral inhabitants pleaded with Cornwallis for help.

"Farmers can't live within their forts," he said. "They must go out in security upon their business to make it turn to any account."

He sent a detachment of troops to offer some shelter. Another ex-patriot Nova Scotian in London told the Board of Trade that many of the promised lots had not been cleared. They sent word to Cornwallis asking why he had not broken the woods yet.

"Indian patrols" comprised of ordinary settlers regularly swept the woods around Halifax. George's Island was heavily armed to protect the settlement. Weary of asking London for more help, Cornwallis sent letters to the governors of the other British colonies to lend him a hand, but they declined. Everybody had his own troubles. He was forced to borrow from Boston and hope that he would one day be able to repay. Nova Scotia's credit was poor, and borrowing cash became more and more expensive. Cornwallis urged London to focus on strengthening what he had built: a strong fort at Halifax to offset Louisbourg and a presence at Chignecto to keep the French out. That was what he had been sent to do, so surely his mission could be seen as a success. Surely he could go home. Halifax would sustain itself with a fishery and small gardens and lie in wait for the next war. "It would be an advantage that would be permanent and sure to the Mother Country," he told London.

Word reached Halifax that a French man-of-war with fifty-six guns had been spotted at the harbour's outer mouth. Another French frigate was seen cruising in Baie Verte. Sources in Boston reported that as many as five men-of-war were travelling together toward Chebucto. Rumours lifted the number to eight and settlers watched the harbour mouth in dread of a French invasion.

"I am a little uneasy for the sloops who are upon a cruise in the Bay of Fundy and Bay Verte that is daily expected," Cornwallis wrote.

The French gunship hung around the harbour mouth for two weeks before vanishing. "With what view I can't judge. As she has not interrupted any vessels coming in or going out, I imagine she has been surveying the coast and harbours. She does have a large schooner in company with her," he speculated.

London wrote back chastising him for the poor quality of his intelligence on French activities in his own territory. "The French have cruised all summer upon your coast and there has not been a man-of-war sent except a ship of twenty guns bound for New York that arrived this month."

Cornwallis was furious. He could not tell them what he did not know. He shot back that he could barely afford to guard the town, let alone patrol the whole coastline. "Did I not acquaint your Lordships of the attack made last fall upon the *Albany* by a ship that was supplying arms and ammunitions to the Indians? Did I not inform you of that black and villainous act upon Captain How? What could your Lordships expect after that? Did I not tell you sending for priests would be necessary and that no good could be expected from French Missionaries?"

He had sent a plan for fortifying the harbour itself and provided an estimate. He had heard nothing in reply. "Has the least notice been taken in any letter?" he asked. He reminded London that all the good done in Nova Scotia had been done by him – and that he had little help. "I have strongly urged the necessity of a lieutenant-governor that in case any accident happened, [command] might not fall into hands you never designed it for," he wrote.

If London appointed a second-in-command, that person could be groomed to succeed him. He could start to plan his return to London.

26
Cornwallis Seeks a Transfer Back to England

The fall of 1751 brought more problems: more English settlers taken hostage, more ransoms to pay. In this case, it was a Lieutenant John Hamilton writing from Quebec to say he and sixty others had been held by Mi'kmaqs for the last two years. So Cornwallis was being asked to pay not only the ransom, but also the room and board costs incurred by the hostages over the last twenty-four months.

Cornwallis brought the matter to council and held a long discussion. It was a cost they could not bear, but the greater worry was the message it would send. Failure to pay would reveal the poor state of Nova Scotia's finances, and it would also further disturb British settlers. The fear of being attacked and carried away by Mi'kmaq was endemic; knowing their own government would abandon them in those dire circumstances would not help. They agreed to pay the full demands. "It appears to be the only means of relieving those unfortunate persons out of this long and cruel captivity," Cornwallis explained to London.

The winter came swiftly. By early November, the settlement had been bathed in its first winter storm. Fortress Halifax sat silent and still as the snow accumulated. Puffs of smoke formed a cloud over the town as each resident huddled inside until the cold snap passed. More than one hungry mind thought of the Mi'kmaq and the strange fact that what was for European settlers the hardest, leanest time of the year was for the Natives a time of feasting on fresh meat and relaxing with families.

182 – Jon Tattrie

George's Island was packed with its temporary population. The new Protestant arrivals were confused and unhappy. The barren island in the harbour did not match the images of rolling farmland that lured them so far from home. They discovered on the voyage over that the linens and clothing supposedly in abundance in the New World were in fact non-existent. Less baggage on board meant there was more room for paying people, so the shipowners lied to maximize their profit.

It was a regular Island of Babel, with French, German and even a little Italian from the Swiss adding to the confusion and mutual incomprehension. English was the closest to a common language, but most communication relied on body language. The island's extensive, expensive fortifications were well established. The indentured labour of the new settlers reduced the bills greatly. But they would have to winter there. A regular ferry shuttled between Halifax and the island to take food, water and other supplies.

Cornwallis was pleased to see the little island fortress bristling with weapons. Rumours regularly reached him that France was settling on the Cape Sable shore. He had sent a team to investigate and it had found nothing, but the province was big and full of little-known coves and harbours. It would not be hard to hide an outpost from Halifax. France had claimed Canso Island near Île Royale and the local commander sent Cornwallis a letter telling him to stop his English fishermen from curing fish on it. Cornwallis rebuffed the request, countering the island belonged to "the king, my master." France wrote back arguing they owned it. After a long back and forth, both sides pledged to prevent their respective settlers from encroaching on each other's territory.

But Cornwallis heard nothing from the Mi'kmaq. Their ghost army had dematerialized. He knew there were thousands and thousands of Mi'kmaq men, women and children in the province, but sending patrols to them was like hunting unicorns. He was compelled to wait for the Mi'kmaq leaders to come to him. It was unclear if they were still at war, at peace, or something else. But he was ready to extend the olive branch. He could not afford to fight them anymore. To that end, he brought in more loyal priests to serve the Mi'kmaq.

"I hope at least this will show them the difference between an arbitrary French government and the longevity and freedom of the English," he told his council. "They may become good subjects – I am certain of that. If only we could keep the French missionaries away from them. But they need priests. We need to send them priests."

He saved more money by spending less on public works, but that slowed the progress of the settlement, and that angered London. Seeing that he could not evict the Mi'kmaq from the peninsula, he changed tactics. The new strategy called for the building of trade posts and forts across the Nova Scotia interior to lure the Mi'kmaq in with trade. Cornwallis spent much of the next year seeking Mi'kmaq partners to use the trade posts and with whom he could negotiate a peace.

Cornwallis received word from London that one of his appointments as justice of the peace was invalid. He had entrusted the critical position to a German man, but London noted you had to be born in Nova Scotia, or a resident for seven years, before you could hold titles or inherit land, let alone be named justice of the peace. Cornwallis and much of his council were exempted from this rule.

In November, he wrote his bosses a long letter laying out in great detail all that he did not know about the state of Nova Scotia. Loose details of the French fort in Baie Verte reached him, but nothing concrete about its size or capability. He had heard rumours of a flour shortage in Louisbourg, but nothing confirmed. Halifax was short on flour, too. Prices in Boston were sky high and he heard repeated reports that unscrupulous businessmen in New England were selling flour to Louisbourg over Halifax, because the French would pay more. He also heard constant reports that smugglers in Halifax were diverting vital goods and selling them on the black market.

Cornwallis signed off with another plea to leave Halifax. "I beg leave to remind your Lordships of my last request for leave to resign my government and return home," he wrote. "I am, Ed Cornwallis."

He no longer even pretended he wanted a brief return to handle business in London. He wanted to leave permanently.

27

Cornwallis Clashes with Joshua Mauger

Cornwallis shivered through the winter, locked into his bed by a vicious attack of rheumatism. He filled his days tracking the colony's financial activity and compiling it for London. He wrote a letter in December, but for the first time in his tenure as governor he forgot to date it. He blamed Little for the fiscal shortcomings and suspended the accountant.

He forgot to date the next letter, too, but it was received in London on January 6, 1752. Cornwallis told his masters that he had struggled over whether to inform them of a certain "transaction" that had recently occurred in Halifax, before deciding to give a full account. He did not doubt it would reach their ears even if he kept silent. Best to get his side in first.

"I hope I shall have support," he implored.

After updating them on the *de facto* peace in the province, he got down to the "transaction." A sloop had landed with goods from Louisbourg in November. It illegally sold them to merchants in Halifax. Cornwallis caught wind of what was going on and got a judge's order to seize and search the vessel, as well as the homes of those he thought had received the goods.

One of those was Joshua Mauger, the slave trader and suspected smuggler. But Mauger was by then a powerful, wealthy man in his own right and when Cornwallis's soldiers demanded he hand them the keys to his storehouse, he denied them access. Even when they produced the warrant, he still refused.

Cornwallis was outraged. The judge represented his own authority as governor of Nova Scotia, and his own authority came from King George. He made this clear to Mauger through his messenger – that to deny Cornwallis access to the storehouse was to deny a direct order from the king. Mauger was unimpressed and kept the doors locked. The messenger rushed back to inform Cornwallis.

"I should be sorry to proceed to violence, but ... if he does not deliver the key, I would have the doors opened!" he shouted.

Mauger wrote back, boldly denying the governor's order in plain ink. Cornwallis blew up. He ordered a civil officer to open the storehouse. "If you meet with obstruction in the lawful execution of your duty, I would support you using force, but do not care to send force without absolute necessity," he instructed.

Before resorting to force, he gave Mauger one more chance. "I desire Mr. Mauger to send one of his people," he said.

But now the officer met with no resistance. Mauger dispatched one of his men to open the storehouse, but the officer found only some casks of French molasses. Mauger insisted it was cargo given to him as part of his stock at the evacuation of Louisbourg. The veterans of the campaign that had captured the mighty French fortress, only to see the English give it back, had never forgotten. Mauger was happy to remind Cornwallis.

Cornwallis stewed. He was certain Mauger was a smuggler and had delayed the execution of the warrant to move his illegal goods to another location. Cornwallis asked London to take action. London wrote back with detailed questions about the timing of the incident. They had received Mauger's account and it disagreed with Cornwallis's: Mauger said it happened after sunset, but Cornwallis had said it happened in daylight. London wanted an explanation of the discrepancy. Cornwallis was baffled as to why the precise timing was relevant, but he bolstered his daylight case as best he could.

"Besides," he wrote, "I have a right to search for prohibited goods at all times. And I have acted with the greatest tenderness in regard to trade and call the whole colony to witness it."

He was not in the business of harassing traders. He only did so in this one case, and only because he had good reason to think Mauger was a smuggler. "I dare say I shall be supported and if their Lordships should be of the opinion that I have acted as becoming my station with regard to my

186 – Jon Tattrie

instructions and the public's welfare, I hope Mr. Mauger will no longer be employed by the victualling board or in His Majesty's employ."

There were bigger issues at stake than a personality conflict. "I am persuaded that this is done for a trial of whether this colony is to be the seat of fair trade and protection to those who pursue it, or a rendezvous for smugglers and people who keep a constant correspondence to Louisbourg with no good design, I firmly believe, to this colony," Cornwallis stated.

He also noted that while he, Cornwallis, was compelled to pay ransom to free captives taken by the Mi'kmaq, Mauger's men were always freed without charge. He implied this showed Mauger was working with the enemy.

In the end, Cornwallis backed down. Cornwallis had London's backing, but Mauger was well connected locally. Mauger continued his work and retained his position until he left for England in 1760. His dubious trade with Louisbourg seems to have gone on until at least 1754.

28

The Struggle for Chignecto

In the spring of 1752, a ship arrived in Halifax harbour bearing an urgent letter from London. Cornwallis broke the seal and sat in his study to read it.

The board had already accused Hugh Davidson, his secretary, of financial malpractice in the colony. Cornwallis had sent him home to answer the charges – but still London was not satisfied. In page after page, his masters castigated him for overspending and underdelivering. The letter ended with some pleasantries congratulating him on what was otherwise a job well done.

Cornwallis was stunned. He glared at the forest city outside his quarters and contrasted it with the luxury he imagined each board member lived in daily. He sat down and wrote back to London. He no longer cared to keep the board's good favour; he was tired of apologizing for his hard work. His spending had exceeded nothing, he said, except the faulty estimations constructed in England. There was little reason for the board to be surprised at his "overspending," he wrote. Britain itself was deep in debt and shovelling deeper. He felt he had been trapped. In his eyes, the board had drawn up plans for Nova Scotia in its comfortable Whitehall salons, but it made no account for extortionate New England traders, misfortune in losing ships, the reluctance of settlers to work for no money and the cost of his quasi-war with the French and the Mi'kmaq. He was waging a war alone on a distant frontier, living in pathetic style, and they accused him of exceedings. The only thing he had exceeded was their false calculations.

"To flatter your Lordships with hopes of savings would be dissimulation of the worst kind," he stated. He set out a long list of what he saw as the unexpected difficulties he had faced, of his careful husbandry of the king's resources, and of the fact that Nova Scotia had stayed in English hands – and that the Chebucto landing had taken root and grown into Halifax.

He said he may as well have spared himself the trouble, given the lack of help coming across the ocean. The duration of his appointment had been vague, but he had been told he would only be stationed on this outpost for two or three years. Well, almost three years had passed. He did not wish to subject his health to another Nova Scotia winter. He asked the board to appoint his successor. He wanted to go home.

"When I set out, they said, 'What has he to contend with but 300 or 400 Indians and no other enemy?' If only that had turned out to be true, I should have been ashamed and confounded to have made such a venture," he declared. "I should have been ashamed not to have given an account of the entire establishment of this province. That this and that settler was employed in such a way, in the fishery, clearing their lands, plowing and sowing their fields in as good land as there is in Europe. But how far different has been the case."

He composed his thoughts.

"The French have not only set on the Indians, but have acted in conjunction with them. They have entered and taken possession of part of the province, drove off the inhabitants and forced them to swear allegiance to the French king. In short, they have acted with as much vigour and done as much harm to us as they could have done in open war. This being the case, the expense is not to be wondered at," he continued.

"Shall I desist from further works? I am not conscious of one man being employed that is not essential. I must postpone taking possession of Cobequid. I must postpone carrying further works at Chignecto. I will endeavour to retrench in every particular. It is impossible to save on the military, unless it is from the Rangers."

He told them he had sent a winter expedition of officers to tour New England and recruit new settlers, but word had spread fast and far ahead of them. The "plantations" were inhospitable woods on rocky soil. No one was safe to venture out of the thin confines of Halifax. Halifax – a mud city of tents and log huts sliding down the slopes of an unprotected citadel. Few expected it to survive. The costly mission brought back only twenty new settlers. Cornwallis estimated that did not even offset the attrition of settlers lost to New England over the same period. As for the latest settlers from Europe stuck on George's Island, he agreed with the board that they would be better placed settling in Chignecto. But he could scarcely afford to give them the tools to break the land and start farms, let alone send enough soldiers to protect them while they worked. "I wish to God they would in time. It will be impractical to settle them at Chignecto now," he replied.

Yes, he knew there were limestone deposits that could be quarried, but it was not as cheap as London's math concluded. It was not merely the cost of extracting the materials, but also the cost of protecting the extractors. It was the same problem that made wood, which was so plentiful, so expensive. Settlers were paying fourteen to sixteen shillings per cord for firewood. "This is amazing," he wrote, but to be expected when the sawmill in Dartmouth was more famous for its cutting of human beings in Mi'kmaq raids than its hewing of logs. Another midnight attack had killed four soldiers and seen six more taken prisoner. Three Mi'kmaq died. The violence badly rattled the settlers. The French constantly harassed Chignecto and would no doubt retake it at the slightest retreat from England. The governor of Canada himself had written Cornwallis, daring to chastise him for taking two French vessels. If they were not attacking King George's land, he would never have touched them, he said, and wrote as much in his reply.

"I told him he should declare war against me," he wrote. "Commence hostilities!"

But in response, he told London, the mighty French fort at Louisbourg captured four New England vessels. The French fort had many English prisoners and paid Mi'kmaq warriors to capture or kill English soldiers. The Mi'kmaq traded English heads like they were pelts, Cornwallis said. "This is so unnatural and inhuman that one could not conceive a civilized nation to be guilty of it," he stated. He did not draw any implications for what this said about his own scalping bounty.

He was convinced the French would attack from Louisbourg and burn Halifax to the ground. "It is very unfortunate to be eyewitness to their treachery," he said. They openly armed the Mi'kmaq and fed them. They attacked English ships. Some of Cornwallis's men were even deserting to throw their lot in with the Mi'kmaq. "What more could they do in open war? I have not the force to prevent it," Cornwallis admitted in despair.

No one left Halifax without protection. "The number of Indians in the province makes it difficult and dangerous to go without parties of soldiers, and I have none to spare," he explained.

He did not trust the Acadians. They were unlikely to remain neutral in the face of French threats to kill anyone who worked for England and regular intimidation from French-allied Mi'kmaq. Cornwallis relayed to London his counter-threat to the Acadians. "I am surprised you hesitate which to obey – the king of England and England's governor, or the Indians," Cornwallis had told the Acadians. "You will be loyal to King George and you will work for King George – or you will face military execution."

He again heaped blame on Commissary Little for his poor accounting skills. "It has been my misfortune to be so ill served in others, but more so in this office," Cornwallis said.

"If the province was secured, there would be no danger of having settlers in abundance," he went on. "There is invitation enough for them, but while they are exposed to the cruelties of the French and Indians, people that have any sustenance will not care to risk it, and such are the people wanted. 1,000 regular troops would sooner settle the province than 3,000 settlers."

He outlined a vague vision for this new soldier-first plan.

"People of substance would follow without expense to the government. They work cheaper and could be made to do so at public works. War is not a time to settle inhabitants and that is so here," he explained.

"We can save a little money, but will lose the province. To limit expense is impracticable as it must depend upon events not to be foreseen and the friendship of the French not to be relied upon."

Was he to pretend he could make such savings to win the board's favour, only to show the lie when Nova Scotia fell? It could be settled only at great expense. If the board wanted the original goal – a fort to offset Louisbourg – then he could do that. Bring in soldiers, build a fort, and leave it at that. But to break this hard land and turn it into a viable colony would be no easy task.

"No man living can say what the expense will be, nor the time it may take to accomplish the first great design of making Nova Scotia your own," he wrote.

He knew he was taking a risk in speaking so frankly to his superiors, but he knew also that his twin brother was deep in the King's bosom as his chaplain. He knew his old friends in London and in Parliament would not let him suffer for the incompetence of the board. He knew he was protected at home. He changed his tone for the conclusion.

"It makes me peculiarly happy that I have their Lordships' appreciation of my past service," he noted, in an attempt to keep decorum. "I hope to retain the same generous and good opinion. It would be the height of my ambition and amply reward me for the laborious and heavy task I have met with."

He trusted they would hear the bitter edge to his words.

"I conclude with desiring your Lordships to consider that at my setting out for this province, two or three years at most was the time I was to continue, and that you would intercede that His Majesty would be graciously pleased to allow of my resignation of the government and grant me the liberty of returning home to give an account of my administration and some respite after years of constant service.

"My health of late has been but indifferent and must, by my constant employ, grow worse. I have requested the same favours of His Grace the Duke of Bedford," he concluded.

*   *   *   *   *

While he waited for a reply in the summer of 1752, Cornwallis and the council decided a lighthouse was needed at the entrance to the harbour to help trade navigation and the fishery. It was tricky to find the distant mouth of Halifax harbour along the lengthy, meandering Nova Scotia coast, and dangerous to sail in the waters if you did not know them. Sambro was selected as the best location and council decided to set up a lottery to raise funds. The idea was you could buy a ticket and win up to £500. In the end, the lottery only took in £450 and the lighthouse idea was shelved.

Cornwallis also lifted his bounty against the Mi'kmaq. The proclamation was read out in Halifax and relayed across the province.

"Whereas by the advice and consent of His Majesty's council of this province, two proclamations were, by me, sometime since issued, authorizing and commanding all officers civil and military, and all His Majesty's subjects within the province, to annoy, distress, take and destroy the savages called the Micmac Indians and promising a reward for each one of them taken or killed, and whereas for some time hostilities have not been committed by the said Indians against any of His Majesty's subjects, and some tending to peace and amity have been made by them, I have thought it fit with the advice and consent of His Majesty's council to revoke the said proclamations and every part thereof, and further do hereby strictly forbid all persons to molest, injure or commit any kind of hostility against any of the aforementioned Indians, or any Indians within this province unless the same shall be unavoidable in defence against any hostile act of any such Indian toward any of His Majesty's subjects."

He also noted that the crew of an English ship had captured and killed two Cape Sable Indian girls and one boy. The Mi'kmaq children had come aboard the vessel during the truce and as an affirmation of friendship, but had been killed. Cornwallis offered a reward for anyone bringing those responsible to him to face a trial, but no charges were ever laid for those three murders.

Further to that end, Halifax's first courthouse opened in August.

*   *   *   *   *

Cornwallis received news another ship of pilgrims had been spotted entering the harbour in August. The *Sally* laid anchor and Cornwallis sent officers on board to inspect its human cargo. To his disappointment, they reported back that of the three hundred promised Swiss, only twenty had materialized. The rest were a mongrel mix of Germans, French and other European nationalities. But they were all Protestant and eager to prove their loyalty. Many looked unwell, as they had spent sixty-eight days at sea as the ship heaved and twisted over the mountains of waves. Medical experts recommended sending them to George's Island in the harbour for a period of quarantine. Disease was rampant in Europe and the doctor worried the newcomers might infect the colony. If any of them were harbouring typhoid, or any other communicable disease, it could wipe out the settlement. They would winter on the island, adding to its fortifications before coming ashore.

Cornwallis agreed. The *Sally* transported its passengers to the island to pass through customs. Each entered his or her name, occupation and place of origin. The immigration officer also asked the reason for their travel. All told the clerks it was to escape religious persecution – except for the Bouteilliers of Montbeliard, who said they had come to improve their financial situation. "It's become impossible to make a living in our old home," Mr. Bouteillier explained. "We desire to try the opportunities in the British-American Colonies."

Jean-George D'Attrey spoke no English - few of the Montbeliard refugees did - but he did his best to inform the officials about his party. He was illiterate and could only make his mark on the documents. In the confusion, his name was transformed. It seemed right: a new name for the New World. The clerk wrote down "Dattirai" and it was later changed to "Tatteray" and then "Tattrie." The Frenchman was added to the victualling list, along with his sister Jeanne and wife Elizabeth. Both were in poor health from the long voyage. The Tattries made their way to their temporary lodgings on the island. The Babel of languages warped all of the old names. Grosrenaud became Grono, Lods turned to Lowe, Robert became Robar, Mailliard became Millard.

Cornwallis was disgusted that settlers had yet again arrived too late in the year to be anything but dependents until the next year. "They might as well as not have been sent," Cornwallis griped. "Unless what strength is sent comes in the spring, they are useless."

He watched from the Halifax shore. They were clearly a better batch of settlers than he had previously been stuck with, but he felt Nova Scotia could do better still and attract not refugees, but established people from the middle classes. "Peace with the Indians and there will in my opinion be no want of settlers," he often mused.

But he seemed incapable of acting in a way that brought about peace. His approach was to violently force his will on the province, even in the face of expensive failure. While he did not trust the Acadians, they had even less reason to trust him. It was clear that when enough Protestants were brought over, the Acadians would be expelled from their land. The Mi'kmaq could not see Cornwallis as a partner for peace, either. He was actively driving them off their land and ignored overtures to discuss ways to share the territory and develop trade. He placed settlements and forts by consulting his maps, not by consulting Mi'kmaq leaders. Resistance to his actions was met with lethal force.

London also saw that his decision to pursue a violent occupation of the province instead of a commercial conquest meant Nova Scotia was still costing money and showed no promise of making a profit for the Crown. The *Sally*'s captain brought verbal reprimands from the Board of Trade for overspending and not developing the economy.

But Cornwallis, mindful that signs of a prosperous colony would bolster his chances of returning to England, wrote a glowing review of Nova Scotia for the *Sally*'s captain to take to the board.

"Everything promises well," he insisted. "Did your Lordships consider the difficulties, the distress and the disappointments I have met with and struggled through? I flatter myself you would rather pity and cherish than censure and discomfort me; and that you will intercede with His Majesty to allow of my resignation of the government and grant me liberty to return home, and some respite, after ten years constant service, and my health of late so indifferent and growing worse in my constant employ."

He watched the departing ship with a great longing to join it.

29

Cornwallis Returns to England

In October 1752, Cornwallis's wish was granted.[23] The king had accepted his resignation. He handed over control of the colony in a ceremony with little fanfare. Peregrine Thomas Hopson took charge and moved into the governor's quarters as soon as Cornwallis was gone.

Hopson, a British veteran who had commanded Louisbourg when the English held it from 1745 to 1748, assessed the province. He had clear instruction from London. He was to roll back all public works to the minimum level needed to safeguard the settlement and use only indentured servants for the labour. Cash pay was to be issued only in the "most frugal manner possible." He was to discharge the rangers, "which by the last return appeared to be ineffective."

London told Hopson to make a priority of clearing land and handing it out to those promised estates. Cramming Halifax beyond capacity was to no one's benefit. He was also to prevent any Catholics from purchasing land for fear of "very bad consequences."

Hopson was told to instruct anyone leaving the province to hand over all their arms, tools and goods that came from the public purse. The Acadians were still to be denied permission to leave under any circumstances.

---

23 Britain and its colonies switched from the old Julian calendar to the new Gregorian calendar in the fall of 1752. Officially, September 2, 1752, was followed directly by September 14, 1752, and the first day of the year moved from March 25 to January 1. In practice, different areas made the changes at different times, introducing a good deal of confusion into dates for this period. This book uses the dates provided by the original documents, although whether they refer to the old or new calendar is not always clear.

A plan was growing to deal with the Acadian problem, but it was too soon to execute it.

Hopson was to crack down on excessive rum drinking, which was weakening the colony, and to bring a stop to illegal trading. London noted that while Cornwallis had granted himself two aides-de-camp, it had been done without the approval or consent of the Board of Trade. "But on the contrary, was considered highly improper and that no allowance could be made out of the civil establishment for this service." Cornwallis's two men would leave with him; Hopson was not to replace them.

Hopson wrote a long letter to London. He made it Cornwallis's last duty to Nova Scotia to carry the letter home. "Upon my examining into the state of affairs of the province, I found Mr. Cornwallis extremely distressed, by having on his hands in and about this place all the foreign settlers who arrived the years 1750 and 1751 whom he had not been able to send out from hence to make any settlement at a distance," Hopson wrote.

"This not only through a want of provisions, arms, tools and implements for clearing and cultivating the land and materials necessary for the building of their habitations proper to enable him for so doing, but also on account of there being no place with any sufficient quantity of land near them proper for placing them upon agreeable to the promises which had been made ... before they embarked."

The stress of settling the settlers wasn't Cornwallis's only problem, Hopson went on. "Likewise because he had great reason to apprehend they might have been molested by the Indians wherever they were sent, he not having it in his power to protect them. The great expense was another considerable objection."

Hopson noted that Halifax was overflowing with stranded settlers. The latest three hundred were crammed into the fort with those who had arrived the year before. The annual problem of settlers arriving too late to be sent into the wood to break new ground created a backlog – an expensive backlog, for they all had to be fed and sheltered.

There was simply nowhere safe and fruitful to send them, Hopson said. They built cheap barracks to house them, but could do little more. He learned that a British agent in London had once again lied to the settlers and told them to sell everything they owned – right down to the bedding – before they left England. That meant the settlers slept on bare decks and platforms for the duration of the crossing. That had badly depleted their health and meant the refugees arrived with no bedding and had to continue sleeping exposed and cold. That had killed many on the journey, and many more continued to die ashore. The agents did this simply because less baggage meant more bodies and the agents were paid per person. Hopson requested London take action to prevent a repetition of such lies.

Hopson, like Cornwallis before him, noted the settlers were a sorry lot. He described them as "poor old decrepit creatures" more fit for the almshouses than to be sent as settlers to the New World. Some of the dead were more than eighty years old. Two of the elderly had died en route, and many of them could not stir off the ship. Young people died, too, leaving eight orphans on the ship. Two of them died two weeks later in the hospital, but the ranks of orphans swelled by fourteen as more parents died.

"No mortal that has the least humanity can do otherwise than feel to the very heart at the sight of such a scene of misery as it is, and the prospect there is of its being a much more deplorable one before the severity of the winter, which now draws nigh, is not over," he stated bleakly.

The problem was not new, he said, as Cornwallis could testify. As he hadn't solved it in three years, Hopson asked the lords' forgiveness if he could not solve it in three months.

Those who were fit often fled, which posed a double problem. "It disgraces and weakens our settlement, but at the same time strengthens our neighbours," he observed.

For now, Nova Scotia was full. He asked London to stop sending Foreign Protestants, or any other kind of settler. They were indentured servants, which certainly saved the province money, but it also deprived the more established settlers of a way to make their livelihood. This caused resentment and more desertions.

Hopson concluded that his priority would be to relocate the existing settlers. The poor, hungry refugees would need at least nine months of provisions to get started. If not, they would inevitably starve. Hopson said it was not even clear how much provisions the colony had at all. He handed the letter to Cornwallis. He would take it to London and present it to the board at his debriefing.

Cornwallis boarded a ship sailing out of Halifax. It was the first time he had viewed the coast since his arrival. The shoreline in the harbour was transformed. The large fortress city had outgrown its wooden walls and was rapidly expanding into the forests that surrounded it. Dartmouth was taking root. George's Island stood fortified in the centre of the waterway, but Cornwallis Island, formerly Chebucto Island and later to be called McNab's, showed little change. On its eastern edge, Mauger's Beach was busy with slaves and workers preparing fish for market. At a northern point on the island he glimpsed a Mi'kmaq camp. Nearby he saw the home of Captain Rous. A grazing herd of cattle stared blankly at Cornwallis's ship as it passed.

He smiled thinly. On July 25, 1752, he had carried out one of his last major duties as governor of Nova Scotia by granting the entire island to his nephews. That had sparked anger, as many settlers argued the land should have been used for the common good or divided more equitably among settler farmers. His nephews did not live in Nova Scotia and would never take possession of the island.

Beyond the settlement, the shoreline looked largely the same as it had in 1749. Cornwallis, now thirty-nine years old, let his mind drift to the journey he had made three years earlier. He thought of the thick woods he had observed through his spyglass, and the basin big enough to hold the entire British navy. His mind drifted to the hope he had forced on himself then and how he had commanded a rough group of settlers to turn a patch of trees into a clearing that became a shantytown, which in time became Halifax. Bitterness shivered through his body like a January chill. He could not dislodge it. His mind drifted to the past, but his eyes never once strayed from the horizon. He stared at invisible England as Nova Scotia floated back into the lost fog. He would never again set foot in North America.

30
Nova Scotia after Cornwallis

Winter shocked the new settlers with its brutality. The forty-five shacks clinging to George's Island were well constructed, but the bald island offered no shelter from the fierce oceanic winds. The island's fifty residents were often woken in the dead of night by a gale that had sped over the Atlantic smashing into them in full fury. The Europeans, used to living in the middle of the continent far from any ocean, shivered and shook as the hard wind pushed unremittingly on their shelters. Roofs blew off, windows crashed in, and sickness feasted on the weakened people.

The Montbeliard families stuck close together. Jean-George Tattrie, now thirty, spent the winter fending for himself, his sister and his wife. Women could not be indentured servants, so he carried the burden for all three. He worked unceasingly on whatever his English-speaking masters ordered. At first, he looked perplexed at the settlement in Halifax and the settlement in Dartmouth, unable to understand where his promised land was, or why he and his family were detained on a frozen island. The toll of the physical work focused him on daily survival and he put his hands in the fate of the God who had brought him this far.

In early January 1752, his wife Elizabeth died without ever setting foot in Halifax. A few weeks later, his sister Jeanne died. Both apparently were buried on George's Island. When the victualling list was printed for February, Jean-George was the only Tattrie left on it.

Peregrine Hopson spent the winter upgrading fortress Halifax and stabilizing the outlying forts. Faced with the massive war bills accrued under Cornwallis's governorship, he decided to take a different approach. He sent word to several Mi'kmaq chiefs that he wanted peace and trade. Chief Jean-Baptiste Cope, chief of the Shubenacadie Mi'kmaq, replied to the overtures and met with British officials in September 1752. He was nearing the height of his power then, and the territory he was responsible for included the areas the British would call Halifax, Cumberland, Colchester, Guysborough, Hants, Antigonish, Pictou, Kings and Lunenburg counties.

Cope, or Kopit, was fifty-four years old and well versed in the British-Mi'kmaq wars. The British agreed to begin negotiations for peace with him and asked for his terms. He demanded they pay for the land they had taken. The British rebuffed that condition and the two sides went back to the negotiating table. They eventually came to the Treaty of 1752.

"Treaty articles of peace and friendship renewed," it was headlined, and was signed by Cope and Hopson. It reaffirmed the neglected treaties of 1725 and 1726 and promised a new start. Article two stated "that all transactions during the late war shall on both sides be buried in oblivion with the hatchet and that the said Indians shall have all favour, friendship and protection shewn them from His Majesty's government."

Cope again promised to try to bring the other bands into the peaceful fold, a task that would prove difficult. Cope also pledged to "discover and make known any attempts or designs of any other Indians, or any enemy whatever, against His Majesty's subjects within the province so soon as they shall know thereof, and shall also hinder and obstruct the same to the utmost of their power."

In exchange, the British government promised that if any other Mi'kmaq band made war on Cope's people, he could turn to the British for military assistance. The Shubenadacie band was further guaranteed "free liberty" of hunting and fishing and the ability to establish trading posts. They were allowed to enter Halifax and all other settlements to sell their goods. Each family was granted a twice yearly quantity of bread, flour and other provisions as a backdoor payment for the land. To maintain the tentative good will, both sides pledged to meet every year on October 1, when Hopson and his successors would "gift," or pay, the Mi'kmaq in blankets, tobacco, gunpowder and ammunition.

Article seven said the Mi'kmaq would rescue any Europeans shipwrecked on their coastline and bring them safely to Halifax, where they would be compensated for their troubles. It concluded: "That all disputes whatsoever that may happen to arise between the Indians now at peace and others His Majesty's subjects in this province, shall be tried in His Majesty's court of civil judicature, where the Indians shall have the same benefit, advantage and privilege as any other of His Majesty's subjects." It was signed November 22, 1752.

Hopson issued a proclamation to his own people informing them of the peace deal. He wrote to "strictly charge and command all His Majesty's officers and all others his subjects that they do forbear all acts of hostilities against the aforesaid Major Jean-Baptiste Cope, or his Tribe of Chibenaccadie Mick Mack Indians from and after the day and the date of those present, as they shall answer the contrary at their peril."

Cope was blasted as a traitor by the French. Louisbourg invited other Mi'kmaq chiefs to the French fortress and urged them not to follow his path. An alliance between the British and Mi'kmaq bands would essentially end France's hold on the territory, as they would lose their spies, allies and *de facto* mercenary soldiers against their European rivals. Some Mi'kmaq chiefs sided with France and plotted against the Shubenacadie leader. Others sought to follow his path.

Cope, fearing for his life and the lives of his daughters, sought refuge in Halifax.

Meanwhile, the ordinary settlers continued to be buffeted by forces beyond their control. The widower Jean-George Tattrie married another newcomer, Maria Catherine Mingo, in May 1753 in the new St. Paul's Cathedral in Halifax. They relocated to Lunenburg in December. The new settlement was just down the coast from Halifax and easily reached, but it was far enough from the fort that the settlers were keenly aware of the danger. Tattrie, like most settlers, took a turn on the "Indian patrols" that guarded the town. It is not known if the patrols were passive or actively attacked Mi'kmaq people in the area.

*   *   *   *   *

The new peace treaty was shaky from the start. Word that the scalping bounty was lifted spread slowly in the thick woods. A major breach
occurred on April 1, 1753.[24] A group of English settlers headed by James
Grace and John Conner (a "one-eyed man" who had been Cornwallis's
bargeman) had been sailing the eastern shore in a schooner. The crew
landed at Jeddore and raided a Mi'kmaq camp, stealing forty barrels of
provisions. The hit-and-run robbers fled back to the ocean with their booty, but were shipwrecked in rough seas. The Englishmen were separated.
Two came ashore and were discovered and killed by the Mi'kmaq they had
robbed.

The other two – Grace and Conner – drifted further along the
coast and came ashore near Torbay. They were found by another group
of Mi'kmaq, "drenched with water and destitute of everything."[25] The
Mi'kmaq, knowing nothing of the raid, rescued the men in accordance
with the terms of the 1752 treaty. Grace and Conner were taken into the
Mi'kmaq homes to recover and "cherished and kindly entertained." As
the robbers recovered, most of the men of the camp left to attend to other
business. The rescued remained at the camp to be cared for by the wom-
en and children. The men left their weapons in the camp. It would prove
a fatal mistake. Conner and Grace killed the two women, a newborn infant and a child, then lay in wait for the men. When they returned, the
English guests killed them too. Grace and Conner cut the scalps off their
hosts, stole their canoe, and sailed for Halifax. The raiding party attempted to sell the six scalps (it appears the infant was not scalped), even
though the bounty had been rescinded.

When the attacked Mi'kmaq community found the carnage of the
seven murdered and butchered men, women and children, warriors were
immediately sent to Governor Hopson in Halifax. Settlers routinely raided
and robbed their camps after provisions had been paid, they told him, and
this massacre was just the latest violation of the treaty. The Mi'kmaq demanded the murderers be brought to justice. They also requested the government send a vessel to bring their band into Halifax. Hopson granted
them this protection and the group came into the fort.

---

24 The account of the April 1 incident comes from Chief Surveyor Charles Morris's letter
to Cornwallis, dated April 16, 1753.
25 Paul, Daniel. Page 131.

Grace and Conner claimed they had merely stopped in Torbay harbour and been attacked by the Mi'kmaq band, and had only killed to escape. There is no record of them being charged or punished for the raids or murders and the two men continued to live freely. Thereafter, few Mi'kmaq bands were persuaded to deal with the English and relations began again to deteriorate.

Hopson developed severe eye trouble and returned to England for treatment in the fall of 1753. Charles Lawrence, a veteran of the Nova Scotia wars, was named lieutenant-governor. Lawrence became governor when Hopson finally stepped down in 1755. Lawrence quickly returned the province to the turmoil of the Cornwallis years.

After the brief peace of the Hopson regime, Lawrence resumed hostilities against the Mi'kmaq. Smaller tribes, harried by settlers and British soldiers, sought any peace terms they could get, while others faced oblivion. In 1754, a Council of the Mi'kmaq and Maliseet Nations met at Fort Beausejour and formed a peace offer to end the war with the British. The proposed treaty was taken to Halifax by Le Loutre. In it, the chiefs pledged to not attack subjects of Great Britain, nor trouble them on the highways, but that any subjects who left the highways for the woods would be treated as an enemy.

"In order to arrive at a solid and durable peace there shall be ceded to them a certain space of territory which they only shall enjoy, suitable for hunting and fishing, and for the establishment of a village and a mission as a parish," they wrote. It was proposed that the territory would include at least northern Nova Scotia, and the Gaspé coast. Le Loutre observed it would include his former mission in Shubenacadie.

The offer noted it was "very moderate, and very limited in view of the immensity of the land they did possess, and of the amount at present in their possession." The land would be theirs alone to inhabit in "all possible tranquility" and be kept free from any European fortresses.

Lawrence rejected the offer, describing the proposals for land sharing as "extravagant" and out of his power to comply with. "The council didn't think it consistent to make any answer to, or take the least notice of them," continued his reply. "The terms in which they are drawn up shows that he [Le Loutre] is not serious because he asks what he knows to be both insolent and absurd, but this is no more than a piece with the rest of his conduct."

204 – Jon Tattrie

Lawrence viewed the treaty offer as coming not from the Mi'kmaq chiefs, but from the messenger, Le Loutre, and designed only to sow animosity between Britain and the Mi'kmaq nations. A second Mi'kmaq mission offered to discuss the borders of the proposed new territories, but was again rebuffed. Lawrence replied to the "different tribes of Micmac Indians," calling the terms "exorbitant"[26] and impossible to meet. He said negotiations would only advance if the Mi'kmaq chiefs, rather than their deputies, went to Halifax to talk with him. Then, he could consider allowing them some tracts of land and "other such indulgences."

Soon after, the European capitals of London and Paris resumed their declarations of war, and the battle spread to North America. Talks of peace with the Mi'kmaq were shelved.

---

26 Governor Charles Lawrence in a letter to "the different tribes of Micmac Indians," dated February 13, 1755.

Book Three:
Fall from Grace

A photo taken by Notman Studios of a sketch of Edward Cornwallis that was dated 1764, which was found in the governor's residence on Gibraltar.

I

Cornwallis Resumes Life in London

In the dying days of his service in Nova Scotia, Edward Cornwallis had been commissioned colonel of the 24th Foot Regiment. He returned to London to take up that position and to enjoy the respite he had longed for. The streets and homes of London must have stunned him with their opulence. After three years living in a rugged hut in a forest clearing surrounded by hostile strangers, it would be hard to believe one could sit on a soft sofa and sip tea without fear of attack.

Cornwallis had not been back long when Sir Peter Warren died, leaving vacant his seat in Parliament. In January 1753, King George made it known that he wished Cornwallis to stand for it. When Parliament was dissolved the following year, Cornwallis was returned to the seat. It seemed his hard service in Nova Scotia had planted the seed that would grow into a mighty career.

The former governor's good fortune solidified as 1753 progressed. Cornwallis arranged to marry the daughter of the late Charles Townshend, 2nd Viscount Townshend. Townshend had been a Whig, a political party that had long fought the Stuart pretenders. The Whigs dominated the government. Townshend had been a powerful man, serving as Secretary of State and playing a key role in crushing the 1715 Jacobite rising. Cornwallis's role in putting down the 1746 rebellion gave him common ground with the family.

On March 17, 1753, Cornwallis wed Mary Townshend. In October of that year, he was told his respite had ended. He was to take charge of the 24th Foot and recruit for foreign service. Cornwallis worked quietly for the next few years. He built a close alliance with Thomas Pelham-Holles, Duke of Newcastle. These high connections would prove critical in the disasters that marked the coming decade.

In 1755, major news came from Nova Scotia. British forces had taken the Acadian farmlands. The imported Foreign Protestant population had swelled sufficiently to tend the crops. The peace with the Mi'kmaq was solid enough not to worry about a two-pronged resistance. Lieutenant-Governor Charles Lawrence instructed the Acadians to gather at the church in Grand Pré that September. He had the men of the families brought before him and told them that after fifty years of patience, Britain was patient no more.

"Your land and tenements, cattle of all kinds and livestocks of all sorts are forfeited to the Crown with all other your effects, savings, your money and household goods, and you yourselves to be removed from this Province," Lawrence told the 418 men.

The ships were ready – the Acadians could take what they could carry. They were declared prisoners of the king and immediately deported to various ports on the Atlantic seaboard and the Caribbean. The Acadian problem had been solved. The Foreign Protestants took over the farmlands.

By 1756, France and Britain were again officially at war. This phase of the conflict would eventually take the name the Seven Years' War, the final showdown for ownership of North America. It was a vast, global battle on land and at sea. In North America, England held the most of the eastern coast from Newfoundland to the southern extent of New England, and the northern territory around Hudson Bay. France held the centre – Canada, New France and Louisiana.

This time, Cornwallis's service would be closer to home. He turned his full attention to the coming debacle at Minorca.

2

The Disaster at Minorca

Cornwallis's regiment was stationed in Minorca, a small island in the Mediterranean Sea. He was on leave in London. Minorca had passed back and forth between the European powers before Britain invaded and won it in 1708. The British fort came under siege by French forces in the spring of 1756. France intended to destroy Port Mahon, the capital, and retake the island. It was second in strategic importance only to Gibraltar, a garrison island guarding the entrance to the Mediterranean, and King George II organized a defence of Minorca. The garrison held out, but needed help, so reinforcements were to be sent by ship. Cornwallis was to return to Minorca to take up his command. He had last visited the island in 1755, when he posed for one of the few portraits painted of him during his life.

Admiral John Byng was appointed to command the fleet. Critics said Byng did not have the capacity or experience to relieve the garrison, but he had the backing of the Crown. He and Cornwallis were old friends. They had spent much of the past few years earning a reputation as leading men of fashion in London. Their select and fast set of men were trendy style setters known as the Corinthians. What Byng lacked in experience, he made up for in ferocity. He was a terror of sailors, infamous for his brutal floggings at any sign of disobedience. He knew in Cornwallis, he had a man who could take orders, and who could give orders.

Cornwallis, Colonel Lord Effingham and Colonel James Stuart sailed to Gibraltar to prepare a fleet to relieve the seven hundred men at Minorca. At Gibraltar, the three colonels boarded the *Intrepid*, Byng's flagship. The *Intrepid* was reserved for Byng's close friends and only fellow Corinthians sailed with him. The Battle of Minorca would be the opening sea salvo in the European theatre of the Seven Years' War.

Cornwallis surveyed the ten-strong fleet, which seemed to him shabby and undermanned. They met Minorca's own squadron off the island's coast. Byng learned the island was already overrun by French troops and the fortress was weakening under siege. With twelve ships to Britain's ten, France's fleet intercepted Byng's, preventing it from going directly to Minorca. Byng ordered his ships to keep a safe distance and did not directly communicate with General William Blakeney on the island.

The next day the French fleet again confronted the British ships. Byng signalled to engage, but in a manner that threw his fleet into confusion. The captain of the *Intrepid* begged permission to join the battle, but Byng would not allow it. With Cornwallis at his side, he watched the slow-starting sea fight. A second ship, headed by Rear-Admiral West, attacked France and drove several ships out of line. But West found himself adrift alone, as Byng did not send any support, and he retired back to the British line. France pounded his ship with cannon fire as he retreated. Byng and Cornwallis stayed out of cannon range the entire time.

When the firefight subsided, Byng called a council of war. Sitting with Cornwallis at his side, he declared his ships were in poor condition and in no position to damage the French fleet. Cornwallis agreed. The council of war was swayed – the fleet would return to Gibraltar. Blakeney's garrison, including Cornwallis's regiment, watched in horror as their relief sailed away. They managed to hold out for five more weeks, but then capitulated. Britain had lost Minorca.

Byng's enemies opened fire on him when word of the battle reached home. The retreat was called a disgrace and England was in a fury. It was an especially bitter pill to swallow because media reports had erroneously reported a major British victory at Minorca and the British public had discovered a new love and pride for the island.[27]

---

27 Plank, Geoffrey. Page 150.

Byng, having returned to Gibraltar, wrote to assuage them with his account of the battle. He explained that upon arrival, it was clear there would be no safe place to land on Minorca to relieve the garrison – France had it too well guarded.

"The *Intrepid*, unfortunately, in the very beginning had her fore-topmast shot away; and as that hung on her fore-topsail, and backed it, he had no command of his ship, his fore-tack and all his braces being cut at the same time," Byng explained of his captain.[28]

"I found the enemy edged away constantly; and as they went three feet to our one, they would never permit our closing with them, but took advantage of destroying our rigging; for though I closed the Rear-Admiral fast, I found that I could not gain close to the enemy, whose van was fairly drove from their line; but their admiral was joining them, by bearing away."

After the first engagement, he said, he inspected his fleet.

"I found that the *Captain, Intrepid* and *Defiance* were much damaged in their masts, so that they were in danger of not being able to secure their masts properly at sea; and also, that the squadron in general were very sickly, many killed and wounded, and nowhere to put a third of their number if I made an hospital of the forty-gun ship, which was not easy at sea," he said.

"I thought it proper in this situation to call a council of war, before I went again to look for the enemy. I desired the attendance of General Stuart, Lord Effingham, and Lord Robert Bertie, and Colonel Cornwallis, that I might collect their opinions upon the present situation of Minorca and Gibraltar, and make sure of protecting the latter, since it was found impracticable either to succor or relieve the former with the force we had. So, though we may justly claim the victory, yet we are much inferior to the weight of their ships, though the numbers are equal."

A further French advantage was that they could send their wounded to Minorca, which would also replace them with reinforcements. In his further defence, Byng offered the minutes from the council of war. "There was not the least contention or doubt arose," he noted.

---

28 The Trial of the Honble. Admiral Byng: At a Court martial held on board his majesty's ship the St. George, in Portsmouth Harbour, Tuesday Dec. 28, 1756.

In short, it was a tactical retreat to secure a greater future victory. He asked for reinforcements to try again. But then the French account of the battle trickled in. A different picture emerged – one of a too-cautious defence, and a flight that came too swiftly.

Byng was arrested, along with Cornwallis and the other colonels who had voted for the retreat. Upon their arrival in Portsmouth, a large, unruly crowd attacked them and almost tore them to pieces. Their guards dragged them through the mob to the safety of prison. Denied the chance to destroy the men who had lost Britain Minorca, crowds throughout the kingdom gathered in town squares and burned effigies of Cornwallis, Effingham and Stuart.[29] The Crown issued a warrant to examine Byng's conduct. Cornwallis, Effingham and Stuart were all charged with failing to join their respective commands at Minorca.

Cornwallis's court martial was a long, tedious affair. The main charge was that he had been ordered to join his regiment on Minorca but had not done so.

"Whereas it now appears that the said Major General Stuart, and Colonels Cornwallis and Earl of Effingham did not join their respective commands, whence arises suspicion of disobedience of orders and neglect of duty," the court martial noted.[30]

Blakeney, who had once sat on the same court as Cornwallis during the trials that followed the Pacification of Scotland, now testified that he had heard nothing from his old colleague, nor from Byng. "Admiral Byng made no signal perceived by the garrison, nor sent anybody off towards Fort St. Philip," he said.

The court heard that instead of advising immediate action to take the fort on Minorca, Cornwallis had assisted Byng in the council of war in his determination to avoid the enemy. He was charged with abandoning Blakeney to his fate and returning to Gibraltar. The question at the heart of the trial was that if Cornwallis was only a passenger, as he claimed, and was therefore not responsible for the decision to retreat, why then was he invited to the war council?

---

29 MacDonald, James. Page 13.

30 The quotes and account of the court martial come from The Report of the General Officers, Appointed to enquire into the conduct of Major General Stuart, and Colonels Cornwallis and Earl of Effingham, Dec. 8, 1756.

Cornwallis told the court he wished for an opportunity to offer some matters in the justification of his conduct. He was allowed to speak. He defended himself robustly, writing a long paper representing the difficulties he had found in the situation, the length of his service to the Crown, and his own great distress at the gravity of his position.

"I received no written orders for my going to my post at Minorca at any time," he began. "Being confined to my house by a severe illness for five weeks, I had heard that the officers belonging to the garrison were ordered to their posts. As soon as I could possibly go out, I did wait upon His Royal Highness the Duke to know his commands. His Royal Highness told me it was His Majesty's pleasure that I should set out for my post at Minorca. I kissed His Majesty's hand and set out ... in a state of health that an officer less desirous or less willing of going to his duty might have pleaded incapacity."

Cornwallis said he hoped that answered the charge he had disobeyed orders. He had not disobeyed, he insisted. As to the question of if he threw himself into Fort St. Philip with his best endeavours, he declared he had. "I went on board the fleet as early as possible with the full intention of going into Fort St. Philip and never perceived any disinclination in the admiral to endeavour to land me."

Cornwallis said he saw no need to ask the admiral to land him, as he trusted there was no question he would do so if it was possible. He went on to lay out a series of times it was not appropriate to ask the commander about going ashore: when the fleet came in sight of Minorca, when the enemy's fleet was spotted and when the two sides lined up against each other.

"After that unhappy engagement, it was impracticable, as the enemy's fleet was between us and St. Philip. An application then would have looked more like a bravado than any real intention to the service," he said.

He then addressed the subject of his claim to have been a mere passenger on the fleet, and yet also a voting member of the council of war. "I think I cannot be deemed a passenger, but an officer actually upon the King's service, having both officers and men of my own regiment under my command and destined for Minorca," he reasoned. "I looked upon myself as under the command of the admiral and should have thought it my duty to have obeyed him."

He continued: "I conceive I behaved like an officer in obeying the summons of the commander in chief to assist at the council of war, the declining of which might, as I apprehend, have been construed as disobedience of orders and a backwardness in assisting upon the king's service."

When it came to his opinion to return to Gibraltar instead of attacking as ordered, he said he had decided "unbiased and uninfluenced" that it was not practical to land.

He summed up his defence with a reminder of his long service and an open appeal to his friends conducting his court martial. "May I be permitted to say that I have been now upwards of 26 years in His Majesty's service and employed upon more service and greater variety than perhaps any officer of my years and standing in the army; that it has been my good fortune during the course of my service never to have had a reprimand, or even rebuke, from any superior officer; and that I have had the honour to serve under several general officers appointed for this inquiry, and I flatter myself they will bear testimony of my zeal for, and forwardness in, the king's service upon all occasions," he concluded.

This was his trump card, he hoped. He knew the king personally, and had since he was a boy. He knew many of the men trying him, both personally and professionally. He bolstered his case with the testimony of Captain William Parry, commander of the *Kingston*, the ship Cornwallis sailed on. Parry told the court Cornwallis had many times expressed "great desire" to be at his post and did not care how difficult the landing might be. He also quoted Cornwallis as having told him, "I wish to God I had been with my regiment." Parry agreed it was not practicable to land the officers.

In the end, Cornwallis got the verdict he wanted: he was just following orders. He was judged to be, along with the other colonels, merely a passenger on the fleet and entirely under the control of Byng. He was freed to resume his service. The other two colonels quietly resigned, but Cornwallis was determined to forge ahead with his career.

Newspapers mocked him as an effete fool who was more interested in fashion than fighting. A cartoon depicted Cornwallis, Byng, and the other Corinthians in poor light.[31] They were shown wearing elegant velvet and satin robes. The robes did not have pockets, so the men sported muffs, which were fur pouches designed to carry snuff-boxes, a lace handkerchief and perfume. These were all essential tools for a gallant Corinthian, but

---

31 MacDonald, James. Page 15.

utterly ridiculous for war. Most Britons saw a muff as women's clothing. The sight of it on the arms of military leaders – even if only in cartoon form – enraged the public.

Things got worse when it was alleged that Byng had made a mistake while packing for the Battle of Minorca and accidentally brought his good china with him. It was valued at £5,000 and was extremely rare.[32] He had amassed it in recent years in emulation of the French fad. When he discovered it was onboard his ship, he became very cautious in battle, lest the old china be damaged. His disgraceful abandonment of the Minorca garrison, and for such trivial matters, sealed his fate.

His court martial found him guilty and sentenced him to death. In March 1757, he was shot dead on HMS *Monarque*. The execution of an admiral sent shock waves across Europe. Many of Britain's enemies were enthralled and horrified by the idea one of her commanders had been killed for cowardice. Not everyone celebrated. Byng's family called it a grave injustice and rang the bells in his home of Southill, Bedfordshire, each year on the anniversary of his death. The French writer Voltaire was inspired by the execution to write some of his most famous scenes in *Candide*, his bitter satire of European war and avarice. He described a continent where "a million regimented assassins, from one extremity of Europe to the other, get their bread by disciplined depredation and murder, for want of more honest employment." Voltaire's naïve hero follows the European war to North America, where France and England "are at war for a few acres of snow in Canada."

Byng, Voltaire concluded, was killed "because he did not kill a sufficient number of men himself." A shocked and bewildered Candide learns the admiral is being executed because "in this country it is found good, from time to time, to kill one admiral to encourage the others."

Voltaire meant it sardonically and prior to the execution sent Byng a letter of support. It was intercepted and used against Byng – surely any action of a British naval commander that won approval from French writers was bad. The execution did indeed encourage the other admirals, who saw clearly that while much could go wrong in battle, the only error that was certain to be fatal was declining to fight. Britain surged ahead towards ruling the waves. Byng was the last man of such high rank to be militarily executed in Britain. His family would continue to seek a pardon for generations. The last effort was made in 2007, and was refused.

---

32 MacDonald, James. Page 14.

In February, the month before Byng's execution, Cornwallis was promoted to major general. Despite the advance, it was a dark time for him. James Wolfe, his one-time subordinate, was on his way to glorious death in Quebec. Before the Plains of Abraham, Wolfe wrote to his father to express his concerns for Cornwallis. It seemed to Wolfe that Cornwallis would never recover, either emotionally or professionally, from the scandal of Minorca. "There is a storm gathering over the head of my unfortunate friend," Wolfe wrote, "such a one as must necessarily crush him; though, in my mind, he acted in this affair but a second part. That, as far as I am able, I shall always be ready to assert, and will give him the best hints in my power for his defence ... I know he is ill-used and artfully ruined, after suffering himself to be misled by an over-fair opinion of his guide."[33]

Future promotions and coveted job postings passed Cornwallis by.

---

33 James Wolfe, in a private letter to his father, dated Oct. 12, 1757.

3

The Rochefort Retreat

Cornwallis was again summoned to action later that year. It was a chance to redeem himself after Minorca – to show he really had just been a passenger following orders. In 1757, he was promoted to major general and remained in command of the 24th Foot. The Seven Years' War was raging on multiple fronts. Cornwallis's target was in mainland France, the French naval arsenal at Rochefort. His commanders were Admiral Edward Hawke, head of the naval forces, and General Sir John Mordaunt, head of the land forces. Cornwallis was appointed to brigade commander under Mordaunt. James Wolfe was named quartermaster general.

A strong force massed on the Isle of Wight in the summer of 1757: ten regiments of foot, two regiments of marines and a great train of artillery. It was a major enterprise – a £1 million mission. The orders were to destroy the docks, shipping and magazines of Rochefort. It was part of Prime Minister William Pitt's harassment strategy in the war. The new prime minister knew France was planning to invade Hapsburg territory. He wanted to harry them on the coast to pin their troops there.

The surprise attack started in September. It began successfully for the British, who caught France unawares. The British quickly captured the satellite island Île D'Aix, but found shallow water prevented the ships from getting closer than a mile offshore of Rochefort. That would require a long, hazardous landing by boats. Heavy fog clung to the water, and worsening autumn weather was arriving. Mordaunt, hanging off the coast and poised to strike, hesitated. The French fortifications looked stronger than depicted in the intelligence reports. Instead of attacking, he called a council of war. Hawke, seconded by Wolfe, voted to attack Rochefort as ordered.

"If we do so, Rochefort can be carried by storm in forty-eight hours," Hawke declared.[34]

It would be a major win for Britain and a large setback for France. The port was a key connection in France's ability to provision the American colonies. Putting Rochefort out of business would cut the legs and stomach out of its forces in New France.

All eyes turned to Cornwallis. With little hesitation, he backed Mordaunt to retreat without firing a weapon. The debate carried on for a week, with two meetings. The council of war met on the *Neptune* on September 25 and on the *Ramilies* on the 28th. The Honorable Major General Edward Cornwallis was marked in attendance for both. Mordaunt advocated abandoning the expedition and sailing back to England. At the first meeting, he said the defences had evidently been improved and a landing would be foolhardy. At the September 28 meeting, he argued for a night attack downriver, led by himself, but the discovery of strong winds caused him to change his mind. Despite Hawke and Wolfe's hunger to attack, Mordaunt and Cornwallis carried the day and the massive fleet sailed back to England without attacking. Mordaunt was arrested when he made land on October 6.

Prime Minister Pitt was furious at the wasted £1 million expedition. At his urging, King George II appointed a board of inquiry to test Mordaunt's claims. "It does not appear to us that there were then, or at any time afterwards, either a body of troops or batteries on the shore sufficient to have prevented the attempting of a descent," it found. It did not believe the defences of Rochefort had been so improved as to repel an attack.

After this devastating finding, Mordaunt was tried in a general court martial in December 1757. He was charged with disobeying the king's orders and instructions. Mordaunt defended himself on the grounds there had been no place to land the troops in bad weather or with a swelling sea. Any landing would be so rough that the troops would be helpless before the French guns.

---

34 This account comes from The Proceedings of a General Court-Martial held at Whitehall on Wednesday the 14th, and continued by several adjournments to Tuesday the 20th of December, upon the Trial of Lieutenant-General Sir John Mordaunt.

Cornwallis was called to testify at the court martial of his superior. He was sworn in and asked what he knew about the opinions of the sea officers as to the difficulty of landing on the night of September 28. He testified that he went on board the *America*, the ship appointed for the rendezvous, at ten p.m. that night. "I was there some time before Sir John Mordaunt came aboard," he said. "There were several captains of Men of War on board and I found that the landing, in their opinion, would be dangerous, almost impracticable and madness in a manner to attempt it."

Cornwallis told the court martial that the war council said it would take six hours of rowing to get the first 1,800 troops to the shore and another six hours before a second embarkation. It would have taken four or five trips to get everyone on land and the boats would be under the enemy's batteries for a considerable time, harming their ability to support the landing. "Sir John Mordaunt came on board the *America* and heard the general opinion as to the difficulty of landing," Cornwallis said. "They all agreed that the attempt would be wrong as the wind then was. Sir John Mordaunt thereupon ordered the troops to reimbark from the boats."

Cornwallis testified he had stayed at his post until daylight. On September 29, he got a letter from Mordaunt desiring his attendance that afternoon on the *Ramilies*. Cornwallis went and, after a long wait, Mordaunt arrived. So did a letter from Hawke. He said if Mordaunt had no further military operations to propose, Hawke would leave for England.

"I told Sir John he knew pretty well my opinion, for I had constantly been against landing, since the council of war on the 25th, and that every day and every hour we stayed, I should be more and more against it. There was no service of consequence to be done, and therefore I was of the opinion to return," Cornwallis said. "Sir John said that if it was the general opinion, he should concur in it."

Cornwallis went on to say that the next day he joined Mordaunt and the other commanders on the Isle of Aix, where they used spyglasses and telescopes to see what they could of the defence at Rochefort. "I could make nothing of it myself as so great a distance," he said. "I asked Sir John if he had any commands for me. He answered that he did not, and so I returned to my own ship."

The court martial heard a summation of the "heavy charge" of criminal disobedience of the king's orders. Mordaunt defended himself. "I did everything in my power to execute faithfully the instructions given me, the trust reposed in me," he said.

The military judges deliberated long hours before declaring Mordaunt was not guilty. The court martial agreed the mission had been badly conceived.

In public squares, the fiasco was repeatedly compared to Byng's dismal showing at Minorca the year before. The execution of the admiral echoed across the land. The exoneration enraged King George II, who wanted Mordaunt dismissed, at the very least. He was deeply disappointed in the leadership of the expedition. He removed Mordaunt, Henry Seymour Conway and Cornwallis from his staff in July 1758. Wolfe and Hawke were widely acclaimed for their efforts. Wolfe, at least, had gone ashore to scout the terrain and constantly urged action. He had even boldly declared he could capture Rochefort himself if he had just five hundred men, but Mordaunt refused to let him try. Wolfe became a favourite of the Crown and was called on to attack Louisbourg in 1758, when his role in the victory recapturing the French fort made him a hero in England. He was sent to Nova Scotia to continue the expulsion of the Acadians, where he won further acclaim. He died the next year in the battle on the Plains of Abraham in Quebec. Quebec fell in the battle, and Britain finally won North America. Mordaunt retained his commission, but never again held a senior field command. He was promoted to general in 1770 and died serving as the governor of Berwick-upon-Tweed, his small home village in northern England.

Cornwallis escaped the fiasco at Rochefort without official approbation, but he would linger in royal purgatory for the next five years before winning another appointment – and it wasn't one he wanted.

4
The Struggle for Nova Scotia Continues

Back in Nova Scotia, geopolitics had dramatically changed life for almost everyone. Much as Cornwallis had predicted, the securing of Nova Scotia for Britain acted as a landing ground for the larger invasion and conquest of riches in British North America. Cornwallis's old comrade, James Wolfe, defeated France in Quebec at the Battle of the Plains of Abraham in 1759. The victory cost Wolfe his life and he was lionized in British history. France was routed and eventually lost all of its claims to the continent. Britain seemed poised to rule the land in perpetuity until the American Revolution took half the continent away from King George III. Lord Charles Cornwallis, Edward Cornwallis's nephew, had arrived in 1776 to lead the British forces. He lost and surrendered the colonies in Yorktown in 1781, thereby ending the Revolutionary War.

For the Montbeliard refugees, life continued to be uncertain and full of upheaval. Most spent several years in Lunenburg before making one last move. In 1765, Lieutenant Joseph Frederick Wallet DesBarres was given 20,000 acres in a royal grant in Tatamagouche.[35] The land was originally a Mi'kmaq settlement and "Tatamagouche" is their word for "a meeting of the waters." French settlers had claimed the land, but lost it when the Acadians were expelled. It was then handed to DesBarres.

---

35 Patterson, Frank. A *History of Tatamagouche*. Halifax, Nova Scotia: Royal Print & Litho Ltd., 1917.

DesBarres was a cartographer from an old and honoured Montbeliard family and he was anxious to fulfill the grant's requirement that he settle the land. He turned to his fellow Montbeliardians and invited them to move to Tatamagouche. By 1771, he had convinced many of the families to trek 142 miles across the heart of Nova Scotia to resettle as his tenants on the now peaceful isthmus that Cornwallis had fought so hard to control. DesBarres offered farm stock in exchange for half of their takings, after the fashion of a European manor. Jean-George Tattrie was by then mostly known as George Tattrie and spoke his native French, as well as some Gaelic, and English. Tattrie, then in his fifties, moved to Tatamagouche with his second wife, Catherine, and settled near French River on land that had been cleared by the Acadians. It was a hard first year, with the settlers surviving on boiled marsh greens. Any extra supplies had to be carried on their backs along the thirty-two-mile trek from Truro. The Tattries had had no children, and Catherine died a few years after the last migration.

Tattrie's life took a dramatic turn when the twice-widowed man married again in about 1776. He was sixty; his bride was sixteen-year-old Maria Elizabeth Langille, a daughter of an old Montbeliard family. Tattrie went from having no children to having three boys and seven girls. In a 1795 survey, Tattrie and seventeen other original settlers were recorded as living on the farm in Tatamagouche. Tattrie was about seventy-three, and a new father to a boy aged five, and one or two babies. Tattrie lived another thirty years and died in 1827, aged one hundred and two.

For the Mi'kmaq, the decades following Cornwallis's land and sea invasion, followed by extensive settlements and fortresses built in their territories, had been harsh. The loss of their Acadian allies and family members in the expulsion left them isolated. Some Mi'kmaq warriors fought alongside the Acadians who resisted, burning a village at Chipoudy, present-day Shepody, New Brunswick, while others helped them escape into French-controlled territory. For many years, several hundred Acadians hid in an area later called Kejimkujik National Park until they were allowed to return to open life in Nova Scotia. In 1756, Governor Charles Lawrence offered a new scalping bounty and once more, the woods were filled with British adventurers killing Mi'kmaq families for cash. Lawrence used the same language of Cornwallis, ordering people to "annoy, distress, take and destroy the Indians," and all of those who help them in any way. He offered £30 for every live man above the age of sixteen; £25 for every dead man; £25 for each woman and child brought in alive. While Lawrence would later move toward peace with the Mi'kmaq, the proclamation was never formally revoked.

When France lost Louisbourg in 1758, the Mi'kmaq were left alone with the British. Successive treaties and agreements corralled the dwindling population of Mi'kmaq people into smaller and smaller parcels of land. Lawrence died in 1760 and the following year his successor, Jonathan Belcher, negotiated a last peace with the Mi'kmaq. On June 25, 1761, a Burying of the Hatchet Ceremony was held at the governor's farm in Halifax.

"Brothers, I receive you with the hand of friendship and protection in the name of the great and mighty monarch, King George the Third, Supreme Lord and proprietor of North America. I assure myself that you submit yourselves to his allegiance with hearts of duty and gratitude as to your merciful conqueror," Belcher said.[36] The Mi'kmaq would retain their Catholic religion, and their priests, and in exchange for surrender, they would get what protection the British Crown offered. They also swore to take up arms against any British enemy. With that, a hatchet was physically buried.

"You now, sir, see us in your presence. Dispose of us as you please," the chiefs said in response to the governor's speech. "We account it to our greatest misfortune that we should so long have neglected to embrace the opportunity of knowing you so well, as we now do."

In the difficult decades that followed, the Mi'kmaq lived "on the fringes of civilizations."[37] Having lost their old world, and being denied access to education or employment in the new world, they fell between the deep cracks of the two civilizations. Many went south to fight on the rebel side of the American Revolution, and others incited rebellion in Nova Scotia, but little came of it. Mi'kmaq communities were compelled to move to poor land in several reservations amounting to 18,105 acres out of the province's 13.5 million acres. The once vast territory collectively known as Mi'kma'ki was further hacked apart when New Brunswick and Nova Scotia became separate provinces in 1784 and when the United States drew its borders through former Mi'kmaq territory in Maine. The scattered remnant tribes were isolated and with few friends.

---

36 Burying of the Hatchet Ceremony, Governor's Farm, Halifax, June 25, 1761, PANS RG1 Vol. 165, p 162-65.
37 Paul, Daniel. Page 179

The Mi'kmaq were pushed to the edge of extinction. Losing their vast hunting and fishing territory took food from their mouths and many starved. It also stole the clothes off their backs, and many froze. In the land their ancestors had thrived in for millennia, they now died in large numbers. By 1780, the government began sending relief packages to the dying families. Many European settlers, shocked by the desperation, petitioned their government for better care. One sent a letter in 1812, saying, "game has become so scarce that they cannot live in the woods. Several of them are widows or old and infirm persons, who live chiefly by begging."[38]

By 1827, the Nova Scotia Legislature openly discussed the possibility that the Mi'kmaq could become extinct in the province. This had been official government policy during Cornwallis's reign just seventy-eight years before, but now the government felt a responsibility to prevent it from happening. The urgency of the situation was revealed in Newfoundland in 1829, when the last Beothuk person died and the ancient race went extinct.

In 1843, Joseph Howe, then Indian Superintendent, said that without relief, the Mi'kmaq, too, would die out within forty years. Before European arrival, there had been 200,000 Mi'kmaq people in Mi'kma'ki. A survey in 1838 found just 1,425 Mi'kmaq men, women and children left in the entire province. Many of those were reported to be starving, malnourished and sick. The Mi'kmaq would begin a long, slow rebuilding from that low point. By 2006, there were 24,175 Mi'kmaq in Nova Scotia – and they were one of the fastest growing segments of the province's population.

38 Miller, Virginia P. "The Decline of the Nova Scotia Micmac Population, 1600-1850." *Culture* Vol. 2 No. 3 (1982). Pages 107-120. As quoted in Daniel Paul, page 197.

5

Exile on Gibraltar

Edward Cornwallis had been returned unopposed to his seat in West-minster in 1753, but faced competition in 1754. Fighting for his position in Parliament proved expensive and he asked the government to pay his costs. He was discreetly given some money.

When he ran again in 1761, he encountered stiff opposition from Sir George Vandeput. Cornwallis wrote to the Duke of Newcastle to express his concern. "Indeed, my Lord, if some care is not taken of Westminster there will be more trouble. I before told your grace of what Sir George Vandeput said – I hear today a Mr. Scot, a brewer in Westminster, in-tends to declare himself a candidate. I can only say I am ready to support or willingly decline. It is the government's interest to support this election and they only can do it," he explained.

Lord Fitzmaurice noted Cornwallis was disliked at Parliament, but he was returned nonetheless. The Parliamentary records indicate he spoke only once: January 29, 1762. The house was embroiled in a confused de-bate on a technical point about the papers concerning the employment of German soldiers. "Generals Cornwallis and Griffin both spoke ... twenty others spoke ... Each had his own scheme, which came to nothing by the immediate proposal of a fresh one," it was noted.[39]

On that note, his career in Parliament ended. He formally resigned his seat later that year to take up a post as governor of Gibraltar. King George II, Cornwallis's long-time friend and supporter, had died in 1760

---

39 House of Commons 1754-1790, Sir Lewis Namier & John Brooke

and been succeeded by his grandson, George III. In later years, George III suffered severe mental health problems. Despite growing up on the same street as Cornwallis, George III was not friendly toward his grandfather's favourite. The new king plotted to get Cornwallis out of Parliament. His removal would be "cruel and unjust," the king admitted, but "if some great [seat of] government were to be vacant, he might step into that: Cornwallis may be removed, but I believe Mr. Fox will cry out for he has always been his friend."

Cornwallis was not pushed out in the end, but did not re-offer. He was quietly released from his post at the king's bedchamber with no notice. So quietly, in fact, that he went on being paid for some time before the error was noticed. His supporters tried to figure out why he had fallen from grace, but failed to learn anything. "I own I do not perfectly understand upon what foundation" he was removed, wrote George Grenville, a nephew of Cornwallis and friend of Lord Townshend. Cornwallis arrived on Gibraltar in the summer of 1762. He toured the fortifications and found "everything here is in good condition." The Moors in Barbary were growing "troublesome," he was told, and he spent much of the next three years negotiating with them for peace and building relations with the Emperor of Morocco.

Cornwallis's performance on Gibraltar was later noted for his sense of disillusionment, a loss of energy and a decline in his enthusiasm for the imperial cause.[40] The fifty-year-old's power diminished. In February 1763, he wrote to London to inform them that a man he had personally given a pass to permit his safe travel through Morocco had been captured.

"He was assured he would be set at liberty as soon as the Emperor was made acquainted with the affair, but to his great disappointment and mortification, the Emperor ordered him to be sent as a slave to Morocco, where he still detains him and has never vouchsafed to give any answers to the repeated demands and solicitations of the consul for obtaining his liberty," Cornwallis wrote.

Cornwallis later noted that his corrupt predecessors had issued passes to "very improper" persons, thus devaluing them to the point where they lost power to guarantee safety. He saw Britain's hold on the island and on trade to North Africa was feeble. Most of the trade to provision the fort was done by ships purported to be loyal to the British Crown, but piloted by Spaniards, Genoese and other foreigners. "When those vessels are

---

40 Plank, Geoffrey. Page 185.

trading to the Spanish coast, in case of meeting with a Moorish cruiser, they are detained, and sometimes plundered, and ill treated, under pretense that they are not English, but enemies to the Moors. If, when they are trading to the Barbary coast, they meet with a Spanish cruiser, especially if they have Moors, or Moorish effects aboard, they are seized, carried into a Spanish port, and sometimes confiscated, under pretext of their carrying on a contraband trade or of the Spaniards having a right to seize Moors, and their effects, whenever they meet them," he wrote.

He needed an influx of British Protestant settlers to Gibraltar, but had little appetite to pursue that plan, which must have seemed very familiar. London had little interest in his work, and so did he. He despaired of the prospects for peace in Gibraltar because "the inveterate enmity subsisting between the Spaniards and the Moors" and the fractious merchant community meant there would always be arguments. The only way he saw peace coming was if "native British subjects" came in great numbers, but he expressed no hope that he could draw them to his island. Britain was then at war with Spain. Gibraltar remained a centre of corruption, Cornwallis believed. While he described his own post as one of the most lucrative available, he was unhappy in exile. He complained of his isolation from power and his being left "totally ignorant of all public affairs."

The alienation was exacerbated by the absence of his wife Mary, who remained in England. By 1765 she was loudly taking up his case in London, asking for his return to England. Cornwallis was despondent and complained he felt a "decline in vigor of body and mind" since moving to the island. He suffered from a "disorder in my head" that left him "incapable of doing any business." In the same year, his old friend and benefactor William, the Duke of Cumberland, died unexpectedly. He was forty-four. Cumberland was buried in Westminster Abbey. Cornwallis had lost one of his few remaining high-level friends and protectors.

Cornwallis wrote long letters to London asking that he be relieved of his post. "After mature deliberation I have determined to ask His Majesty's leave to resign the government of Gibraltar or at least the command of it. I solemnly assure your Lordship I do not do this out of any whim, discontent or uneasiness," he wrote on March 4, 1765. "I have had too recent proof of His Majesty's goodness to me not to wish to serve him in any station I was capable of to the end of my days, but I find I decline both in vigour of body and mind and the trust of Gibraltar is so important that I should not act honourably or even honestly if I did not inform my sovereign of it, that his service may not suffer through my imbecility."

Cornwallis argued it would be in the best interests of the kingdom if a more capable man took his post. He showed little indication he hoped to advance his career by stepping down from Gibraltar. He once again reminded the king of his long, dutiful service.

"Your Lordship may well conceive how painful it is to me to be under the necessity of asking to relinquish a command the most honourable and lucrative a military man can enjoy, but it is conformable to the sentiments I ever held. If my past services of 35 years should be thought to merit any reward His Majesty will grant it; if not, I am sure he will be gracious and merciful as to permit me to retire upon the small pittance I shall then have."

He followed that up with another letter May 17, 1765. He complained that Lord Halifax's last letter to him had come after his letter requesting to be released, but had not addressed his request. He reiterated his desire to retire. He begged for swift release, so he wouldn't have to sail back to London in the winter. Cornwallis was desperate.

"A disorder in my head which has plagued me several years at times is grown so much worse as often to stupefy me and render me incapable of doing any business. It affects my strength and makes me truly incapable of executing the trust reposed in me," he wrote. "I do trust, my dear Lord, that this matter will be forwarded that I may not have a winter passage home. There can be no greater anxiety of mind that where a person is stationed in a trust that he is conscious he cannot properly execute. Think of this, my good old friend, and release me."

He was granted a leave to return to England later that year. It was offered as time to recuperate and to put his personal affairs in order. He did so, but returned miserably to Gibraltar in 1768. In that same year, his twin brother Frederick turned his long friendship with Augustus Henry FitzRoy, Third Duke of Grafton, and then prime minister, into a major promotion when he was named Archbishop of Canterbury, the head of the global Anglican Church. Archbishop Cornwallis was in the prime of his career, married to the love of his life, and highly popular in the highest circles of London.

Back on Gibraltar, Cornwallis wrote to the Earl of Egmont, who was Secretary of War, and complained about being passed over in a recent bout of promotions. He wrote about his extensive services and sacrifices for his country and his disappointment at being dealt with unfairly. But he had few old friends left in government and little lingering influence in the royal court after Minorca and Rochefort. His pleas fell on deaf ears. In 1771, he was reappointed to another term as governor. In January 1772, he again wrote to the War Office seeking a promotion off the island and asking that his case be taken to the king. Cornwallis detailed his service and sacrifices and his long exile from home on an island that was for him unhealthy.

"No notice appears to have been taken of his request," writes historian James MacDonald. Cornwallis would spend more time as governor of Gibraltar than he did at any other post, but his time there would be reduced to two cursory lines in *The Rock of the Gibraltarians*, William G.F. Jackson's definitive history of the island.

Cornwallis did not write again to the War Office. On January 14, 1776, Cornwallis died on Gibraltar. He was just a few weeks shy of what would have been his sixty-third birthday. The British records of his life and work for the Crown close with a final note: "DD," or "discharged dead." His body was brought back to England and buried in the family crypt. Records for his wife Mary vary, but indicate she died in December the same year. His brother Frederick died at Lambeth Palace in March 1783 at the age of seventy. Frederick was buried in St. Mary's Churchyard near London. A simple rectangular tablet on the north wall of the organ chamber records his name, along with the arms and mitre of the archbishop and a plain shield with drapery in folds.

The twins Edward and Frederick, and their nephew Charles, were the last generation of Cornwallises to hold such high offices. The family name faded in the decades to come. The barony was extinguished in 1823, and the earldom and marquisate in 1852. Edward Cornwallis's name would disappear almost everywhere, except in one small city on the far shore of the Atlantic, once a distant outpost in a vanished empire.

Epilogue:
Tales from the Cryptkeeper

When Lesley Robinson answers the phone in Suffolk, England, in the fall of 2012, it's clearly not the first time she's had to answer for Edward Cornwallis.

"Is the abolish Cornwallis movement still going?" she asks, before adding, "He didn't do so well with the Mi'kmaqs."

Robinson is the archivist at Culford School. It has seven hundred students ranging from age three to eighteen and sprawls over the nearly five hundred acres that once comprised the Cornwallis family estate. The mansion Edward Cornwallis once lived in is now filled with school children. The family church, St. Mary's, nestles in a copse of trees at the edge of the estate and the village. A church has stood there since the thirteenth century, but the new one was built in 1674 for the third baron Cornwallis. It's a beautiful stone building set in an ancient graveyard. Today, it is shared between the Anglican village and the Methodist school.

Robinson describes it as a serene place where only birdsong and the hum of mowers break the silence. "So calm is it here, so delightfully free of the modern age, that I have already booked my space in its graveyard," she tells me.

She'll be in notorious company. Robinson is the unofficial cryptkeeper for the one-time governor of Nova Scotia, Edward Cornwallis. I tell her the books I've read have him variously buried in Gibraltar or London, and some people imagine he rests in Nova Scotia.

St. Mary's Church, 2010, where Cornwallis is buried.

"No, he's here," she assures me. I ask her to take a photo of his grave. She obliges, heading into St. Mary's Church and descending under the vestry into the crypt. It measures nine metres by three and a half metres. The barrel roof is barely a metre off the ground, so she has to bend double to shine a flashlight into the crypt and take a few photos. They reveal a desolate, forgotten vault. Many of the "ovens" are empty; one is stacked with debris. In the corner, next to an empty oven, is a familiar name: "In Memory of The Honble. Lieutenant General Edward Cornwallis, Governour of Gibraltar, who Died January, 14th, 1776, in the 63rd Year of His Age."

No mention of Halifax. "I can only presume that his cruel treatment of the indigenous Indians was something the family wanted to forget, too, and by not including it on the oven-end inscription, I get the impression that they hoped he would not be remembered for his cruelty by later generations. No such luck, unfortunately," Robinson reflects.

In Memory of
The Honble
Lieutenant General
EDWARD CORNWALLIS
Governour of Gibraltar,
who Died January, 14th, 1776
in the 63^d, Year of
His Age

Cornwalllis's burial vault in the crypt of St. Mary's Church, 2012.

Cornwallis is forgotten in England. His family titles are long gone and his estate passed out of Cornwallis hands in 1823. It went through other families before the school bought it in 1935. There is little mention of the man so famous across the ocean on the grounds he once called home. I lived in Scotland for seven years. I visited Culloden and toured all over the Highlands. I never heard his name once. It was only a passing reference to Michael Hughes's A Plain Narrative and Authentic Journal of the Late Rebellion that tipped me off to his deeper role.

When I contacted the government of Gibraltar, the name Edward Cornwallis meant nothing to the press officer. She forwarded me to the archivist, who answered my questions with silence. The island's main history book contains two lines noting his years in office. The archive was unable to provide more information on him, so I turned to historian Geoffrey Plank and he forwarded me his copies of the letters Cornwallis wrote during his long tenure at the British outpost.

But Robinson remembers Cornwallis. She talks easily about the events of his life and mentions in passing that she once saw the arthritic hip of his twin brother Frederick preserved in a jar. She's spent a lot of time thinking about how you deal with such a troubling historical figure.

"As I say, to you, to the Mi'kmaq, to anyone, history is what has been done and it can't be undone. Bad things committed centuries ago are not the fault of later generations, but neither is it their right to expunge history from the records; the idea is that we learn not to do the bad things again," she says. "Hitler, Pol Pot, Cornwallis: all names that bring loathing to some and admiration to others. It all depends which side of the fence you were on at the time."

Like many Britons today, she understands that the violent empire building of her ancestors often left bitter scars and lasting damage around the world. Some estimates say Britain has invaded nine out of ten countries around the world, with only twenty-one nations having never known a British military presence. In countries where the indigenous people still form a majority – India, South Africa, Malaysia – the British "heroes" have been removed from their pedestals. Streets and buildings named for them have long been renamed. Entire cities have new, post-colonial identities.

Empire heroes linger in lands where the settlers became the majority. Five hundred years ago, Mi'kmaq people made up 100 percent of Nova Scotia's population. Today, they account for about one percent. Nova Scotia is, as Cornwallis intended, overwhelmingly populated by people of Protestant European descent. But we are not the same as he. Robinson says something that sticks in my head for months. "If you accept him as a man of his time, then we must accept ourselves as people of our time."

For men like Cornwallis, "king and country" were the only things that mattered. God appointed the British king and if you obeyed him (and his subordinates) you were safe. But if you rebelled, you excluded yourself from humanity.

"If you weren't prepared to be peaceful, he killed you," Robinson says of Cornwallis. "Peaceful on his terms. That's how they kept order. That's why they got sent out to these places, isn't it? Because they stamped their hot little foot and said, 'It will be done this way,' and that was that. If these people didn't learn about or accept God, then they had to be controlled."

234 – Jon Tattrie

The way Cornwallis treated rebellious people abroad was similar to how he treated his social inferiors at home. The villagers of Culford were at the mercy of the aristocrats. Ordinary people were not permitted to own greyhound dogs, because they were deemed royal animals. If you rolled your eyes and got one anyway, the Cornwallises could have you executed, decapitated and peg your head on London Bridge.

"I don't think we can understand Cornwallis today. I mean, they didn't really know the meaning of the word democracy, did they? Not then. Even in the village here – it was the estate workers and the family, and never the twain would meet," Robinson says. "A lot of these men from these high families, I imagine they were terribly snotty and demanding. We would probably think they were ghastly people today."

I love Nova Scotia and am deeply connected to it. I feel a profound kinship with Mi'kmaq people today and love to hear their ancient legends about the long human history of our land. But I am also the descendent of European refugees, and so feel drawn to the Old World. During my years living in Europe, I travelled by land all the way to the ruins of ancient Greece, passing through the land my ancestor Jean-George Tattrie fled 260 years ago. I found the roots of the European part of my Euro-Nova Scotian heritage, but did not find home. That's why I came back to Nova Scotia – back home.

Robinson, Cornwallis's cryptkeeper, offers some sage advice. She says Cornwallis's story should be told in full – his role as founder of Halifax, and his role as invader of Mi'kma'ki. If we, today's Nova Scotians, wish to honour him with statues and street names, we must do so based on our values today. You now know Cornwallis's full story: is this a man you wish to honour?

Robinson suggests putting the Cornwallis statue into a history museum. Placing him on a pedestal in a park implies we celebrate him as a representative of our province today. Installing him in a museum telling the full story of Halifax would allow us to understand him in his own context. It would also free us up to explore the open question of how we want future generations to understand us.

Jon Tattrie
Halifax, Nova Scotia
November 13, 2012.

Acknowledgements

D igging into the life and times of Edward Cornwallis required the help of many. I'd like to thank the staff at the Nova Scotia Archives and Records Management for helping me locate and understand documents about Cornwallis's time in Halifax.

Geoffrey Plank, professor of American Studies at the University of East Anglia, shared his copies of Cornwallis's Gibraltar letters and spoke to me at length about Cornwallis's time there.

Daniel Paul did much groundbreaking research on Cornwallis for *We Were Not The Savages* and has shared ideas and information with me over the years. He first brought Cornwallis to my attention as a figure worth investigating, and I thank him for that.

Lesley Robinson, Culford School archivist, helped me understand Cornwallis from an English perspective and provided the photos of his final resting place.

Peter Landry, the Dartmouth lawyer and enthusiastic Nova Scotian historian behind Blupete.com, proved a great resource for gathering information about the minor figures in this book. He also provided the final, critical piece of information that helped me track down Cornwallis's body in Culford.

Thanks also go to Lesley Choyce, my publisher, for his constant encouragement and support of my writing, and to Julia Swan and Peggy Amirault, the outstanding Pottersfield Press editors who helped me get my facts straight and greatly improved the quality of the writing.

Jeff Freisen is a talented photographer and he took the photo of the Cornwallis statue on the cover and provided the basic concept. You can see more of his work at jeff-friesen.com.

My parents, Jack and Gail Tattrie, have always supported my writing. My father did most of the research on our family history. My aunt, Marge Ferguson (née Tattrie), taught me the family history from a young age and helped me make sense of the early years of the Tattries in Nova Scotia.

Most of all, thanks to my wife, Giselle, who spent a full year listening to every detail about the life of Edward Cornwallis and, instead of screaming, offered useful criticism and suggestions.

Sources

Grenier, John. *The Far Reaches of Empire*. Norman, Oklahoma: The University of Oklahoma Press, 2008.

Haliburton, Gordon M. "George Tattrie: A Nova Scotian Pioneer From Montbeliard." *Nova Scotia Historical Review* Vol. 1 No. 2, 1981. Pages 74-90.

Hawkins, John. *The Founding of Halifax*. Halifax, Nova Scotia: Goldcloth Publishing Company, 1999.

Hughes, Michael. *A Plain Narrative and Authentic Journal of the Late Rebellion*. London: Henry Whitridge, 1747.

Jackson, Sir William G.F. *The Rock of the Gibraltarians*. Madison, New Jersey: Fairleigh Dickinson University Press, 1987.

Jobb, Dean. *Bluenose Justice*. Halifax, Nova Scotia: Pottersfield Press, 1993.

MacDonald, James. *Hon Edward Cornwallis, founder of Halifax*. Halifax, Nova Scotia: The McAlpine Publishing Company, 1905.

MacKenzie, Sir George, of Coul. *A General View of the Agriculture of Ross and Cromarty*. London: George Ramsay & Co., 1810.

McLeod, Donald. *Gloomy Memories in the Highlands of Scotland*. Glasgow: A. Sinclair, 1841.

Miller, Virginia P. "The Decline of the Nova Scotia Micmac Population, 1600-1850." *Culture* Vol. 2 No. 3 (1982). Pages 107-120.

Patterson, Frank. *A History of Tatamagouche*. Halifax, Nova Scotia: Royal Print & Litho Ltd., 1917.

Paul, Daniel. *We Were Not the Savages*. Halifax, Nova Scotia: Fernwood Publishing, 2000.

Plank, Geoffrey. *An Unsettled Conquest*. Philadelphia: University of Pennsylvania Press, 2003.

Plank, Geoffrey. *Rebellion and Savagery*. Philadelphia: University of Pennsylvania Press, 2005.

Prebble, John. *Culloden*. London: Secker & Warburg, 1961.

Raddall, Thomas H. *Halifax: Warden of the North*. Halifax, Nova Scotia: Nimbus Publishing, 2010.

Salusbury, John. *Expeditions of Honour*. Newark, Delaware: University of Delaware Press, 1982.

Wilson, Isaiah. *Geography and History of the County of Digby*. Halifax, Nova Scotia: Holloway Bros., 1900.

The Nova Scotia Archives.

The Report of the General Officers appointed to enquire into the conduct of Major General Stuart, and Colonels Cornwallis and Earl of Effingham. London: M. Cooper, 1756.

The Proceedings of a General Court-Martial for John Mordaunt. London: A. Millar, 1757.

House of Commons 1754-1790, Sir Lewis Namier & John Brooke

"Culloden: The Jacobites' Last Stand." *Battlefield Britain*. Dir. Ian Lilley. Presenters Peter and Dan Snow. BBC Two, 17 April 2004. Television.

BluePete.com